STRINDBERG
AND THE
POETRY OF MYTH

STRINDBERG AND THE POETRY OF MYTH

Harry G. Carlson

University of California Press | Berkeley | Los Angeles | London

UNIVERSITY OF CALIFORNIA PRESS
Berkeley and Los Angeles, California

UNIVERSITY OF CALIFORNIA PRESS, LTD.
London, England

COPYRIGHT © 1982 BY THE REGENTS OF THE UNIVERSITY OF CALIFORNIA

In slightly different form; first published in Swedish as *Strindberg och myterna*,
trans. Sven Erik Täckmark (Stockholm: Författarförlaget, 1979).

Library of Congress Cataloging in Publication Data

Carlson, Harry Gilbert, 1930–
    Strindberg and the poetry of myth.

    Includes bibliographical references.
    1. Strindberg, August, 1849–1912—Criticism and
interpretation.   I. Title.
PT9816.C37   839.7'23   81-12989
ISBN 0-520-04442-8   AACR2

PRINTED IN THE UNITED STATES OF AMERICA

1 2 3 4 5 6 7 8 9

FOR CAROLYN

Contents

Acknowledgments

Parts of this book have appeared in magazines and I am grateful to the editors for permission to use them here: a section of the chapter on Strindberg and myth is reprinted from "The Unknown Painter of Myth," *The Scandinavian Review* 64, no. 3 (September 1976): 32–38; and a section of the chapter on *Easter* is reprinted from "Strindberg och mytologierna—en studie i 'Påsk,' " trans. Herbert Grevenius, *Signum* 4, no. 3 (1978): 73–77.

The book itself was first published in Swedish in 1979, in a slightly different form, as *Strindberg och myterna*, and I am especially grateful to the staff of the Stockholm publisher, Författarförlaget, in particular, Rut Jonsson, Nils Leijer, and the translator, Sven Erik Täckmark.

I am indebted to people on both sides of the Atlantic who facilitated my research: in New York at Queens College, Bertram L. Joseph, Saul Novack, and Mimi Pechansky; and at the Swedish Information Service, Marna Feldt and Bertil Hökby; in Stockholm at the Strindberg Museum, Harald Svensson; and at the Swedish Institute, Lena Daun.

My gratitude goes to a number of friends and colleagues who read the manuscript in whole or in part and made valuable

suggestions: Marianne Ahrne, Elinor Fuchs, Herbert Greven-
ius, Eric O. Johannesson, Bettina Knapp, Olof Lagercrantz,
Sven Rinman, Carl Reinhold Smedmark, Hjalmar Sundén, and
Leif Zern.

My students at Queens College and The City University of
New York Graduate Center contributed much as we studied
this material together, but I am particularly grateful to Gloria
Horowitz for bringing Joseph Campbell, C. G. Jung, and Erich
Neumann to my attention.

My warmest thanks go to my best friend and severest critic,
my beloved wife, Carolyn.

Landfall   H. G. C.
East Hampton, New York
August 1981

Textual Note

Two chief sources are cited throughout the book: Strindberg's collected correspondence (*August Strindbergs brev*, ed. Torsten Eklund [Stockholm: Bonniers, 1948–76, 15 vols. to date]), hereafter referred to in notes as *Brev*; and his collected works (*Samlade skrifter*, ed. John Landquist [Stockholm: Bonniers, 1912–21, 55 vols.]). In references to the works, the volume number appears in italics, the page numbers in roman (i.e., *15*, 33 means volume 15, page 33). All translations, except where otherwise indicated, are by the author.

In several instances, a recent, more complete edition of the plays is cited: *August Strindbergs dramer*, ed. Carl Reinhold Smedmark (Stockholm: Bonniers, 1962–70, 4 vols.).

All Biblical quotations are taken from *The New English Bible*, standard edition (New York: Oxford University Press, 1971).

The transliteration of Sanskrit characters in the references to Indic mythology follows that of Monier-Williams's *Sanskrit-English Dictionary*, rev. ed. (Oxford: Oxford University Press, 1899).

Introduction

There are curiously contradictory aspects to the position August Strindberg occupies in modern literature. In Sweden, he is the national author, a titan who established landmarks in drama, fiction, and poetry and left his stamp on the language. Yet he is more respected than beloved. He spent a good portion of his creative life abroad, in exile, drawing sharp, often unflattering portraits of his countrymen and lecturing them on their shortcomings. As with other contemporary exiles—Ibsen, Synge, Joyce, O'Casey—the mention of his name arouses mixed feelings in his homeland.

In the world, Strindberg challenges Ibsen as the most influential of modern playwrights, a precursor of expressionism, surrealism, and the theatre of the absurd. But despite the fact that more than sixty years after his death his plays continue to fascinate, they also puzzle and disturb, perhaps almost as much as they did when they first appeared. We are just beginning to recognize the true breadth of his genius. The most hostile of critics acknowledge the presence in his work of an extraordinary power—raw and sometimes primitive—while the most sympathetic ones confess to having difficulties describing the nature of that power and how it functions.

The artist himself contributed to some of the problems in interpretation. He liked to boast that he was a disciple of naturalism, but the kind he practiced was uniquely his own, bearing only a general resemblance to the more programmatic variety associated with dramatists like Becque, Hauptmann, and Gorky. While three of the plays discussed in this volume— *The Father*, *Miss Julie*, and *Creditors*—do approach the cherished "scientific" naturalistic goal of an objective portrayal of the pincerlike movement of the forces of heredity and environment, Strindberg rendered this movement in poetic dimensions rarely present in other examples of the genre. In later plays, also discussed in the pages that follow—*To Damascus*, *A Dream Play*, and *The Ghost Sonata*—he virtually invented a new kind of drama: densely symbolic action set in dreamlike states or situations. Stubbornly, however, he declared even after this radical change in style that he was still a naturalist and would always remain so.[1]

The common factor in these varieties of naturalism was his insistence on realistic detail as the point of departure. "A writer is only a reporter of what he has experienced," he proclaimed in an 1875 letter.[2] And he drew the raw material for his prodigious reportage—fifty-five plays, fourteen novels, novellas, or romans à clef, eight collections of short stories, and numerous poems and essays—directly from the life he knew best: his own. For models, he used anyone he considered appropriate—himself, his three wives, his friends, his enemies—often doing little to disguise the original sources. In his borrowings from real life he was candid, ruthless, and frequently indiscreet, but he could be as hard on himself as on others. At one point, he referred to his approach as vivisection (*40*, 46); understandably, many of those he operated on howled in protest.

One consequence of Strindberg's predilection for autobiographical writing is that critics have found in him an easy target for charges that he was too subjective.[3] According to this view, because everything he wrote was colored by the most intense of personal feelings, his plays fall short of greatness since they are comprehensible only as mirrors of a private fantasy world. The weakness of this argument is that it does not explain why the power in his work remains undiminished, attracting audiences today who know little, if anything about the playwright or his life.

What led me to search for other ways, apart from biography, to explain the power in Strindberg's work was my curiosity about his life-long preoccupation with mythology. Mythic images are scattered not only throughout his plays, novels, and poems but in letters and his diary as well.[4] Scholars noted the preoccupation early. In 1926 Strindberg's first important biographer, Erik Hedén, pointed out the author's particular fondness for Heracles; references to the Greco-Roman demigod, explicit or implicit, appear in many places.[5] Until recently, these various mythic images have been regarded as of superficial importance, either as decorative touches or as signs of Strindberg's megalomania—daring to identify himself with the gods. Eric O. Johannesson, in his pioneering study, *The Novels of August Strindberg* (1968), was the first to explore in a comprehensive fashion the notion that the images are not decorations but structural elements pregnant with meaning.[6] Other critics who have found significance in Strindberg's use of myth are Pavel Fraenkl, Sven Delblanc, Stephen Mitchell, and Olof Lagercrantz.[7] The present study is an effort to carry earlier explorations further.

In the background of the cover portrait is a statuette of Jason carrying the Golden Fleece. Strindberg purchased it on May 6, 1901, the day of his wedding to his third wife, Harriet Bosse; it stands today in the living room corner of the apartment in Stockholm that is the main feature of the Strindberg Museum. The original of the statuette, a gigantic work by the Danish nineteenth-century romantic sculptor Bertil Thorwaldsen, played an important role in Strindberg's life: its creation was the subject of his first produced play, *In Rome* (1870).

Based on an 1803 incident in Thorwaldsen's life, *In Rome* presents a mythic theme, a young hero at a crossroads. After a study period abroad, the sculptor must decide whether to follow the calling he feels to be an artist or to yield to his father's urgings that he abandon such high ambitions and settle for being a craftsman instead. Working on an early version of the

statue, he is filled with doubts and stares at his creation critically
and questioningly.

> THORWALDSEN: Is this truly the beautiful image
> of the son of Hellas I glimpsed upon the
> journey
> when my soul, separated from its earthly
> bonds,
> ascended on gossamer wings toward the spirit
> world,
> and at the sight of which every fiber quaked
> and heartstrings trembled with enchantment
> when I spied, above the highest vaults of
> heaven's reaches,
> a distant glimmer of God?
> Oh, no! It is only a dim shadow
> of the ideal which floated before me (*I*,
> 185 – 186).

Behind the youthful hyperbole is a context rich in mythic
resonances. Strindberg's Thorwaldsen, who wonders whether
to smash his work with his hammer, is more than just another
artist plagued by uncertainties. His very name suggests a different hammer wielder and doer of great deeds, the god Thor. And
the statue is more than an art work that falls short of the vision in
the artist's imagination. Portrayed is a prototypal hero at the
moment of triumph: the attainment of the splendid treasure at
the conclusion of the quest. Jason is the mythic hero as primal
model, as repository of all human awareness and achievement,
as touchstone to remind men today, as it reminded the Greeks,
of the outer limits of human potential.

Ultimately, the protagonist of *In Rome* does not have to
destroy his statue. As his friend and confidant Pedersen observes, a deus ex machina saves the day. A wealthy Englishman
arrives to commission a marble version of Jason, and Thorwaldsen's career is launched. Strindberg's modest, little verse play
demonstrates that its author had learned early and well how to
make mythic images cast long shadows.

But there is also a dark side to the Greek hero's story. Jason
betrayed and was betrayed in return by a woman whose revenge

cost him his sons. Like many mythic characters, he is a complex symbol: noble and treacherous, glorious victor and tragic victim. It is not difficult to imagine the several reasons that might have attracted Strindberg to Jason and compelled him to purchase the statuette on that May morning at the turn of the century. It must have reminded him not only of his first youthful triumph but of the difficult, stony path of the hero's quest, which he too had trod. At age thirty, he had been lionized as the most promising Swedish author of his generation. In his midforties he saw his career in tatters, and he was bankrupt financially and emotionally. Now, just past fifty, he was beginning to receive the international renown that would earn him a permanent place in the history of world drama.

One solace had never abandoned him: the ambiguous, multivalent eloquence of mythic imagery, investing pain with hope and hope with resignation. The title of his autobiography, *Son of a Servant Woman*, carries more than an echo of the shame and humiliation of Ishmael and his mother, Hagar, cast out into the desert. Ishmael's destiny (of which Strindberg, as a student of the Bible, was surely aware) was to rise to an exalted position: forefather of the Arabs and Moslems, who honor him as the Jews honor Isaac.[8]

Like his predecessors in the practice of mythopoesis (Goethe and Dante come to mind—he admired them both), Strindberg had a relationship with myth that was personal and complex. He shaped and reshaped the traditional stories to fit a variety of expressive purposes, adding emphasis here, deleting it there, until he had evolved his own individual mythic grammar or mythic landscape. Sometimes an image is conspicuous to the point of being too obvious, such as the many references to the passion of Christ in *Easter*. At other times the image is so subtle or disguised as to be almost obscured, such as the implicit references to the legend of the Wandering Jew in *To Damascus*.

Again like Goethe and Dante, Strindberg, especially in the late plays, was polyphonic in his approach. A single character may contain resonances from two or more mythic sources, such as the Stranger in *To Damascus*, who resembles not only the

Wandering Jew but Christ, Lucifer, Everyman, and others as well. The frequent result of this polyphony is a richness of poetic texture unparalleled in modern drama; not chaotic or incoherent, as might be expected, but with unity in diversity. The following chapter is a discussion of the diverse sources of this unity.

1

Strindberg and Myth

One of the most revealing letters in Strindberg's voluminous correspondence was addressed from Austria to an old college friend, Leopold Littmansson, in Paris, during a period of extreme financial and emotional distress. The year was 1894. Strindberg at forty-five was in exile, at the nadir of his life, personally and professionally. Celebrated by the French as the notorious Swedish misogynist, alchemist, and playwright (*Creditors* had recently opened at the Théâtre de l'Oeuvre), yet the celebrity's coffers stood empty. Behind him were two broken marriages and a career that most knowledgeable contemporaries regarded as wasted and lost. Reviled in Sweden as a dangerous writer, who corrupted and subverted the young with his sexual candor and his attacks on the decadence of bourgeois society, he had abandoned belles lettres for the life of a dilettante scientist, hoping to create gold and to demonstrate that the element theory of matter was a fraud. Five years later, a new career would open for him as he would startle and puzzle the world with the bursts of creative energy that helped to revolutionize modern drama—*To Damascus*, *A Dream Play* and the chamber plays—but for now he had a great need of money.

The letter proposed that Littmansson act as agent in the sale of a small collection of Strindberg's own paintings, and enclosed was a catalogue of sorts. For each painting, Strindberg provided an "exoteric" and "esoteric" description, explaining that "each painting is, so to speak, double-bottomed: having an exoteric side which everyone can discern, albeit with difficulty, and an esoteric, for the artist and the initiate":

No. 1

Exoteros!   A man in a blown raincoat is standing on a beach cliff which is washed by ocean waves; far out on the horizon the three white-painted, unrigged masts of a stranded bark.

Esot.   On closer observation one sees that the man on the cliff has a slouch hat like Vodan (Buddha); that the crests of the waves resemble monsters, the clouds demons, and in the middle of the sky is a remarkable likeness of Rembrandt. The three masts with three top cross bars look like Golgotha or three crosses on graves and might be a trimūrti, but this is a matter of taste (subjective).

No. 2

Exot.   A dense forest interior; in the middle, a hole opens out into an idealized landscape where sunshine in all colors pours in. In the foreground, rocks with stagnant water in which mallowworts are reflected.

Esot.   The wonderland; the battle of light against darkness. Or the realm of Ormuzd opened with the exodus of the liberated souls into the land of the sun. . . .

No. 3

Exot.   It has rained in the Alps which lie half-veiled in clouds and vapors. In the foreground, desert with slates and broom [shrubs].

Esot.   The desert wanderer's longing for wet rain, cool snow, clean ice. My eyes turn toward the heights, but the weary ones remain in the desert.

No. 4

Exot.   The greening island. The sea tranquilly smooth before sunrise. The sky yellow and rose-colored. Morning mists lie on the horizon, but above them the treetops of the greening island are visible and are reflected in the sea.

Esot.	Life's meridian (For me, Kymmendö Island 1880) therefore the island itself veiled, in white, yellow and rose.
No. 5	
Exot.	Flood on the Danube.
Esot.	The water is rising. Where is the ark? etc.
No. 6	Landscape.
	Ad libitum.
No. 7	
Exot.	A shit-green landscape, with shit-red rocks, a shit-yellow sky and shit-black fir trees.
Esot.	Sweden![1]

Strindberg's repudiation of art and poetry was more tenuous than even he realized. What started as a random series of associations almost immediately took on form and coherence. Symbol evolved into myth, and myth into cosmogony, all in the space of a few lines. Vodan (i.e., Odin) evoked Buddha, who in turn evoked Christ; the Crucifixion evoked the Indic trinity (trimūrti): Brahmā (the creator), Visnu (the preserver), and Śiva (the destroyer). The rich panorama offered included a dualistic version of the Creation (Ormuzd and Ahriman, the Zoroastrian gods of good and evil, respectively);[2] Eden as a "greening island"; the desert and the outcasts after the Fall; and the Deluge, this time without an ark in sight. But the flow of associations seemed to shut off after the mention of paradise lost. The beached poet had been set afloat again by the wave of images that flooded his mind, and old energies were quickened, but only briefly. Perhaps the journey back into memory was too painful, threatening to carry him onto dangerous shoals, and so he felt it necessary to cut it short with a sardonic parting shot at the country whose failure to understand him he blamed for much of his troubles.

That Strindberg should compose such a document in the middle of his half-decade flirtation with natural science is indicative of the attraction the world of symbol and myth had for him, like a magnetic field whose power was irresistible once he came under its sway. The nautical image he used of a "double bottom" was an apt one. Like the air space at the bottom of a ship's hull, there is a buoyant, mythopoeic layer in Strindberg's work, rich with meaning, beckoning us to exploration.

There are several probable reasons why Strindberg's interests in mythopoesis have not been investigated more extensively than they have up to now. Because he was so consistently autobiographical in his writing, his own life has been the primary model used to interpret his art and several generations of scholars have assiduously tracked down the real-life inspirations for countless elements. The result is a considerable and invaluable body of evidence detailing the relationship of the artist to his work. But good biography does not necessarily make good criticism and there have been too many formulary observations such as character A is really a portrait of Strindberg's wife, or character B's feelings are actually the artist's own. This kind of critical analysis becomes less a search for intrinsic meaning than for biographical revelation.

Another probable reason why Strindberg's mythopoeic interests have not been analyzed closely is the persistence of a skeptical attitude on the part of many scholars toward myth criticism. According to this view, mythological thinking is "primitivistic" or "prerational" or "prescientific" or "mystical"; or what is even worse, to paraphrase James Joyce, myth is a happy hunting ground for many minds that have lost their balance. A good example of the attitude is Gunnar Brandell's contrast of Strindberg's labors in alchemy and mythology: "When he was busy over his crucibles, Strindberg was freer— was further from psychotic experience—than when he was studying primitive mythologies."[3]

It is possible, as Eric O. Johannesson has noted, to take a more positive view of Strindberg's approach to myth.[4] Though by conviction an autobiographical artist—he liked to boast that as it was with Goethe his works too could be read as one long confession—he was convinced that his private visions had universal relevance and application, and he was strongly drawn to the traditional poetic images of this relevance.[5] Several decades ago it was fashionable in the Swedish theatre to have the actor playing the Stranger in *To Damascus* costumed and made up to resemble Strindberg as closely as possible, thus canceling the effect of a more important analogy. The Stranger has much in common with the morality play character Everyman: their anonymity suggests that they are both inhabitants of a mythic land, where the laws of time and space have been suspended, enabling us to witness primordial man confronting ageless problems.

As for the connection between mythological thinking and primitivism or insanity, if we discount mythic resonances in Strindberg's work as signs of derangement, we are then also obliged to discount similar resonances in some of the greatest artists of the past two centuries: Goethe, Wordsworth, Balzac, Wagner, Emerson, Poe, Melville, Mann, Joyce, Yeats, and Kafka. In any case, the essential thing is, not whether the artist's mind is coherent, but whether his work is. The only issue we need clarified about Strindberg's relationship with myth is whether the mythic resonances present in his work are integral parts of patterns that reveal meanings not otherwise apparent.

There are at least two possible approaches in evaluating Strindberg as a mythopoeic writer. We can examine mythic images and symbols solely in the contexts of the fictional works in which they appear, or we can try using his letters and essays to incorporate what the author knew and said about myth into our analysis of how he used it. The observations made above about the limitations of the biographical approach to Strindberg criticism should not be construed as censure of the important biographical research already done. The very nature of the man's genius demands that we depend heavily on this research. Because creative currents tended to flow in both directions for him—from life into art and from art into life (it was typical of him to remark that often he could not decide which he perceived as more real, his life or his art)[6]—I have chosen the second approach: to examine both his attitude toward myth, to the extent it can be determined, and the uses he found for it. Consequently, the first questions are: How much did he know about myth, and when did he know it?

The answer is that his knowledge was broad, if often shallow, and that he began accumulating it early in life. With myth, as he was with many of the sources he tapped for poetic inspiration, Strindberg was a dilettante, choosing to assimilate and exploit only those ideas and images that interested him, ignoring the rest. This explains why, although it may be easy to detect a variety of literary or philosophical influences in his work, it is equally easy to point out contradictions, to demonstrate that his borrowings lack systematic consistency. As an artist, however, he was more interested in poetic than philosophic truth. He respected myths as powerfully evocative, sacred stories, but he could separate them from the religions with which many were connected. He was fascinated, for example, by the striking images Swedenborg used to depict the infernal nature of earthly life but grew bored with Swedenborg's theology.[7]

His first and most enduring source of mythopoeic inspiration was the Bible. From the time of his first contact with a stern Christianity in his Pietistic childhood home to the period of desperate spiritual torment he underwent during what is referred to as his "Inferno Crisis" years (1894–97), Biblical imagery exerted an extraordinary effect on his imagination. One of his habits late in life was to throw open the Bible at random and find comfort in the fates of the martyrs—Job, Jacob, Jeremiah, Saul—who struggled as he did to find meaning in their sufferings.[8]

As a student at Uppsala University in 1870, Strindberg's interest in Norse mythology was stimulated when he helped to organize a literary group, the Runa Society. One of the society's enthusiasms was for the rediscovery of the glories of the old skaldic literature in an atmosphere Strindberg described as a "prevailing neo-Nordic renaissance" (18, 360). Records in the Uppsala University and Royal libraries between 1867 and 1871 reveal that Strindberg was an avid borrower of the Icelandic sagas,[9] and in 1872 he wrote glowingly of

> the rich treasure of poetry that lies hidden in the hoary, shadowy, derided songs, and sagas of the fatherland. May the day not be far off when our schoolboys will tell with pride how many sagas by Snorri they know instead of how many books by Livy they have explicated. Only then will the people's spirit be stirred to life, and only then will we know what the word *Scandinavianism* means (54, 179).

The familiarity with Norse mythology and Viking culture that he acquired through sources like Snorri's *Prose Edda* is apparent in an assortment of literary forms: from the poem "Loki's Blasphemies" in 1882 to the short story about the Viking hero Starkodd in "Stig Storverk's Son" in 1903. The dark, pessimistic world of these myths was a congenial environment for him, and he admired the "Nordic stoicism," as he called it, which he found expressed there (*18*, 422).

Another mythology that attracted his attention in the early 1870s was that of ancient Greece and Rome, probably as a result, as least in part, of the research he conducted in classical sources for *Hermione* (1870), his tragedy about the last days of Athens. As we shall see, Greco-Roman mythology was to become almost as important for him as the Bible, and here, too, he identified with the martyrs and rebels: Prometheus, Heracles, and Orpheus.

By the early 1880s Strindberg had become sophisticated not only about mythology but also about the associated field of folklore research. One of the reference sources he most admired, not only then but later as well, was *Värend and the People of Värend*, by Gunnar Olof Hyltén-Cavallius, the first significant attempt in Sweden to examine folklore materials in a scientific manner.[10] In Strindberg's *The Swedish People*, a two-volume historical-ethnographical study published in 1881–82, Hyltén-Cavallius is described as being "able to speak where the flint-stones are silent" (*8*, 182). In the same work the eccentric seventeenth-century Swedish scholar Olaus Rudbeck is criticized for theorizing that Sweden was the location of the lost continent of Atlantis and thus the cradle of European civilization. Even as Strindberg faults Rudbeck for chauvinistically motivated speculation, he finds especially telling the analogies drawn between Norse and Greek mythology and gives examples to illustrate how an enlightened age might have become persuaded by Rudbeck's theory:

> Mimir's head spoke; Memnon's did likewise. Frodi could transform himself through all kinds of guises; so could Proteus. According to Ovid, Lycaon was an enemy of mankind; Loki was an enemy of Aesir [gods]; Lycaon was transformed by Jupiter into a wolf; Loki was the father of the Fenrir wolf. . . . Whereas

Greco-Roman mythology has a golden age, Norse has the same, and they are depicted in the same colors and words [in Ovid's *Metamorphoses* and the Voluspá] (180).

Evident in this appreciative statement is an absorption in comparative mythology that would deepen considerably over the next two decades, especially during the mid-1890s, the psychologically turbulent Inferno Crisis years. In an 1896 letter to Torsten Hedlund, Strindberg declared in a burst of syncretistic enthusiasm: "There are . . . no more mysteries in the world: all is written in the Mythologies or the Skaldic writings. . . . All cosmogonies are in general, mutual agreement and are true."[11] Some of the same faith in the continuity and harmony of all legends and myths can be found in Hyltén-Cavallius's study, where the author states that he can demonstrate that certain features of Swedish folk beliefs

> can be traced back historically not just to the distant point in time where the heathen systems of the Norse peoples and the peoples of antiquity have their common source, but to the golden age of the childhood of the human race, where the traditions of the peoples of the West and the East meet and where the first signs of humanity stir in forms, which, on a certain primitive level of development, seem for all the peoples of the earth to be analogous.[12]

Brandell asserts that "Strindberg's preoccupation with mythology grew directly out of his [mental] crises."[13] I must disagree. It is true that in the hectic Inferno period his interests in myth intensified, but so did all other interests and perceptions: life itself became almost unbearably intense for him. Thinking mythopoeically was not a momentary, periodically recurrent aberration, it was as natural for him as thinking dramatically. Ostensibly, his primary occupation at this time was scientific experimentation and research, but interspersed among the formulas, notes, and observations in his letters and secret diary are scores of mythic images. The most common of these are Greek and Biblical, but by 1894 and 1895 there were signs that he was deepening his acquaintance with a mythology that he had previously known only indirectly: Indic, particularly Hindu and Buddhist. In an 1895 letter to Hedlund Strindberg confessed: "I

was educated by three Buddhists: Schopenhauer, v[on] H
mann and finally Nietzsche. Perhaps that is why we have points
in common. . . . As a Buddhist, I am, like Buddha and his three
great disciples, a woman-hater, for I hate the earth because it
binds my spirit and because I love it. Woman to me is the earth
with all its splendors, the tie that binds . . ."[14]
    The reference to Buddha is revealing in several ways. First, it
demonstrates how responsive Strindberg was to myth as metaphor. Buddha is not just a fellow misogynist: if woman is the
lure that binds man to earth, that traps spirit in matter, then
Buddha represents the longing of spirit to escape the earthly
prison that is at once so seductive and so painful. Martin Lamm
is among the critics who have warned against overestimating
Strindberg's knowledge of or insights into Buddhism on the
grounds that the reference sources he used were popular studies
and not scholarly ones.[15] The warning might be well worth
heeding if one were trying to establish Strindberg's credentials
as a serious student of comparative mythology, but this is not
my intention. Here is an artist, responding to an eloquent
image. Regardless of how he acquired the insight, whether from
a secondary source or through an intuitive flash, he understood
the symbolism in the Buddhist attitude toward woman, who
because she is the creator of new life becomes the chief obstacle
to redemption.[16]
    The second revealing aspect of the reference to Buddha is the
link to Schopenhauer. According to biographical scholar Torsten Eklund, Schopenhauer's ideas did more to shape Strindberg's understanding of metaphysics than the ideas of any other
single individual, including Swedenborg, whom Strindberg
himself referred to as his chief spiritual guide. Strindberg's first
acquaintance with Swedenborg, says Eklund, "dates from the
last phase of the Inferno Crisis, whereas Schopenhauer's philosophy followed Strindberg in every period of his life from the
1870s on."[17] In a review of an Asiatic art exhibit in 1876 Strindberg spoke of his admiration for the "religious philosophy of
India [which] was capable of inspiring as profound and modern
a spirit as Schopenhauer."[18] Eklund notes the influence of the
German philosopher's mythic orientation but seems to take

much the same dim view of the value of this kind of thinking as Brandell does, interpreting it as a symptom of mental illness: "Like Strindberg, Schopenhauer was personally addicted to superstitious and magical lines of thought, which grew out of a neurotic's view of the world, out of a neurasthenic egocentric's perception that he was being obstructed and persecuted."[19] What Eklund fails to see is Schopenhauer's mythopoeic importance to Strindberg: as a model who demonstrated the great poetic potential that lay in the power of myth as metaphor, who showed that one could believe in the truths that myths express without having to believe that the myths themselves were true. One could be a skeptic or even an atheist and still be a "true believer" when it came to myth.

It is not surprising that the mythology Schopenhauer found most vital was Indic; he was in college when the exaltation of Indic religion by German romanticism was at its height. In 1813, as a student of the great Indic encyclopedist Friedrich Majer, he embarked on a study of the Hindu *Upanishads*; later he came to regard Buddhism as closely parallel to his own philosophical orientation. He saw Buddhism using myths as educational tools, bringing to common people truths that they would not ordinarily comprehend: "[All] that can be thought only generally and in the abstract is quite inaccessible to the great majority of the people. Therefore, in order to bring that great truth into the sphere of practical application, a *mythical vehicle* for it was needed . . . a receptacle, so to speak, without which it would be lost and dissipated. The truth had therefore everywhere to borrow the garb of fable . . ."[20]

Schopenhauer was unimpressed for the most part by Old Testament mythology, which he found too realistic and optimistic. The exception he singled out was the image of the Fall: that he admired. In contrast, "the basic character of Brahminism and Buddhism," he asserted, "is *idealism* and *pessimism*, since they 'allow the world only a dream-like existence and regard life as the consequence of our sins."[21] This could well be a summary of what were to become the basic elements of Strindberg's metaphysics: that the world is "only a dream-like existence" and that life is "the consequence of our sins." Schopenhauer also spoke of the world "as a place of atonement, a sort of penal colony,"[22] an image Strindberg was to repeat, sometimes verbatim, in a variety of contexts. In an 1895 letter he wrote: "I hope that if this life is a time of punishment, and the earth a penal colony where one serves time for unknown crimes from another existence, that my time is soon done."[23] In Schopenhauerian terms, there is only one salvation in this world of illusion, this earthly hell: "*denial* of the will to life and redemption from a world in which death and the Devil reign."[24] Another Strindberg letter, this one from 1896, declares: "The world outlook that has developed within me is closest to that of Pythagoras and adopted by Origen: We are in Inferno for sins committed in a previous existence. Therefore: pray for nothing other than resignation! and ask nothing, absolutely nothing of life!"[25]

Strindberg's readings during the Inferno period included, in addition to Schopenhauer, a wide variety of religious, philosophical, and occult sources: Swedenborg, Plato, Éliphas Lévi, the Kabbalah, the tarot, and Gnosticism, to name the most prominent. What all these sources have in common is a mythic basis or orientation. For Swedenborg, myths were projections of eternal truths, "representations from heaven," as he called them, which demonstrate that the minds of the ancients "were nearer to heaven than ours, which do not even know that such representations exist, still less that they signify such things."[26] On one of the cover pages of Strindberg's *Occult Diary*, the secret journal he kept between 1896 and 1908, is the extravagant declaration: "The explanation of this diary, including all signs and symbols, can be found in Eliphas Levi [sic], *The Key of the Mysteries*."[27] The dominant feature of Lévi's book on occult secrets is the use of myths as sources of allegorical revelations: "The Bible is not a history, it is a collection of poems, a book of allegories and images"; "the fables of Homer remain truer than history."[28]

Favorite mythic reference sources for Strindberg both during and after the Inferno Crisis were books by Viktor Rydberg, a Swedish poet, novelist, and comparative mythologist. In an August 1896 letter Strindberg wrote: "In [Rydberg's *Teutonic*

Mythology] is everything I have been groping for. The World Tree . . . the creation of the first couple out of wood (Ovid's metamorphosis!)."[29] In an *Occult Diary* entry made the same day, Strindberg stated that he had read Rydberg's book "and felt liberated."[30]

Ovid's *Metamorphoses* was only one of a number of literary sources in which Strindberg found mythopoeic inspiration during the same period. A letter in October 1896 described excitedly how he had read the "secrets" in "Hesiod, Ovid's cosmogony, Homer, the Bible, the Eddas!"[31] As we have seen, with the exception of Hesiod, evidence of the sources listed can be traced back to Strindberg's earliest years as a writer.

To further catalogue examples of Strindberg's interests in myth would depart from the chief purpose of this book. Myth played a very important part in the way he thought and worked as a playwright, but he never became a scholar in the subject. His library as it stands today in the Strindberg Museum in Stockholm contains more than half a hundred books on myth, but the many marginal notations in them attest to an enthusiasm that was motivated more by personal artistic considerations than by scientific ones. Even when he worked as a scientist, he was a mythopoeic artist, his own proclaimed intentions to the contrary notwithstanding. To object that his knowledge of myth was often derived from secondary rather than primary sources—his well-marked copy of the Finnish myth epic, *Kalevala*, for example, was an edition intended for primary schools—is beside the point. Like other borrowers from mythic sources—Dante, Shakespeare, and Goethe—he was hunting for expressive metaphors to turn to his own purposes, and he took them where he found them. We need now to address more important questions: How did he use mythic resonances in his work, and how do they add to meaning?

Myths fall into two general categories, and Strindberg dealt expressively with both of them: (1) cosmogonies—creation tales of origins and beginnings; and (2) hero quests—stories of warriors and world redeemers, individuals who serve as exemplary models for more ordinary mortals. Although many of Strindberg's references to myth are subtle and even hidden, he wrote one undiluted creation play, inspired by and imitative of medieval drama: *Coram Populo, or De Creatione et Sententia vera Mundi (The Creation of the World and Its True Meaning)*, a brief "mystery," as he called it (2, 313-318). Written in 1877—78, it was published as a play-within-a-play in the epilogue to the verse version of the history play *Master Olof.* The author thought so highly of it that almost twenty years later he revised it into a kind of prologue for the original French version of the novel *Inferno*,[32] the epochal work with which he returned to belles lettres after his sojourn in the physical sciences.

Too slight to be important as drama, the modest, little creation play is nevertheless vital to an understanding of Strindberg's work; it is his Book of Genesis. Throughout a playwriting career of almost four decades, he adhered with amazing consistency to the metaphysical principles implied in *Coram Populo.*

In six acts and three settings (heaven, earth, and hell), the play includes the same cosmogonic panorama—Creation, Fall, Deluge, and coming of the Savior—mentioned earlier in the exoteric-esoteric catalogue of Strindberg's paintings. In the opening scene in heaven, the stage directions in the French version (a more complete play than the Swedish version) describe God as "an old man with a stern, almost wicked mien . . . and small horns like the Moses of Michelangelo." Lucifer, in contrast, has a halo over his head, is "young and handsome," and resembles Prometheus, Apollo, and Christ. God is bored and decides to create a new world.

GOD: From Nothingness it will be born and to Nothing-
            ness it will one day return. The creatures who live
            there will believe they are gods, like ourselves, and
            our entertainment will be to see their battles and
            their vanities. Its name will be the world of mad-
            ness. What says my brother Lucifer who divides
            with me these domains of the southern Milky Way?

LUCIFER: Sire, brother, that evil will of yours craves suffer-
            ings and misfortunes. I detest your idea
            . . .

            I arraign you before the tribunal of the Eternal One.

GOD: Well, I'm waiting! When do we ever see the Eternal
            One except during his visits to these regions once
            every tens of myriads of years?

The basic conflict is set in motion between a capricious,
sadistic Creator and his brother, the light bringer, who attempts
to thwart the evil design. The concept of such a conflict was
almost certainly derived, as Torsten Eklund has pointed out,
from Schopenhauer, where we find passages like the following
from *Parerga und Prolegomena*: "the world is Hell, and men are on
the one hand the tormented souls and on the other the devils in
it . . .; that a god like *Jehovah* should create this world of want
and misery *animi causa* and *de gaieté de coeur* and then go so far as
to applaud himself for it, saying it is all very good: that is quite
unacceptable."[33]

The reference in the scene to the Eternal One, a deity superior to God, indicates a relationship that brings to mind at least
two sources that might have been influential in the modeling of
the creator figure: the world artificer of Plato's *Timaeus* and the
demiurge of Gnosticism. In each instance the deity responsible
for creating the earth is of a lower order and ultimately answer-
able to a higher authority. Strindberg's God, as we see, is
hubristically contemptuous of the Eternal One and curses his
brother when Lucifer responds impertinently.

GOD: Thy place shall be under the world of madmen so
            that thou shalt see their torments, and men shall call
            you the Evil One.

In act two, on earth, Lucifer, in the guise of the Serpent,
persuades Adam and Eve to taste the forbidden fruit in order to
understand the terrible place they have been consigned to.

LUCIFER: You will become aware of good and evil. You will
            know then that life is evil, that you are not gods . . .
            and that your existence unfolds only to serve as a
            laughingstock for the gods. Eat of it, and you will
            possess the gift of deliverance from anguish: the joy
            of death!

Back in heaven, God counters by preventing men from
taking consolation in the fallen angel's message. He plants an

instinct that will prevent humanity from perishing: "They shall propagate before they die. Let there be love!"

Lucifer tries to fulfill his promise to men by destroying all life with a Deluge, but in the Ark God manages to save two of the "least enlightened," who will surely forget Lucifer's example. Before God can rejoice in his victory, however, bad news comes from below through a messenger angel.

URIEL: Lucifer has given them a plant called the vine, whose juice cures ignorance and confusion. One drop of wine and men see things as they are.

GOD: The fools! They don't know that I have endowed their plant with strange qualities: madness, sleep, and forgetfulness. With this plant, they will no longer remember what their eyes have seen.

But there is more bad news: Lucifer has given men other "gifts" of liberation: war, pestilence, hunger, storm, and fire. Moreover, he has taught them to question, and they have built a tower to storm heaven for answers. God retaliates by cursing men with a love for life and by afflicting "their tongues so that they will ask questions without answers." Lucifer, in turn, sends his "only son," whose mission is to "liberate men, and with his own death aspires to abolish the fear of death."

At this point the original Swedish version ends with God's angry reaction: "They still don't know anything, the madmen!" The line is missing in the later French version, and the scene continues with God ordering the angels to spill the globe into the abyss and turn it into a penal colony: "Fix on the brow of this cursed planet the gallows, token of crime, punishment, and anguish." The results of this action, according to the angel Egyn, are catastrophic:

The earth bolts in its orbit, the mountains crumble, the waters flood the land; the axis aims to the north, toward cold and darkness; plague and famine ravage the nations; love has changed to deadly hate, filial devotion to parricide. Men believe they are in hell, and you, Sire, you are dethroned.

God sees that his authority has been undermined by his own creations, and he regrets having started the whole business: "I have deposited sparks of my soul into impure beings whose fornications degrade me as the wife defiles her husband by defiling her body." To the amazement of the angels, who believe the whole universe is going insane, God prostrates himself and begs forgiveness from the Eternal One, whose power he had earlier scoffed. The play ends with Egyn's somber observation: "Thus goes the world: the gods at play lead mortals astray."

Because the little creation play is filled with lively, outrageous humor, one is tempted to dismiss it as a sardonic joke, but it is far more important than that for several reasons. In spirit it is generally faithful to the Gnostic *Weltanschauung*, with a view of the earth as a prison created by the evil underling demiurge, a place of darkness and suffering where mortals are the containers of sparks of divine light that have been trapped in matter.[34] Men can be liberated, however, to the transcendental "other world" of their origin through knowledge, *gnosis*, of that luminous realm whose ruler is a supreme god representing absolute good. What Strindberg adds to the Gnostic metaphysical design is a marvelous tension. Each of God's curses and Lucifer's gifts is made ambivalent, either because of the essential nature of the curse or gift in question or the motivation of the sender. For example, love of life, isolated, can be interpreted as a blessing, but as part of a scheme to trap man in worldly delusion, it is an evil; conversely, death may be a blessing because it comes from a compassionate source as an offer of liberation from the delusion, but it is also a fearful enemy. Consequently, each curse contains a positive charge of energy, and each gift a negative one, and the incongruity produces flashes of grim comedy: comedy filled with pain, but comedy nonetheless. In this way, a line like God's command "Let there be love!" turns Him into a parody of the Creator God, Yahweh, of the Book of Genesis, but the joke is on man as well as God. In later plays—*Creditors* is a good example—Strindberg employed the same kind of tension to produce the variety of comedy that made him the most important precursor of the theatre of the absurd: black metaphysical farce.

The creation play is also important for the adversary relationships established between Lucifer and God and between God and the Eternal One: they are models for character relationships that served Strindberg well from the beginning of his career to the end. As we shall see later, the major difference between the Swedish and French versions of the play—God's repentent declaration of obedience to the Eternal One—reveals a profound change in outlook that contributed much to Strindberg's development as an artist.

In Lucifer's decision to risk the wrath of the demiurge and attempt to liberate mankind is reflected the dangerous journey implicit in the second category of myth: the hero quest. Strindberg's interest in the concept of the mythic hero appears even earlier in his writings than his interest in cosmogony. Two of the references are to the Norse Thor: Thorwaldsen, the sculptor—protagonist of *In Rome*, and the central figure in a painting by M. E. Winge, which Strindberg reviewed in an essay in 1872. There Thor is shown charging in his chariot, preparing to slay some of his enemies, the giants, with his mighty hammer. The young critic quickly made clear that he was more interested in the theme than the artist's technique, and, not surprisingly in an incipient playwright, his focus was on the action:

> Who is this who rides through the dark clouds, his wheels shooting sparks? It is . . . the first manifestation of the Eternal Spirit, it is the light! . . . He is calm in his wrath because he is certain of his triumph. And these heavy bodies, difficult to distinguish from the clods and stones that follow them as they fall, are they evil spirits? No, they are great children, conscious of their own strength but not how to use it. Why must they fall? They are born to die, and they are lighthearted in the moment of death as if they had a presentiment of better things to come. It is today's childhood that has to die; adolescence is setting in; the Spirit has awakened and with the recklessness of youth he storms ahead over the bodies of the fallen—it is the day that follows the night; it is a victory cry, a mighty "let there be light!" (*54*, 177–178).

On one level, we can read in the passage projections of the young writer's personal enthusiasms, ethnic and political. Like many students and intellectuals of the day, he was an avid supporter of the revival of Pan-Nordic ideals; and "The Spirit has awakened" was one of his favorite rallying cries, reflecting his strong antiestablishment sentiments. On another level, we see Strindberg being drawn inexorably into a larger, more universal arena, into what he himself called the "dark world of myth, where fantasy was allowed to play unrestrainedly" (179).

Thor comes charging out of the dark clouds on a special mission; he has a calling; he swings his hammer not just to protect himself but to save mankind. The explicit enemies are the forces of reaction, the decadent ideas in the social canon, which must give way to new truths. The implicit enemies are, first, the hero's own fears, which, as the author indicates, Thor has already conquered, and second, the darkness. The god not only brings light; like the Lucifer of the creation play he personifies the light of consciousness that must and will triumph over the darkness of the unconscious. And the victory is a glorious one. The fallen are not even in pain, partly because their consciousness is so limited, and partly because they sense that their dying implies a rebirth; when they revive they will be part of the light instead of the darkness. What we have is a classic inventory of the mythic hero's attributes—courage, strength, self-sacrifice, and wisdom. The obstacles he must overcome are as much within as without. These are the secrets Strindberg said he found in myth: poetic insights into the evolution of human consciousness, psychic/spiritual truths about man's search for self-realization, framed in such striking images that their power to compel our attention survives the disappearance of the civilizations that once believed in them as literally true. Many years after the Winge painting review, in his essay "In the Cemetery" (1896), Strindberg defended the telling of fairy tales and legends to children on the grounds that "they let the child in his imagination undergo his phylogenesis, in other words: to experience the earlier stages of his existence, just as the foetus in the womb passes through the whole line of its evolution as an animal" (27, 604).[35]

In his plays Strindberg used mythic structures as blueprints for the search for self-realization, interpreting the conflict in the search as an intrapsychic dialogue in which confrontations are staged, as in the description of Thor and the giants, between forces representing the conscious and the unconscious. Over the past half century research into the psychological and literary values in myth by C. G. Jung, Erich Neumann, Northrup Frye, Bruno Bettelheim, Joseph Campbell, Mircea Eliade, and others has demonstrated that the hero-quest structure is a common form for the expression of intrapsychic confrontations.[36] More than a century ago Strindberg began a career of experimenting with the poetic and dramatic possibilities present in the various components of the quest theme: the knight errant who must answer a calling; the dragons and trolls he must battle; and the maiden he must liberate from her prison in a tower or a castle. Maiden and tower imagery play especially important roles as early as 1872 in *Master Olof* and as late as 1907 in *The Ghost Sonata*, as we shall see. In psychological terms, the knight, dragon, and maiden can be thought of not as separate entities but as disparate, alienated aspects of a single individual. The calling, then, is a challenge to the hero to conquer his own fears and selfish instincts and to liberate his creative potential.

Although quest and cosmogony are separate myth categories, they are interrelated. If the quest depicts the struggle of the hero to achieve a new vision, a new world, the creation myth reveals the origin and dynamics of the social matrix from which the hero developed and against which he must rebel. One of the tasks a hero is sometimes expected to perform is the restoration of a condition of existence that once prevailed but has been lost. A common feature of many creation myths is the emergence of a dualistic world of opposites and multiplicity where originally there had been a unifed oneness. The paradisiacal state Adam and Eve know in Eden implies an absence of conflict, a harmonious, eternal unity. But then they taste the fruit of the Tree of Knowledge. The light of consciousness enables them to distinguish good from evil, to know the world of opposites, but the unity is shattered. Consciousness, therefore, is a mixed blessing. With it, man can separate light from darkness and bring order out of chaos, but nothing can totally compensate for the loss of the original harmony. In Eden the garden is full and luxurious and there is understanding between man and God; outside is a thorny desert where life is a struggle and God is often an intimidating, fearful puzzle. In this context the hero myth can be thought of as an extension of the creation myth. The hero has the skills and courage necessary to restore the oneness, but microcosmically instead of macrocosmically, by making himself a whole person.

Strindberg returned to these two basic mythic patterns again and again in questions that are at once mythic, metaphoric, psychological, and metaphysical: What are the hero's responsibilities, and how must he fulfill them? How can man become reconciled to the loss of Eden, and more importantly perhaps, how can he become reconciled with a Creator who banished him from the oneness into a world of disharmony and yet left him free to dream, painfully, of the time before the Fall?

Existential alienation and the attendant search for reconciliation of the human and the divine are the most powerful themes in Strindberg's drama; man and God are the central characters, usually in a metaphoric sense, though sometimes literally. Some scholars and critics have regarded the themes as fundamentally religious, asking whether Strindberg ever found the faith he searched so long for, whether the many references in his work to figures such as Christ constitute primarily evidence of religious conviction or an artist's fascination with symbols or both. Other scholars, emphasizing psychological implications, have interpreted the suggestion of man-God confrontations as simply symptomatic of the emotional stress the author was suffering. I have chosen an eclectic approach, drawing insights from a variety of sources that focus attention on the interplay so characteristic in myth between psychological and metaphysical meaning. On the whole, the sources chosen are more Jungian than Freudian. In my view, strict Freudian interpretations often reduce meaning to a single dimension: biology. Myth offers an instructive example here: the Greeks perceived in the concept of Eros, more than a blunt personification of sexual desire, the entire driving, generative force of the universe. In his handling of the theme of the psychology of eroticism, Strindberg, like all the great dramatists, was a master, and in his plays, as in myth, sexuality has a metaphysical as well as a physical dimension.

It is customary to divide Strindberg's artistic career into two parts: before and after the Inferno period. It is also customary to describe the first part as basically naturalistic and the second as basically symbolistic, or at any rate nonrealistic. It is also possible to define the parts as different phases in the relationship between the mortal and the divine. The differences become apparent when one examines creation-myth and hero-quest resonances in two plays, *Miss Julie* and *To Damascus* Part One, written a decade apart.

In *Miss Julie* (1888) Strindberg effected a brilliant interpenetration of myth, fairy tale, the psychology of eroticism, and the socioeconomic implications of class conflict. Julie's butler Jean tells how as the poor child of a servant he worshipped her from afar; she was the lonely little rich girl whose elegant gardens contained the golden apples he sorely longed for. He admits, however, that as a child he feared the guards who were like cherubim protecting the gate to Eden, and his confession of timidity, as we shall see, is a very telling dramatic foreshadowing. On a sensuous midsummer eve, wine and beer are the forbidden fruits Julie and Jean taste, and the knowledge they subsequently acquire about the devastating power of sexual attraction and the insuperable barrier of class differences is too much for them to assimilate. This Adam and Eve are totally lost, and Jean's kitchenmaid mistress, Kristin, becomes a dark angel of the Lord, condemning their transgression. In the end, Julie is a suicide and Jean is reduced to a whimpering lackey. Neither was equal to facing the consequences of the Fall.

The Stranger in *To Damascus* (1898) is another kind of character in another kind of drama. At the beginning of the play he is a lonely man, adrift from family and society. A writer who was made a pariah because he outraged the cultural canon of his day by revealing its corruption, his creativity has run dry. Even more than Julie and Jean, he is alienated and an outcast, but in contrast with them he has the courage to take the long journey to find himself; on the way he may be struck with divine lightning—as Saul was struck on the road to Damascus and transformed into Paul—and reacquire a calling, able once again to perform great deeds. At the start of the journey he picks a new mate and names her Eve; it is the dawn of a new Creation. When he learns that she is captive in an unhappy marriage to a Doctor nicknamed the "Werewolf",[37] the Stranger steals the damsel away from the dragon. By the end of the play he has learned something about himself: that the search for self implies the necessity of confronting a concept or entity larger than one's own ego, whatever name or supernatural identity is assigned to it. Although the Stranger discovers that he risks hubris in the search, he also discovers that through expiation he can approach reconciliation with the suprapersonal power whom he respects but before whom he is not prepared to cringe, as Jean cringes in *Miss Julie*. For Jean, the servile valet, all orders come from above, literally and figuratively. Although his master, the Count, never appears on stage, he hovers over the action like a forbidding Yahweh figure out of the Old Testament. When the Count summons Jean with the ringing of a bell, the hapless servant is incapable of anything but obedience. The Stranger, like Jacob, however, is prepared to wrestle the angel all night long, even if it means paying for his arrogance with an injured hip.

In *Miss Julie* the divine force suggested is without and above: an unapproachable and unforgiving Yahweh. In *To Damascus*, the divine force is mystically within, an immanent God, and the most important confrontations the central character has are with doubles who represent his innermost self. The two plays thus imply not only two different concepts of God but two separate and often conflicting *Weltanschauung*, the first occidental and the second oriental, symbolized in the figures of Yahweh and Buddha.

There are significant female mythic figures in Strindberg's plays in addition to the males. Perhaps the most obvious ones are Eleonora in *Easter* and Agnes in *A Dream Play*, both examples of the godhead incarnate as victim/redeemer. Another female is prominent from first play to last, the Great Goddess in her maternal aspect: the Great Mother. If the Count in *Miss Julie* and the Doctor in *To Damascus* resemble Father Heaven, the Nurse in *The Father* and Mrs. Heyst in *Easter* represent Mother Earth. Here, too, as with the paternal figures, there is metamorphosis. In early plays such as *Master Olof* or *The Father* the Great Mother is the male protagonist's most potent enemy; the Captain's mother-in-law in the latter, although unseen like Julie's father, broods over the action offstage. In later plays like *To Damascus* and *Easter*, Great Mother characters function, not as enemies, but as chastisers who mean the heroes well and prepare them for decisive confrontations with paternal mythic figures.

In 1886, the year before he wrote *The Father*, Strindberg came in contact with the theories of one of the most important nineteenth-century interpreters of myth, the Swiss jurist and would-be philosopher Johan Jakob Bachofen (1815—1887). In a preface in the second of two volumes of short stories, *Getting Married*, Strindberg approvingly cited a passage from "Le Matriarcat," an essay in *La Nouvelle Revue*, by Paul Lafargue, a sociologist and disciple of Bachofen: "The patriarchal family is consequently a comparatively recent form of society, and its rise was marked by as many crimes as we may perhaps expect in the future, should society attempt to revert to matriarchy."[38] Reflected is the central theme in Bachofen's theory of the development of society, that a matriarchal system, an age of "mother right," preceded the existing patriarchy. The increase in social instability that Lafargue feared would accompany a retrogression to an earlier system is in harmony with Bachofen's belief that "every change in the relation between the sexes is attended by bloody events; peaceful and gradual change is far less frequent than violent upheaval."[39]

Most of the conclusions in Bachofen's major work, *Mother Right: An Investigation of the Religious and Juridical Character of Matriarchy in the Ancient World* (1861), were based on extensive research in Greco-Roman myth. In contrast to modern theorists, who do not regard myth and history as equally valid tools for analyzing the continuity of human development, Bachofen expressed his confidence that myth could "provide as definite and secure results as any other source of historical knowledge. Product of a cultural period in which life had not yet broken away from the harmony of nature, it shares with nature that unconscious lawfulness which is lacking in the works of free

reflection. Everywhere there is system, everywhere cohe-
sion . . ."[40]

At the time Strindberg read "Le Matriarcat," he had been
under attack for several years from influential quarters in
Swedish society. In the first volume of *Getting Married* (1884), he
had offended religious conservatives, through a casual reference
to Christ as a revolutionary, and feminists, through such statements in his introduction that "The Woman Question, upon
which the foundations of our society are now said to rest, seems
to me to be overrated."[41] When criticized, he responded in the
introduction to the second volume by using Lafargue's essay as
supporting evidence for his contention that the inevitable result
of attempts to emancipate women would be a disastrous return
to matriarchy.

Until now, scholars have interpreted Strindberg's references
to Lafargue and Bachofen[42] as simply indications in his polemical
writings of the contempt for feminism that was to emerge in his
drama and fiction and earn him the still unchallenged title as one
of the most prominent misogynists in the history of literature.
But this judgment fails to take into account the differences
between the polemicist and the dramatic poet. While the first,
especially in this period, seems ill-tempered, inconsistent, and
biased, the second was passionate, coherent, and above all
emotionally involved. By nature he was able to identify with
each of his characters, female as well as male, and made them all
come alive as believable people. It is possible that the polemicist
thought he had mounted a telling indictment of feminism in *The
Father*, but the text does not support his argument. Examined as
a piece of propaganda, the play is strident and unconvincing;
examined as a work of art, it is overwhelmingly powerful and
absorbing.

Anthropologically, Bachofen's theory of matriarchy preceding patriarchy was discredited by the turn of the century, but
his ideas about the stages through which mythic and religious
concepts evolve have had a continuing influence in comparative
mythology and religion and depth psychology. Erich Neumann, for example, saw the matriarchal stage not as a historical

entity but as a psychological reality "whose fateful power is still alive in the psychic depths of present day man."[43] And the most recent archaeological research, such as at the neolithic city unearthed in the last several decades at Çatal Hüyük in southern Turkey, sustains not only Bachofen's belief that a religion of the Great Mother preceded the great patriarchal religions of Judaism, Christianity, and Islam "but also his recognition of Syria and Asia Minor as the proximate Asiatic provinces from which the agriculturally based mother right culture complex came to the isles and peninsulas of Greece and Rome."[44]

Bachofen's stages in the transformation from mother to father right have astronomical designations: earth, moon, and sun, "the tellurian, corresponding to motherhood without marriage; the lunar, corresponding to conjugal motherhood and authentic birth; the solar, corresponding to conjugal father right."[45] The lowest stage of tellurian life is described as "Aphroditean," "characterized by unregulated sexual relation . . . by the communal holding of women, children, and consequently of all property."[46] Associated with nomadic life, the Aphroditean stage "knows no stable resting place other than the tomb." The Great Mother dominant in this stage is the Terrible Mother and her mythic embodiment is the Sphinx, representing "the feminine right of the earth in its dark aspect as the inexorable law of death. . . . She sends forth matter from darkness to light, and she will again consume it."[47] Pure tellurism "subordinates the male to the female principle, the ocean to the *gremium matris terrae* ('womb of mother earth'). The night is identified with the earth and interpreted as a maternal chthonian power; here the night is the oldest of deities and stands in a special relation to woman."[48]

The next stage begins with the transition from a nomadic to an agricultural life; Aphrodite is transformed into the Earth Mother, Demeter—Terrible Mother into Good Mother, one might say—or, to use Bachofen's vegetative imagery, the self-generating swamp growth, the Aphroditean "*creatio ultronea* ('wild plant life')", gives way to "*laborata Ceres* ('the tilled soil')."[49]

The earth becomes wife and mother, the man who guides the plow and scatters the seed becomes husband and father. The man is joined in wedlock with feminine matter, and this provides the model for an intimate, enduring, and exclusive relation between the sexes.

Woman has risen from pure tellurism to the lunar stage of existence. . . . The children now have a father as well as a mother, they are legitimate offspring.[50]

Only by degrees does the final, solar stage of father right gain ascendency and achieve total liberation from the maternal bond. In mythic terms Nietzsche was later to borrow for *The Birth of Tragedy* (he was a frequent guest in the Bachofen home in Basle in the early 1870s), Bachofen described the last two stages of solar development as Dionysian and Apollonian: "Dionysus merely raised paternity over the mother; Apollo frees himself entirely from any bond with woman. His paternity is motherless and spiritual, as in adoption, hence immortal, immune to the night of death which forever confronts Dionysus because he is phallic."[51]

Two of Strindberg's plays offer interesting parallels to Bachofen's stages in the mother- to father-right evolution: the pre-Inferno *The Father* and the post-Inferno *Easter*. I said earlier that the Nurse in the first play and Mrs. Heyst in the second were Mother Earth figures, but there is a difference: the Nurse is Aphroditic-tellurian and Mrs. Heyst Demetrian-lunar. Appropriate is the season of the year in which each play is set: in *The Father* it is the winter solstice, and the language of the play is heavy with ominous images of darkness and doom; in *Easter* it is the time of the vernal promise of rebirth, and the language is lush with vegetative imagery and references to the sun and hope and atonement. In the first play the hero, a cavalry captain, like an ancient warrior battling an enemy whose power he cannot comprehend, at least not rationally, faces a conspiracy of women, of mothers, led by his wife who seems bound to deny him his only link to immortality by suggesting that he is not his daughter's biological father. According to Bachofen, in the earliest stage of mother right only the mother's parenthood was unquestionable.[52] In the end the Captain dies in the arms of the childhood nurse who has always been his surrogate mother and who actually participates in his destruction. To paraphrase Bachofen: she who sent forth matter from darkness to life has again consumed it.

The male protagonist in *Easter* is also surrounded by women. In contrast to the Captain, however, he not only survives, but, thanks to the women, ascends to a higher level of self-awareness and fulfillment. Significantly, his name, Elis, links him with the sun symbols Helios and Apollo, reinforcing the mythic movement in the play from lunar to solar. As in *The Father*, a mother and daughter are closely connected to the play's central theme, but whereas in that play the emotional bond between Laura and her daughter, Bertha, generates conflict and alienation by opening a gulf between mother and father right, the bond that is reestablished in *Easter* between Mrs. Heyst and her daughter Eleonora contains the same healing power as the reunion of Demeter and Persephone and sets the stage for general reconciliation.

This is not to suggest, of course, that the first play is a simple repudiation and the second a simple affirmative of matriarchal power; as we shall see, Strindberg's handling of mythic themes was much more subtle and complex than that. The Captain may struggle against the authority of the old religious forms represented by the women in his home. He succumbs however, not because of the conspiracy but because he lacks the will to throw off the net closing in around him. Even as he complains about the tyranny of the women, he needs them and calls them to him. Joseph Campbell, writing as Bachofen did about the transformation from matriarchal to patriarchal symbolism, remarked on how tenaciously the old myths survive in the new; his comments can be applied to the Captain's fate as well:

> There is something forced and finally unconvincing about all the many moral attitudes of the shining righteous deedsmen, whether of the biblical or of the Greco-Roman schools; for, in revenge or compensation, *the ultimate life*, and therewith spiritual depth and interest, *of the myths in which they figure continues to rest*

with the dark presences of the cursed yet gravid earth, which, though defeated and subdued, are with their powers never totally absorbed. A residue of mystery remains to them; and this, through the history of the West, has ever lurked within, and emanated from, the archaic symbols of the later, "higher" systems—as though speaking silently, to say, "But do you not hear the deeper song?" (Italics added.)[53]

The demiurge and the Great Mother: they are but two of the archetypal figures who appear and reappear in Strindberg's plays in imagery drawn from that ancient and hallowed tradition, the "dark world of myth, where fantasy was allowed to play unrestrainedly."

The plays selected for discussion in this volume represent a compromise of sorts. To analyze all the implications of the use of myth in Strindberg's works would necessitate a study many times the size of this one. Among the items omitted from consideration are some of his most mythological plays: *The Crown Bride*, *Swanwhite*, and *Lucky Per's Journey*. Discussion is limited primarily to ones that established Strindberg's international reputation, with one exception, *Master Olof*, which signaled his arrival as an artist of major talent and reveals so clearly his mythopoeic instincts.

This book is motivated by a hope, persistent and perhaps vain, that a study of Strindberg's mythic imagery can be useful not only to the reader who pores over the text in his study but to the actor, director, or designer preparing a production; vain because we have lost the preconditions that once allowed mythic resonances to inform and enrich performances of drama with great power. Aeschylus and his actors and audiences, Shakespeare and his actors and audiences: in each instance, writer, performer, and spectator shared a common storehouse of mythic and religious associations that allowed subtle meanings to be exchanged quickly and easily between them. In our day, this kind of easy interplay is impossible: even people educated in the classics strain to remember the characters and plots of the old myths. But as Jung and others have so eloquently demonstrated, even if individual myths have been forgotten, the ancient structures of meaning that they represented reappear continually in the most modern of the arts. Question: If actors, directors, and designers can be made more aware of these structures, might they not be able to create richer, denser productions? It is in the belief that an exploration of the mythopoeic dimension in Strindberg's plays can help produce such results that this book is grounded.

2

Master Olof

Given Strindberg's interest in myth, the choice of dramatic form for what was to become his first important play seems a natural one. The history play lends itself readily to enrichment by mythic resonances. The mythic hero has two tasks: to save himself and to save mankind, and success or failure at the one is inseparable from success or failure at the other. Playwrights from Shakespeare to Goethe to Brecht have found the form an expressive vehicle for exploring the interaction between man, the psychological animal, and man, the political animal: man with responsibilities to himself and his individual destiny and man with responsibilities to his fellow men and to the renewal of the cultural tradition that is his legacy.

The setting of *Master Olof* is Sweden in the 1520s, at the dawn of the Reformation. For his central character Strindberg picked a historical figure at the center of a storm of conflict: Olaus Petri, later called Master Olof, a Catholic clergyman who turns Protestant reformer, the Swedish Luther. Olof, to accomplish his goal of bringing Luther's message to Sweden, must contend with a variety of forces: the Church, which is trying to silence him; ordinary churchgoers who resent the corrupt activities they see practiced by the clergy but who resist change; and King Gustav Vasa, who, less interested in spiritual goals than political ones, wants to cancel the power enjoyed by the papacy in Sweden and to acquire its resources for national, secular purposes.

The incident that starts Olof on the road to rebellion at the opening of the play is set in the town of Strängnäs, where the clergy have locked the doors to the church because the required tithes have not been paid. On the important eve of Pentecost the people are denied religious services. The time is ripe for a leader to galvanize their discontent into action. Olof seems an unlikely candidate at this moment. He is busy rehearsing a play with a group of young confirmands. The play's theme is the plight of the people of Israel in the Babylonian captivity, praying for God's pledge to Abraham to be redeemed. A friend and colleague of Olof, Lars Andersson, chides him for only "playing" about the needs of an imprisoned people; a greater task of real liberation awaits him. The mythic structure of the hero quest is easily discernible: a national crisis demands a liberator who must answer a call to action. Lars Andersson is the herald who brings the call. But Olof hesitates. He feels he is too young and his faith has been undermined. Lars responds with the admonition Jeremiah received from God to gird up his loins and advance to preach His word. Apprehensive, but with an almost adolescent eagerness for the struggle, Olof accepts the call.

But another herald comes to complicate things: the rabble-rousing revolutionary, Gert Bookprinter, one of Strindberg's outstanding, early dramatic creations. Where Lars suggested the bright, if rather vague healing prospects presented by the coming of a new order, Gert suggests the specific dark violence that may be necessary to destroy the old one. He points out that there are two enemies, not one. The first is the pope, author of spiritual repression; the second is the emperor, author of political repression. Vasa, according to Gert, is as great a threat to freedom as the Church. The Reformation in the spiritual realm must be accompanied by a revolution in the political realm.

Luther was satisfactory as far as he went, says Gert: "He made a beginning. We have to continue!"(2, 21). Olof is faced with a difficult decision: spiritual freedom seems to be inseparable from political freedom, but the destruction of the old order, no matter how justified, threatens to unleash chaos.

Behind Olof and Gert's relationship is a mythic model: Adam and Lucifer. "I am the cast-out angel," Gert boasts (19). He has recently been released from an insane asylum, in which he says he was confined for having received the Holy Spirit. "Just now," Olof says to him," "you look like Satan . . . where did you learn to be so shrewd?" Gert replies, "In the mad-house"(23, 25). Questions arise that weaken Olof's resolve: Is Gert an ally or an enemy? His person is mysterious and his message unnerving. Finally, however, infected by Gert's strange energy and power, Olof overcomes his apprehensions and takes a momentous step: he defies the clergy's ban, rings the vesper bell, and offers to conduct services.

The last important figure to appear in act one is the king, who has no knowledge of Gert's political ambitions and only little of Olof's spiritual ones. But he knows an opportunity when he sees one: the young heretical Olof can be used as a weapon against the Church, so Vasa appoints him to an important government post in Stockholm. "I've acquired a pointer who can raise the game," the king is heard to say. "We'll have to see if he comes back when I whistle"(37).

The situation in *Master Olof* offers splendid mythopoeic opportunities: a hero at a crossroads of history, struggling for self-realization in a larger context of great potential social and spiritual realization. Like many another Renaissance religious reformer, Olof has a vision of men free to respond to the dictates of their own consciences instead of the rule of religious author-ity. But to battle the pope he must make league with the emperor, and even as one tyranny is broken, another is estab-lished. Under Vasa, Swedish citizens do gain more spiritual freedom, but far less than Olof had hoped for. And although national unity is achieved, Vasa is ruthless and the costs of unity are high in terms of the loss of individual liberties. In the end Olof is denied the satisfaction enjoyed by the mythic hero. He has neither forged a new condition of freedom for man nor restored a paradisiacal golden age. He has only assisted in the creation of a new kind of prison. But the mythic resonances inform the play with a marvelous tension produced by the discrepancy between the hope and the reality, between the lofty goals toward which Olof strives and the distance by which he falls short. He may be an imperfect mythic hero, but an important dimension has been added to the characterization, like a template against which we can measure Olof's strengths and weaknesses.

In some instances, the mythopoeic template used is too obvious, a fault Strindberg learned to avoid as he matured as an artist. For example, in the rowdy tavern scene that opens act two Olof enters and defends a prostitute against attacks from self-righteous clergymen. He becomes the Christ who invites those who are without sin to cast the first stone and who advises the woman to go and sin no more. More subtle is a mythic resonance evoked at the end of the scene through an old theatrical convention, a tableau. As Olof is about to lead the prostitute out the door, two women enter: Olof's mother and Kristina, Gert's daughter, whom Olof later marries. When the old woman catches sight of her son with the prostitute, according to the stage directions, she is "beside herself" (59). "Olof! Olof!" she reproaches, and exits. He rushes to the door, but it is slammed in his face, leaving him to shout helplessly, "Mother! Mother!" as the curtain falls.

There is a strangely unreal quality to this brief moment, as if an image were flashing by in a dream. Although brief, it is important preparation for what is to come; Olof's pained response to his mother's disapproval casts a long shadow. The three women present are more than flesh–and–blood figures, they are three of the symbolic faces of woman as the eternal feminine: the siren or temptress, the mother, and the maiden or beloved. Part of the mythic hero's task is to overcome his fascination with the power of the first two in order to unite with the third. Here is Olof's main stumbling block: his mother's power is awesome. As the play develops we see her come to symbolize all the reactionary forces Olof must battle, both outside himself and within, religious as well as political. She wants him to remain a Catholic and a priest and does everything she can to bend him to her will. She is mother and Mother Church. Above all she is the Great Goddess, *Magna Mater*: the Great Mother of myth and legend. Olof's plaintive "Mother! Mother!" echoes Faust's cry "The Mothers! Mothers—sound with wonder haunted." According to Jung, the "realm of the Mothers," which so fascinates Faust, "has not a few connections with the womb, with the matrix, which frequently symbolizes the creative aspect of the unconscious."[1] But this creative aspect is like a prize or treasure that must be fought for to be won. The Great Mother is at first the Good Mother, the source of all sustenance and comfort. But there comes a time, says Erich Neumann, when the Great Mother no longer appears as friendly and good, but becomes the hero's enemy, the Terrible Mother, and this enemy must be vanquished if he is to succeed in his quest.[2] Olof confronts this necessity when he proceeds to the threshold of adventure: the antechamber of Stockholm's Great Church, where he will preach the new Lutheran doctrine and risk provoking the hostility of parishioners and religious and secular officials alike.

Strindberg chose an appropriate place for his hero's first test: a church chamber is a traditional vessel of transformation and rebirth and in this way related to caves, cauldrons, ships, and even great fish. As Noah journeys in the ark to find a new Creation, Heracles and Jonah each travel in the bellies of sea creatures and emerge more complete human beings. In many myths such transformation chambers have guardians who stand at the entrances to prevent the heroes from gaining access to the treasure. Olof also encounters a guardian, his mother. She appears as he is about to enter the pulpit and tries to intimidate him with news of the terrible consequences he will suffer if he preaches: church authorities are negotiating to bring the Inquisition to Sweden to deal with heretics. But Olof will not be deterred. The God who protected Daniel in the lion's den will also protect him. He goes to preach. The guardian has been bypassed; the Great Mother has been thwarted, at least temporarily, and the hero has passed his first major test.

When Olof returns from his ordeal in the pulpit, having been
stoned by angry parishioners, Kristina is there to comfort him.
Quickly they realize how much they love each other, but a
discordant note is struck. Whereas she is happy that she did not
wait for the dashing knight she dreamt of as a child, he visualizes
her as the embodiment of a romantic fantasy. "You were the fair
maiden of my dreams," he tells her, "imprisoned in the tower by
the stern lord of the castle, and now you're mine!"(82). This is
the image configuration of maiden and tower. Kristina responds
with a warning: "Beware of dreams, Olof!" She seems to feel
that Olof does not understand all the implications of freeing the
maiden, and she is right. Shortly thereafter, they are married,
and Olof tells her of the price of the maiden's liberation.

OLOF: Why are you so happy today?
KRISTINA: Shouldn't I be happy when I've escaped from bond-
             age by becoming your wife?
OLOF: Forgive me if my happiness is less joyful, since it
             cost me—a mother! (118).

Later in the same scene Kristina is emboldened in Olof's
absence to say to his mother the things for which he lacks the
will: "Do you believe that it's your child's mission to sacrifice his
life just to show you gratitude? His calling urges: 'Go!' You
shout: 'Ingrate, come here!'" (122). Olof is not happy, however,
when he returns and finds his mother leaving the house in anger,
vowing never to forgive him.

It is not long before Kristina and Olof are estranged from
each other in their own home. She complains to Olof's brother,
Lars: "He wants me to be like a saint, standing on a shelf" (136).
Olof did not realize that saving the maiden entailed accepting
her as a simple human being.

Olof's marital difficulties are not an isolated issue, they are
part of a larger problem: an inability to cope with the guilt that is
part of the hero's destiny. He feels guilty for defying his mother's wishes by marrying Kristina as he feels guilty for having
turned his back on the Catholic church. Later the guilt becomes
an almost impossible burden when he is summoned by the news
that his mother is dying.

The mother's deathbed scene in act four brings about the final confrontation between the hero and the great goddess, and nothing in Strindberg's early work demonstrates more convincingly the sureness of his instincts as a dramatist than this brilliant, chilling scene. Although the old woman is dying, she controls the situation with supreme authority. She knows the persuasive force she has at her disposal, and she exploits it to the full. Wisely, she banishes the independent Kristina from her sight. When Olof arrives, he is powerless to wrest an advantage. As his mother lapses into semiconsciousness, he kneels by her bed to ask forgiveness. The mood of the confrontation becomes eerie, like the meeting of a suppliant and a primitive goddess.

> OLOF: Mother, Mother, if you're still alive, talk to your son! Forgive me . . . Do you want me to obey you and so destroy what cost so much pain and tears? Forgive me!
>
> MOTHER: Olof! . . . turn back, sever the unclean bond your body has entered into. Take up again the faith I gave you, and I'll forgive you! . . .
>
> OLOF: [after a pause]: No!
>
> MOTHER: God's curse upon you! . . . Cursed be the hour I gave you birth! [She dies.]
>
> OLOF: Mother! Mother! [taking her hand] She's dead! Without forgiving me! (145–146).

Olof's refusal at this crucial moment to return to the old faith is his most courageous act against his mother, but it is a Pyrrhic victory. He seems to realize that her death means that ultimate forgiveness and reconciliation are forever out of reach. Pathetically, he lights the consecrated candles, which he despises as symbols of an obsolete faith, and begs her spirit for forgiveness.

Recovering after a short time from what he calls a "moment of weakness"(147), Olof horrifies his brother by exulting in their mother's death: "She was too old, and I thank God she died. Oh, now I'm free—for the first time! It was God's will"(150). The mother's death has had an effect like that of the death of the fairy tale dragon's: a spell has been broken and vital energies released. Olof is able to express the dread he has felt:

> OLOF: If she hadn't died now, I don't know how much more I would have had to sacrifice. Brother, have

you seen in the spring how last year's fallen leaves
cover the ground and try to smother the young
plants coming up? What do the young ones do?
They either shove the dry leaves aside or go right up
through them because they *have* to come up
(150–151).

But this heroic outburst smacks of bravado. Why is it that only
after her death is he able to repudiate what she stood for? His
mind may accept the justice that demands that new plants force
their way if necessary past last year's dead leaves, but his heart
knows that it is all a lie.

This is not the only scene in a Strindberg work in which the
image of a dead or dying mother dominates. In his autobiography, *Son of a Servant Woman*, there are two such scenes: one
involving the narrator's foster mother and the other his real
mother; and in *A Dream Play* a flashback to the Officer's childhood returns him to the time when his mother's death was
imminent. An expressive example of the image appears in the
novella *The Romantic Organist on Rånö*. The organist of the title
has never really recovered from the loss of his mother, who died
under mysterious circumstances when he was a boy.

Whatever it was that had happened during that difficult winter
when his mother died seemed in the youngster's mind to demand
a burial, a thick covering of earth and stones, an entire cairn of
other memories to prevent it from rising up again. And when the
trivial events of his tedious little life could not supply material
fast enough, he invented things, masses of impressions, and piled
up fabrications, hallucinations, imagined sounds in order to
construct a thick layer that would cover the dark spot (*21*, 245).[3]

In each of the scenes mentioned the maternal figure retains her
power over her son, for even as her image recedes beyond the
grave, it sinks simultaneously deep into his unconscious, there
to lodge as an autonomous force, independent of his will.

Whatever energies were released by Olof's mother's death,
their effect on him is devastating. He throws himself full force
into the conspiracy against the king, which is given new impetus
when Vasa, although finally succeeding in nullifying papal
power in Sweden, gives no firm support for the goal Olof
considered most important: recognition of the legitimacy of

Luther's teachings. At the opening of act five the conspirators meet at night in the ruins of a convent in a scene that has the quality of a Judgment Day panorama. The playwright, borrowing the apparatus of gothic melodrama—moonlit ruins, open graves, torchlight processions, and conspirators gathered in a tomb—orchestrates a coda of the themes and conflicts in the play, religious, political, and psychological. In accordance with the king's orders, church property is being confiscated and converted to secular purposes. As royal workmen dismantle papal power, Olof, Gert, and others plot the destruction of royal power. Destroying the old order seems indeed to have unleashed chaos because Olof's actions as a member of the conspiracy are so indiscreet and reckless that he seems to be actually inviting arrest, as though he were compelled to act out personally the consequences of his mother's curse. But he is still ambivalent about his commitment; even as he urges that the king be killed, he says "Let's go before I regret it"(2, 167). Olof's basic problem remains unresolved: because he has never really accepted the task of finding himself, he is an incomplete hero, unable to be devoted unequivocally to any cause.

The conspiracy is short-lived, and in the final scene, set in Stockholm's Great Church, Olof and Gert are strapped in a pillory, disgraced, waiting to be executed for treason. Olof is told that his life will be spared if he publicly repents his subversive actions. At first he refuses but then yields to the Lord High Constable's argument that he is needed by the church, his parishioners, and especially his young wife. By contrast, Gert goes to his death with his integrity intact, and Strindberg gives him the last line in the play, an accusation shouted to Olof from offstage: "Renegade!"(184).

It has been argued that in yielding Olof was finally responding to earlier appeals made to him by Kristina to be more human: "You won't fall from your heights," she said, "if you put away your solemn talk and for once let the cloud fade from your brow. Are you too great to look at a flower or listen to a bird?"(119). His action in the pillory, however, comes too late. He is not triumphing by realizing another dimension in himself; he is surrendering his ideals in order to survive. Responding earlier might have brought about a heroic transformation within; now he is simply accepting a dictum from without. If Olof's story is ignominy in victory, Gert's is triumph in death. One leaves the play, especially a production of it, remembering Gert's voice as much as or more than Olof's. Gert may not be the central character, but he is the most striking and complex invention in the play. On a realistic level the figure can be viewed as an accurate, straightforward portrait of a revolutionary type, resembling a participant in the Paris Commune, the violent destiny of which was played out only months before Strindberg wrote *Master Olof*. Part zealot, part scoundrel, part radical, and part madman, Gert is a member of that special breed that every revolution needs.

On a mythic level, Gert evokes several images, one of which, as mentioned earlier, is Luciferian. In the sketches and outlines for the play, Strindberg experimented with several last names for him: Cooper, Powdermaker, and Potter.[4] The name he finally selected, Bookprinter, is almost too obviously symbolic of Gert's role as the bringer of light and truth. The other characters sense in him a frightening, supernatural quality; he seems possessed of divine energy. A clue to the nature of his mysterious presence is contained in the seriousness with which he treats the concept of Pentecost.

> GERT: You see, Olof, it's Pentecost now. The time when
>   the Holy Spirit descended and poured over the
>   Apostles—no, over all humanity. You can receive
>   the Holy Spirit; I've received it because I believed
>   it. God's spirit has come down to me, I feel it; that's
>   why they locked me up as insane, but now I'm free.
>   Now I'll speak the word, for you see, Olof, now
>   we're on the mountain!(21–22).

Pentecost—regarded as the origin, the birthday of the Church—is a spirit of new beginning. As such it resembles both the spirit of the Reformation, when *Master Olof* takes place, and the spirit of revolution, a concept much on Strindberg's mind at the time he wrote the play. Here, too, there is a mythic structure. Like its religious counterparts, the spirit of revolution contains the promise of a day of reckoning—a Deluge, or a

Ragnarök to destroy the corruption of the past—and the dawning of a golden era; and it creates icons of its saints and martyrs. In *Master Olof* the modern political radicalism ignited by the American and French revolutions reverberates behind the Reformation fever of the sixteenth century.

At one point in the play, when, momentarily, the spiritual revolution seems to have been accomplished, Olof expresses disappointment: "It wasn't victory I wanted, it was the struggle"(128). What he fails to see is that Gert's call to him to join the revolution is not only an invitation to an outward journey to adventure but a true quest: an inward journey to self-realization. The revolution—spiritual and political—must begin and end within, and Gert articulates this message through the expressive symbolism of Pentecost and the Holy Spirit, especially in his final speeches to Olof: "Even if the whole world says you're wrong, believe your heart, if you have the courage. The day you deny yourself, you're dead, and eternal damnation will be a mercy to the one who has sinned against the Holy Spirit"(179). In the Gospel of John, Jesus promises the Apostles at the Last Supper that after he is gone the Father will send in his name a *Paraclete*, the Holy Spirit, who "will teach you everything, and will call to mind all that I have told you."[5] In Strindberg's novel *Inferno*, the narrator speaks of someone coming as "a messenger from Providence, a Paraclete"(28, 82). The word is from the Greek *parakletos* and can be translated as "advocate," in a juridical selse, suggesting a public defender who represents the common people. Jesus assures the Apostles that though their faith will be tested—"They will ban you from the synagogue"—the Paraclete-advocate "will confute the world, and show where wrong and right and judgment lie." And when he comes, this "Spirit of truth," "he will not speak on his own authority, but will tell only what he hears; and he will make known to you the things that are coming."[6]

There are interesting parallels between the Paraclete and Gert Bookprinter. It is on the eve of Pentecost that Gert first brings his message of truth to people who have been banned from the temple. Later, when the conspiracy against the king is at its height, Gert shows Olof a book in which he has collected

masses of testimony to demonstrate that Vasa's new tyranny is
as corrupt as the old papal variety:

OLOF: Who wrote this book?
GERT: The people! . . . I've asked them: Are you happy?
             and here are the answers. I've held court sessions,
             and the verdicts are inscribed here (2, 165).

Like the Paraclete, Gert is a defender of the people, an advocate,
and as a spirit of truth, he "will not speak on his own authority,
but will tell only what he hears." In one of Strindberg's character outlines, Gert is referred to as "pure spirituality,"[7] and his
resemblance to the Paraclete lends special meaning to his warning: "The day you deny yourself, you're dead, and eternal
damnation will be a mercy to the one who has sinned against the
Holy Spirit." Denying oneself and sinning against the Holy
Spirit are synonymous in this context. Olof denied himself by
compromising his calling and so incurred the one unforgivable
sin, mentioned not once but three times in the New Testament
gospels: "No sin, no slander, is beyond forgiveness for men; but
whoever slanders the Holy Spirit can never be forgiven; he is
guilty of eternal sin."[8]

The symbolism of the two polar forces working on Olof's
will—his mother and Gert—reveals deep affinities with mythic
and mystic traditions. Olof can be seen as a divine spark trapped
in matter, represented by the feminine authority of his mother
and the Mother Church, and he is urged to seek liberation by
Gert, who is the masculine force of spirit. As Gert is about to
die, he scoffs at those who think that because the conspirators
have been caught the revolution is over: "There are conspirators
all around us—in palace chambers, in the churches and out on
the town squares"(179). In other words, there are potential
recruits everywhere for the revolution of spirit. The gift of the
Holy Spirit was a guarantee that despite the Crucifixion there
would be continuity in the new harmony between man and
God. Gert offers a new continuity: out of the old view that held
that the road to spiritual fulfillment was through religious forms
and practices comes a new vision in which spiritual fulfillment is
inseparable from the goals of freedom and social justice. Gert

finds all violence, spiritual as well as physical, equally abhorrent and calls for a new allegiance, not to outside authorities, religious or secular, but to one's own inner resources, resources epitomized in the example of the mythic hero. The implication is that, though God may be dead and the church only a vestigial institution, the symbol of the Holy Spirit can still serve to energize psychic potential for self-realization.

If Olof's mother represents that aspect of the past that is a deadening burden to him rather than a fruitful heritage, Gert is the future, not as a romantic promise of wish fulfillment, but as a challenge, as a difficult, but ultimately rewarding road toward self-understanding. Olof unfortunately never learns the true nature of the choice confronting him. Like Lot's wife, he is unable to resist the temptation to look back and so never escapes the prison of the past.

The opposing archetypal extremes of Kristina and the mother also pose an impossible choice for Olof: he cannot reconcile the debt he owes his mother with the fulfillment he owes his wife. The fact that they are both named Kristina underscores the difficulty he faces trying to separate the demands each woman makes on him: the beloved beckoning the hero toward maturity, the mother striving to keep him her obedient child.

Olof fails to secure the "treasure" selfhood, so often associated with the hero quest. The psychic blueprints for the meaning of this failure Strindberg found in a variety of mythic models, some general, some specific: the liberator and the maiden in the tower, Adam and Lucifer, the Fall, the Deluge, Christ and the Pharisees and, perhaps the most important, the Great Mother. The author had found new energy and significance in an ancient symbolic language, and we shall see how he continued for the rest of his life to explore its eloquent potential. In *Master Olof* a victory for the power of the Great Mother is reflected in the humiliation of a would-be hero. Next, in *The Father*, we see how a would-be hero is literally destroyed by the same power.

3

The Father

Nearly everything about *The Father* is paradoxical. It earned
Strindberg his first international recognition as a playwright,
but in a time of no copyright laws, virtually no money. It
brought him to the attention of important people, such as Guy
de Maupassant, Nietzsche, and Zola, and after several years
made him a celebrity in Berlin and Paris, but performances
alienated audiences: frequently the theatre was empty before
the final curtain. Strindberg regarded the play as a contribution
to the vogue of naturalism sweeping Europe, but Zola, despite
being moved by it, objected to what he felt was excessive
abstraction in characterization and skimpy depiction of milieu.
It was roasted right from the first as outrageous autobiographical propaganda in which the author had depicted his marital
problems in a self-serving way. At the same time, it was and
continues to be praised, even by its severest critics, for a raw
power that transcends biography or questions of style. Robert
Brustein exemplifies the frustration and ambivalent feelings
many critics have admitted when confronted with the task of

analyzing the play. On the one hand, he talks about the "futility of trying to extract any logical consistency from this intensely subjective nightmare." And on the other hand, he acknowledges that "like a nightmare, *The Father* does possess a kind of internal logic, which makes all its external contradictions seem rather minor; and it maintains this dreamlike logic right up to its shattering climax."[1]

References to myth in the play are not so much paradoxical as misleading. Most occur in the final act and seem, at least at first glance, obvious and gratuitous. The Captain, carrying an armload of books, breaks out of the room in which he has been confined and proceeds to cite examples of heroic men—some actual people, some figures from myth and literature—who have in common the fact that they recognized the treacherous nature of woman. Later, after he has been tricked into allowing his old nurse, Margret, to confine him in a straitjacket he shouts "Omphale! Omphale! Now you play with the club while Hercules spins your wool"(23, 91). The references are misleading because, despite the impression most of them give of being blatant classical allusions dumped into the text, the last one cited, Omphale and Hercules, is the key to what Brustein calls the "internal logic" of the play.

Most critics when defining the basic conflict have borrowed the Captain's own description of the dilemma in his household: "It's man versus woman, endlessly, all day long"(16). To be sure, a straightforward summary of the plot tends to confirm this definition. The Captain and his wife, Laura, quarrel bitterly over how their daughter, Bertha, is to be educated. Laura learns from a doctor that the power of suggestion can be used as a tool to destroy someone's mind, which is exactly what she does to her husband by allowing him to believe that he is not the father of his own child.

Like many plot descriptions, it tends to obscure deeper patterns and meanings. The Captain's real enemy is not just woman but woman in her archetypal maternal role, and the reference made to the Hercules myth amplifies and illuminates this adversary relationship. Strindberg's interest in this myth of the prototypal hero amounted almost to an obsession, and the many references to the demigod in his works function like barometric readings of Strindberg's response to and feeling for mythic resonances in general.

Omphale's name, meaning "navel", connects her directly with the Great and Terrible Mother: *omphalos* was the sacred stone the Greeks regarded as the navel of the world, and, according to Jane Harrison, was "the very seat and symbol of the Earth Mother."[2] Omphale buys Hercules as a slave and compels him to the demeaning feminine work of spinning wool. Hercules must escape this bondage, since the first priority of the quest is for the hero to tear himself free of the psychic umbilical cord that ties him to the Earth Mother. In a sense, *The Father* is a dramatization of a Hercules unable to take that crucial step.

The Omphale/Earth Mother image is diffused in the play in the persons of four women whom the Captain identifies as his opponents in the struggle over Bertha's future vocation: "My mother-in-law wants to turn her into a spiritualist; Laura wants her to be an artist; the governess wants to make her into a Methodist; old Margret wants her to be a Baptist" (12). One of them, the governess, never appears on stage and plays no influential role in the action, but the mentioning of her adds cumulative strength to the archetypal mother image. Of far greater importance is the other woman who never appears on stage: the Captain's mother-in-law. She is the secret heart of the play, hidden and mysterious. She speaks only a few lines—to call to Laura—but she is referred to one or more times by all the major characters. Ironically, with each reference the image we are given of her grows not clearer but stranger, more shadowy, and more ominous. There is even something curious about her place in the family. Whereas Laura always refers to her as her mother, the Captain and the Pastor, Laura's brother, speak differently about her:

CAPTAIN: It wasn't enough that I married your sister—you had to palm off your old stepmother on me too!
PASTOR: Well, good Lord, a stepmother isn't someone you have living with you.

With the Pastor speaking of Laura as "my own sister" (13) and of
the old woman as his stepmother (14), we have an apparent
discrepancy. Perhaps this was one of the details in the play Zola
found lacking in naturalistic consistency. But note that the word
stepmother appears not once, but twice, as if the playwright
wanted to assure us that he did not make a mistake. Moreover,
the distinction between Laura's term and her brother's makes a
great deal of sense when interpreted in the symbolism of fairy
tale language. To Laura the woman is simply "mother"—at best
a positive image, at worst a neutral one. To the Pastor she is the
familiar villainess of countless tales, and he knows very well that
"a stepmother isn't someone you have living with you."

Because the other characters always go to her room to serve
her needs, the implication is that the old woman is infirm in
some way. But whatever the infirmity, it does not prevent her
from attempting to exercise great power, particularly over her
granddaughter, Bertha.

> BERTHA: Help me! I know she wants to hurt me!
> CAPTAIN: Who wants to hurt you? Tell me—who?
> BERTHA: Grandmother! But it was my fault. I played a trick
>   on her! . . . In the evening she likes to turn the lamp
>   down and have me sit at the table holding a pen over
>   a piece of paper. And then she says the spirits are
>   going to write.
> CAPTAIN: What? Why haven't you told me about this before?
> BERTHA: Forgive me—I didn't dare. Grandmother says the
>   spirits avenge themselves on people who tell. And
>   then the pen writes, but I don't know if it's me. And
>   sometimes it goes well, but sometimes not at all.
>   And when I get tired, nothing comes, but some-
>   thing *has* to come anyway. And tonight, I thought I
>   was writing well, but Grandmother said that it was
>   copied . . . and that I had tricked her. And then she
>   got terribly angry (35–36).

Spiritualism and automatic writing: the old woman is teaching the girl the languages of the dead and of the dark world of
unconscious impulses. According to Bertha, the woman also
claims oracular power: "Grandmother says," she tells her
father, "there are things she can see that you can't see"(37).

Stepmother, communicant with the dead, believer in the miraculous powers of the unconscious, oracle: these witchlike characteristics are all attributes of the negative component of the Great Mother configuration: the jealous, suffocating, cannibalistic Terrible Mother.

Another ominous presence in the play is the house—the most powerful central symbol of female domination. Characters sense the force of this presence, and they describe it in vivid terms. The Captain talks about entering the house interior as equal to entering "a cage of tigers" (13); Bertha complains that "in there it's always gloomy and as terrible as a winter night" (38); and the Pastor says that Laura has supporters "in there" (16), pausing before uttering the phrase as if to give it greater weight. The most evocative description of the house interior is contained in a night-time scene between Bertha and the Nurse.

BERTHA: I don't dare sit up there all alone. I think it's haunted.
NURSE: Did you hear something?
BERTHA: Oh, do you know, I heard someone singing up in the attic.
NURSE: In the attic! At this time of night?
BERTHA: Yes, it was so sad; the saddest song I ever heard. It sounded as if it came from the attic storeroom. Where the cradle is . . .(51).

Bertha is not just a fanciful young girl who resents being forced to learn spiritualism and feels uneasy in a cold, dark house. She is a reluctant initiate in an ancient ritual; and the house, in which singing can be heard in the attic "where the cradle is," is the sacral precinct of the Great Mother.

The symbolic dimension of the house is augmented by what appears to be an ordinary architectural detail. The entrance to the Captain's room is through a "wallpapered door." In act three Laura and the others imprison the Captain in his room, and he is forced to break his way through the door, now barricaded, in order to make his final entrance. Covered with the same material as the wall, the door lacks definition; to an audience in a theatre it would appear to be swallowed up into the background. What could be more suggestive of the Captain's fate? He too is being swallowed up. When he bursts the barricade, it marks his last effort to resist being buried in the enveloping womb-tomb of the Great Mother.

Images of envelopment, entanglement, and entrapment are pervasive in *The Father*, and these too are intimately associated with the Great Mother. The most obvious image is the strait-jacket, which the Nurse manages to get the Captain to wear in the last scene. If Laura's mother represents the negative element in the Great Mother archetype, the Terrible Mother, the Nurse suggests the positive Good Mother. The Captain trusts her as no one else, and their special relationship makes their scene together at the end at once touching and horrifying. As she coaxes him into the straitjacket, she murmurs the same kind of warm, encouraging words she might have used when he was a small boy and she dressed him for bed. When he realizes what she has done, he feels betrayed and angry, but his anger quickly turns to pleas to be cuddled, and a murder scene becomes a grotesque combination of love scene and ritualistic "religious transaction," as Carl Reinhold Smedmark has aptly described it:[3]

CAPTAIN: Now I lay me down to sleep.
NURSE: Listen, he's praying to God.
CAPTAIN: No, to you, to you, to put me to sleep, for I'm tired, so tired. Good night, Margret. "Blessed art thou among women" (94–95).

With these words from the angel's Annunciation message to the Virgin Mary—the prototypal Good Mother—the Captain lapses into the coma that signals his end. In his case, the Good Mother has turned out to be, if anything, more dangerous than the Terrible Mother.

Besides the reference already mentioned to Hercules spin-ning, other images in the play associated with entanglement include actions such as embroidering and objects such as nets, webs, and shawls. The Captain is worried in the opening act that "a web is being spun around him" (34); and in the final scene he observes that whereas "in the past it was the smith who made the soldier's tunic, now it's the seamstress" (94). The most ambiguous object related to fabric imagery is Laura's shawl, which the Captain begs her to throw over him as he lies bound in the straitjacket. For a moment, the smell and feel of the shawl evoke for him warm, sensuous memories of when he and Laura were young lovers, but then, as if he suddenly realizes that the shawl has a predatory quality, he shouts: "Take away this cat that's lying on me! Take it away!" (93).

In a letter written some months after he completed *The Father*, Strindberg described how he expected an actor to perform the role of the Captain: he should go "to meet his fate with rather jaunty courage, shrouding himself in death in these spider's webs that natural law prevents him from tearing apart."[4] The web in which the Captain is caught is not just a house full of maternal females, it is the web of existence, a web spun and tended by woman in her fecund role as Great Mother. In a later chapter, dealing with *A Dream Play*, we shall see how Strindberg developed the image of the web of existence further under the influence of Indic mythology.

Charles R. Lyons has pointed out that the Captain's fate has psychosexual meaning: "a reality of emasculation, castration, impotence."[5] An obvious example of symbolic castration is Laura's ordering that all the cartridges be removed from the Captain's guns and gun pouches (73). But the Captain's troubles have spiritual and metaphysical meaning as well. On a realistic level, he is a dissatisfied army officer, who feels unfulfilled in his career and so conducts independent scientific research, hoping to find signs of organic life in meteorites. Laura thwarts his efforts by intercepting his mail, making it difficult if not impossible for him to obtain the books he needs for his research. On a symbolic level, the Captain is the mythic hero, reaching toward the light, toward a higher level of consciousness, while Laura and the other mother figures are the dragon forces of the unconscious, trying to keep him imprisoned in the darkness. One of the ancient symbols for consciousness is a mirror; Laura says she never uses one (77).

During her marriage, Laura has played a dual role of mother

and wife for the Captain, and the suggestion of incest contributed to the deterioration of their relationship. "Do you remember," Laura asks him,

> that it was as your second mother that I first came into your life? . . .You were a giant child who either came into the world too soon or were unwanted. . . . Yes, that's the way it was then, and that's why I loved you as if you were my child. But you saw, I'm sure, that each time your feelings changed and you came to me as a lover, I felt ashamed. For me, our lovemaking was a joy that was followed by the sense that my very blood was ashamed. The mother became the mistress—ugh! (66–67).

Laura then says something that in a curiously roundabout fashion analyzes precisely why the Great Mother archetype is so important in the Captain's life: "The mother was your friend, you see, but the woman was your enemy" (67). In fact, the reverse is also true. Symbolically and actually the mother has always been his enemy, as the Captain himself acknowledges. He says that his own mother, fearing the pain that would result, tried to prevent him from being born by denying him proper nourishment in the womb. And although he now complains much about the suffering under a yoke of feminine tyranny, the yoke of maternal tyranny he endures is far more serious and he is incapable of throwing it off. He knows it is wrong, for example, to allow his Nurse to treat him as if he were a baby, but he also knows that he needs this kind of attention. His ambivalent feelings for Margret are summed up by him in a single sentence: "She's kind, it's true, but she doesn't belong here." She definitely does not belong there, but the Captain cannot get rid of her. The Pastor's criticism of his brother-in-law—"You have too many women running your house" (13)—needs to be recast: the Captain has too many mothers running his life.

    In her role as wife, Laura is often interpreted as the epitome of feminine treachery. Børge Madsen, for example, describes her as "all that is evil and deceitful in woman, and nothing else . . . no moral scruples whatsoever."[6] In this way, however, she becomes villainy incarnate, the Captain a helpless victim, and the conflict in the play is oversimplified. It is true that Laura is drawn in bold strokes, almost larger than life, but this is in keeping with the style of the play, and Laura is not lacking in the contradictions that suggest very human qualities. She sees her husband as an enemy and her anger makes her vicious, but she also feels compassion, and the battle is taking its toll upon her as well as him. The Nurse indicates that her mistress is considerate with others in the house, and Bertha says that her mother cries a lot. At worst, she is not so much a force of evil as a tool in a process she does not totally comprehend. When the Captain finally lies helpless before her in the straitjacket, she feels safe enough to allow herself a strange, moving statement, part apology, part self-justification, asserting that she did only what she had to do, as a woman and a mother.

> I don't know that I've ever thought about or intended what you think I've done. A vague desire probably did have hold over me to get rid of you, like some obstacle, and if you can see some plan in my actions, it's possible that it was there, even though I wasn't aware of it. I've never given a thought to my actions—they just skimmed along on the rails you yourself laid down. Before God and my conscience I feel innocent, even if I'm not. Your existence has always been like a stone on my heart, pressing and pressing until my heart tried to shake off the obstructive burden. That's how it's been, and if I've tormented you without provocation, I ask your forgiveness.

To which the Captain replies, equally expressively, "It all sounds plausible—but how does it help me?" (92).

The interpretation of the character of the Captain has been similarly skewed. At one extreme we have F. L. Lucas's absurdly reductive biographical criticism that the Captain "can be understood only if it is grasped that he is not a real soldier, but simply the neurotic Strindberg disguised in uniform."[7] At another extreme we have Madsen's opinion that "despite a few minor faults of character, the Captain is essentially a noble, virile, admirable man." I should say that the Captain's faults of character—particularly his psychological faults—are major, the most catastrophic one being his inability to harmonize in his own mind the disparate aspects of the Great Mother: he cannot reconcile his fear of the Terrible Mother with his need of the good one. Is the Great Mother enemy or friend? Strindberg renders a wonderfully equivocal answer to the question through the character of the Nurse. Margret acts out of the deepest of feelings and is totally oblivious to the irony of the role she plays. After first refusing to help get the Captain into the straitjacket, she agrees to do so because she is afraid someone else might hurt him. It has to be done with tenderness—"gently, gently," as she puts it (81). She may be part of the maternal configuration that is devouring him, but she is motivated by compassion, not malice. She is a docile celebrant in the primordial ritual. She treats the Captain as though he were a little boy because that is the way she sees all men. In her youth she bore an illegitimate child, but she seems emotionless about it, as she seems emotionless about the man who made her pregnant. All she knows is mothering, and she pursues her destiny relentlessly, even if it involves unwittingly devouring her young, which calls to mind the ancient circular image of the Ouroboros, the great serpent swallowing its own tail. Margret is the relentless force of life itself, the endless round of creating, nurturing, and destroying, the "Aphroditic-tellurian" mother, as Bachofen might have described her.

The Captain should get rid of her, but cannot. A spiritual dilemma confronts him. He has abandoned one faith for another, religion for science, but the emotional energies generated by the old faith continue to exert their influence, surreptitiously, like a mighty river gone underground. The three other males in the play have found ways of living with the fact that the old energies must be respected. Nöjd, the Captain's orderly, is the male as simple biological creature: the unthinking stud. He is "satisfied" (which, in fact, is what his name means in Swedish) to yield to the seductress Eve, impregnate her, and go about his business. Like Margret, he plays his role in the Great Round without questioning. The Pastor is the male as representative of the orthodox establishment: a conventional guardian and upholder of the rational order so cherished in bourgeois society. Despite his orthodoxy, however, he has learned to respect those women who have what might be called more primitive spiritual commitments than his own. He knows his sister to be a willful and perhaps dangerous adversary, but she fascinates him and he admires her strength and tenacity. The Doctor represents the new, empirical orthodoxy, but like the Pastor he too is limited in his authority and knows it. He is uneasy trying to cope with the manipulative Laura and, although sympathetic toward the Captain, cannot give him much support and assistance. The Captain falls between the positions accepted by the other men in the play. He cannot yield as they have yielded. He sees Nöjd as irresponsible, the Pastor as reactionary, and the Doctor, he fears, is his enemy because he is Laura's tool. At the end, the Doctor and the Pastor are awed and helpless in the face of the Captain's collapse. When Laura asks the Doctor why he has so little to say, he replies: "That's all! I don't know any more. Let him speak who knows more." Bertha then utters the cry which is so much the anthem of this powerful play—"Mother, mother!"—and runs to be embraced by Laura, who seals the moment of triumph with a simple, but stunning possessive claim: "My child! My own child!" The "religious transaction" is complete, and there is nothing left but for the Pastor to pronounce: "Amen" (96).

When the Captain is seen, as Lucas sees him, as an autobiographical extension of his creator, the character becomes a defense attorney drawing attention to the troubles in Strindberg's marriage. What gives the play coherence, unity, and power are not Strindberg's personal problems but the Captain's. And if the Captain resembles Strindberg, he also resembles—in ways more important to dramatic criticism—a number of mythic heroes. He is Hercules in bondage to Omphale and, as scholars have already pointed out, he is Agamemnon trapped in the net and about to be destroyed by that classic example of the Terrible Mother, Clytemnestra. The Captain is also kin to two other heroes who have difficulties with maternal figures: Euripides' Hippolytus and Pentheus.

Not sufficiently clear in English translations of *The Father* is the Captain's branch of service: he is *Ryttmästarn* (a "cavalry officer"). At the end of act one, he is deeply upset and decides to go for a solitary drive in a racing-type sleigh (*kappsläd*) (45). Hippolytus is also fond of racing about in a horse-drawn vehicle, a chariot, and he is even more intimately associated with horses: his name means "of the stampeding horses." Like the Captain, he has problems with a stepmother, his own, and consequently with the threat of incest. Finally, both men are destroyed because of the failure to balance and reconcile responsibilities to two goddesses. Hippolytus' dedication to chaste Artemis causes him to neglect the goddess of love; the Captain's worship of woman as mother—"Blessed art thou among women"—alienates him from woman as lover. When Pentheus in *The Bacchae* rails against the power over women possessed by the cult of Dionysus, and when the Captain complains about the un-justified authority wielded by the women in his house, each is trying to deny the power of the irrational. Nietzsche says in *The Birth of Tragedy* that one of the lessons taught by the Greeks was the certainty that even as the forces of reason and order repre-sented by Apollo must rule over the forces of irrationality and chaos represented by Dionysus, both gods must be honored. The power of neither can be ignored. The tragic fact about the Captain and Pentheus is that each is trying to repudiate with his conscious mind what he is slave to unconsciously. By attempt-ing to ignore the unconscious, they are doomed to be devoured by it. Just as it is appropriate that it should be the Captain's surrogate mother, Margret, who lures him into the straitjacket, so it is fitting that it should be Pentheus's mother, Agave, who tears her own son to pieces. In each instance the final visual grouping of mother and son is striking: a deeply disturbing, but moving Pietà. The power to create has evolved into the power to destroy, same power in the same person; the round is complete. As the Captain lies dying, he wonders what force it is that rules over life. Laura replies, "God alone rules." And the Captain concludes, "The God of strife, then! Or nowadays, the Goddess!" (93).

4

Miss Julie

FAIRY TALE MANQUÉ

No other play is more often described as a masterpiece of naturalism than *Miss Julie*, a work with the objectivity of science, showing in the brief, tragic affair that a young woman has with her servant the results of the awesome power of nature's twin forces, heredity and environment. An uninterrupted flow of action suggests that real life is unfolding before our eyes. But this evaluation does not do justice to Strindberg's achievement, for the play is an abundantly poetic work in which he blended myth, fairy tale, and even dream elements.

It is commonly believed that Strindberg's explorations of the artistic potential of dreams did not begin in earnest until after the traumatic Inferno period in the mid- and late 1890s. A decade earlier, however, he had Miss Julie and Jean telling each other dreams that are microcosms of the play's action, radial centers of its themes. From the dreams, connections can be drawn to many other elements, and the grid thereby constituted shows a mythic structure of great subtlety and density.

The telling of the dreams is motivated in a psychologically

believable fashion. The festive, orgiastic atmosphere of mid-summer eve—a bright, magic time in Sweden—induces two young people to exchange confidences. A titled, unmarried woman, mistress of the manor, who ordinarily would not engage in but a casual or businesslike conversation with her father's valet, proceeds to tell him about a dream she has that confuses and unnerves her. He responds with a description of a dream of his own.

> JULIE: I have a dream which recurs now and then, and I'm reminded of it now. I've climbed on top of a pillar, and I sit there and see no way of getting down. I get dizzy when I look down, and I must get down, but I haven't the courage to jump. I can't hold on and I long to be able to fall, but I don't fall. And yet I'll have no peace until I get down, no rest until I get down, down to the ground! And if I get down to the ground, I'd want to be under the earth. . . . Have you ever felt anything like that?
>
> JEAN: No! I dream that I'm lying under a high tree in a dark forest. I want up, up in the top to look out over the bright landscape, where the sun is shining—plunder the bird's nest up there where the golden eggs lie. And I climb and climb, but the trunk is so thick, so smooth, and it's so far to the first branch. But I know that if I just reached that first branch, I'd go to the top as if on a ladder. I haven't reached it yet, but I shall reach it, even if only in a dream (23, 132–133).

Julie, perhaps sensing that the atmosphere has become more intimate than she intended, that more has been revealed than was prudent, changes the direction of the conversation: "Here I stand, talking to you about dreams. Let's go out. Just into the park." But Jean wants to sustain the intimacy a moment longer, and he replies with one of the many fairy-talelike resonances in the play: "We must sleep on nine midsummer flowers tonight, to make our dreams come true"(133).

The first thing evident about the dreams is their ambiguity. Like prophecies in myths, legends, and fairy tales they are open to several interpretations. The choices favored by critics have been social and/or sexual. Socially, Julie's desire to get down has been seen as the desire of a lonely aristocrat to mingle with commoners, and her fear of descending to their level is a fear of being mocked and humiliated, which, as Jean describes it, is precisely what has happened. As she danced with some of the servants, attempting to share in the midsummer gaiety, other servants made fun of her behind her back. Sexually, her need to get down has been interpreted as a longing to yield to long-suppressed desires. Strindberg himself certifies such a reading in the play's preface where he talks about "repressed instincts breaking out uncontrollably"(105).

Jean's dream has been treated in the same way: socially, the climbing represents his ambitions to rise in the world; sexually, the phallic nature of the tree is obvious and requires no further elaboration.

Beyond the social and sexual meaning of the dreams are other implications. In Julie's desire to get down is the suggestion that she is trapped, a prisoner of some sort. But only part of her wants to be free; another part is afraid that being released will lead to her destruction. Although Jean's longing to find the golden eggs is an integral part of the hero's quest—the search for "the treasure difficult to attain"—he seems reluctant to pursue the quest very vigorously. He has not even reached the first branch and will be satisfied to reach the goal "only in a dream."

Prisoner in a high place, adventurer in search of treasure, the ingredients are familiar: the maiden in the tower and the knight errant. But something is not quite right. She is a prisoner who fears liberation, and he a hero who seems more interested in answering the call in dreams than in reality. On the one hand, the fairy tale atmosphere leads us to expect a happy ending, a union of princess and hero. On the other hand, we are made to feel that the characters are not equal to their tasks. Neither Julie nor Jean has the courage and maturity necessary to become what fairy tale heroines and heroes are supposed to become: complete, responsible, adult human beings. A tension has been created, obliquely, through the ambiguous suggestiveness of the imagery of the world of make-believe.

The author goes to some lengths in the preface of the play to stress the circumstances that have brought Jean and Julie together at this place and time and how the forces of heredity and environment conspire to attract them to each other fatally.

> I see Miss Julie's tragic fate as motivated by . . . her mother's primary instincts; her father raising her incorrectly; her own nature and the influence of her fiancé on her weak and degenerate brain. Also, more particularly: the festive atmosphere of midsummer night; her father's absence; her monthly indisposition; her preoccupation with animals; the provocative effect of the dancing; the midsummer twilight; the powerfully aphrodisiac influence of flowers; and, finally, the chance that drives the couple together into a room alone—plus the boldness of the aroused man (102).

It all sounds very scientific in this statement written after *Miss Julie* was finished. In the play itself, there are indications that a less scientific force is operative, that a mythic destiny had long ago designed and determined the characters' fates. We are reminded of Stanley's line to Blanche in the rape scene in *A Streetcar Named Desire*: "We've had this date with each other from the beginning."[1]

The clues to destiny's design are in a monologue Jean has about his childhood.

> I lived in a laborer's shack with seven brothers and sisters and a pig out in the old crop fields, where not a single tree grew. But from the window I could see the wall around the Count's gardens, with apple trees rising above it. It was the Garden of Eden, and there were many terrible angels with flaming swords to guard it. All the same the other boys and I found the way to the Tree of Life (137).

The simple story of an envious peasant boy is invested with mythic resonances. Echoing under the description of the difficulties faced by poor children growing up under the stultifying burden of class distinctions is the universal lament of man having to endure the discrepancy between the dream of Eden and the barren, thorny field of reality. But we sense also an ulterior motive in Jean's pleading: he is trying not only to gain Julie's sympathy but to arouse her feelings. As he continues his story, all three levels of meaning are mingled: Jean is simultaneously victim of social injustice, mythopoeic narrator, and tentative seducer.

One time I entered the Garden of Eden with my mother to weed the onion beds. Next to the garden plot was a Turkish pavilion in the shadow of jasmines and overgrown with honeysuckle. What its purpose was I didn't know, but I'd never seen such a beautiful building. People went in and came out again, and one day the door was left open. I sneaked up and saw the walls hung with pictures of kings and emperors, and there were red curtains on the windows with fringes on them—now you know what the place was. I . . . *[breaks off lilac flower and holds it under Julie's nose]* . . . I'd never been inside the manor house, never seen anything but the church, and this was more beautiful. From then on, wherever my thoughts ran, they always returned—there. And so, gradually, a longing developed to enjoy—just once—all its . . . comforts. *Enfin*, I sneaked in, saw, and admired. But then I heard someone coming! There was only one way out for the gentry, but for me there was another, and I had no choice but to take it! (137–138).

Jean's pathetic, humiliating, and even blackly amusing account of his daring to use an upper-class outhouse and then having to escape through the excremental route obviously disturbs Julie: she drops the lilac on the table. Jean continues with how he fled in shame and disgust until he arrived at a rose terrace:

There I saw a pink dress with white stockings: it was you. I lay down under a pile of weeds—*under*, can you imagine—under thistles that pricked me and wet earth that stank. And I watched you walking among the roses and thought to myself: if it's true that a thief can enter heaven and be with the angels, then it's strange that a peasant's son here on God's earth can't come into the manor gardens and play with the Count's daughter.

The story has become personal for Julie; their fates are more intertwined than she knew, and she reacts as Jean surely intended she would: "[*Sadly*] Do you suppose all poor children would have had the same thoughts you did?"(138). Naively, she sees a young boy thinking idealistically about social injustice; in fact, Jean's thoughts then and now were about other things as well. Later in the play, after he seduces her, Jean admits: "When I lay in the onion bed and saw you in the rose garden, well—I'll tell you now—I had the same dirty thoughts all boys do"(151).

Although the monologue can be seen primarily as a tool Jean is using to ingratiate himself with Julie, the fairy tale resonances present give it an important psychological dimension. The pavilion and rose terrace story deals not only with an episode in a boy's life but with one of the primary human experiences. The sequence of feelings described from innocence to disgust to awe and fascination, together with the implication of guilt about "dirty thoughts," suggest that Jean's journey from the pavilion to the garden involved nothing less than his sexual awakening. One contrast is striking: the purity of the object of the journey, the virginal little girl, with the humiliating baseness of the route traveled toward the object; the contrast between the brightness of the rose garden of love and the dark, underground origins of desire.

Subtle references bring to mind a particular fairy tale: the swineherd and the princess. Jean says in the monologue that there was a pig in his family home, and Kristin, his mistress, jealous after learning that Jean and Julie went to bed together, boasts that no one can accuse her of lowering herself, of having had an affair with "the boy who takes care of the pigs"(180). Strindberg deals with the same tale much more explicitly in another source: the novel A Madman's Defense. As a number of scholars have pointed out, there are significant parallels between events in Strindberg's life and events in the novel and in three important plays: The Father, Miss Julie, and Creditors. He assembled and reassembled the same biographical details and mythic images in constantly changing patterns, like taking a collection of bones, shaking them up, and throwing them out, again and again, as if to shake out all possible meanings. But although the bones may be the same, each new pattern possesses its own integrity. The ways in which the image of the swineherd and princess are used in A Madman's Defense and Miss Julie are illustrations of this kind of integrity.[2]

The plot of the novel is based rather closely on Strindberg's relationship with his first wife, Siri von Essen, from their first encounters to their marriage and to their eventual separation. When he met her, she was already the wife of a titled army officer and the mother of a small child. Strindberg was of a lower class; to use the title of his autobiography, he was the son of a servant woman. The surreptitious courtship described in the first person in the novel understandably fills the narrator with apprehension and guilt, both of which are expressed in a passage describing the consummation of their affair: "The son of the people had conquered the white skin, the commoner had won a girl of breeding, the swineherd had mixed blood with the princess."[3] The same contrasts that we found in the pavilion/ rose terrace story are drawn. On the one hand, there is the purity of a white-skinned, well-bred princess; on the other hand, the base background of young man associated with an animal traditionally symbolizing impure desires.[4]

There are several fairy tales dealing with swineherds and princesses. One of these, "The Princess in the Tree," from Germany, contains some interesting parallels with *Miss Julie*, especially with Jean's dream of climbing a high tree from which to see the whole world and of longing to reach the first branch of the tree. While a young man, as Jung retells the story,

> is watching his pigs in the wood, he discovers a large tree, whose branches lose themselves in the clouds. "How would it be," says he to himself, "if you were to look at the world from the top of that great tree?" So he climbs up, all day long he climbs, without even reaching the branches. Evening comes, and he has to pass the night in a fork of the tree. Next day he goes on climbing and by noon has reached the foliage. Only toward evening does he come to a village in the branches.[5].

In the world the swineherd reaches at the top of the tree, he finds a girl who has been imprisoned in a castle by a wicked magician. The swineherd liberates the girl, but only for a short time. The magician employs a ruse to escape with her back to earth and the hero takes up pursuit. Finally, with the help of a witch who provides him with a magic horse, the swineherd eventually saves the girl a second time, and they live happily ever after.

The differences between the tale and the play turn out to be as significant as the similarities. The swineherd, for example, keeps pushing on until he gets to the top, despite the shortage of branches; Jean is still waiting to reach the first branch. Despite Jean's claim of confidence that he will eventually achieve his goal, there is nothing that really supports this in either his professional or private life. He boasts of having been a wine steward in one of the largest hotels in Lucerne, and after the seduction he proposes to Julie that they open a first-class hotel together somewhere in Switzerland or the Italian islands. For all his vaunted ambition, however, Jean has chosen to remain a valet up to now in a household where by his own admission he is a lackey who cringes before his master and obeys his every whim. "I think if the Count came down now," Jean says in the final scene, "and ordered me to cut my throat, I'd do it on the spot" (185). Strindberg in the preface says that Jean "emerges from the battle unscathed and will probably end up as a hotel-keeper" (107). This is an example of where, to borrow D. H. Lawrence's admonition, it is better to trust the tale than the teller. After the seduction, when Kristin indicates to Jean that the time might be opportune for them to make their relationship permanent and move on to another job, he rejects the offer: "I couldn't get a position like this if I was married . . . it's not my style to begin so soon to think about dying for a wife and children. I must confess I've set my sights a little higher than that" (170–171). He may have high ambitions, but the inner determination necessary to fulfill them is not in him.

Strindberg also says about Jean that "sexually he is the aristocrat because of his masculine strength" (107), but if this is true, then why has Jean chosen a casual liaison with Kristin, an unattractive woman five years his senior, a liaison in which he willingly submits to indignities? Kristin bosses him about and lectures him on wrongdoing as if she were his teacher or his mother. The playwright is closer to the truth when he says that Jean "is afraid of Kristin because she knows his dangerous secrets" (106). Jean's secrets, both as a servant and as a man, are weaknesses of character that prevent him from pursuing the hero quest to a successful conclusion.

We do not have a witch and a magician in the play as we do in the fairy tale, but we do have a cook, Kristin, and a count, Julie's father. When Kristin leaves for church after she discovers that Jean has been unfaithful, she says: "On the way I'm going to tell the stable boy not to let out any horses—in case anyone wants to travel—before the Count gets home!" (182). This witch (Jean calls her a devil) will see to it that there will be no magic horse available for Jean and Julie to escape on.

If Julie's father is not an actual magician, he has an extraordinary, almost supernatural influence on the action of the play. Like the stepmother in *The Father*, the Count never appears on stage, yet his presence is even more dominating then hers was. At the opening of the play he is absent from the estate, perhaps attending a midsummer eve celebration elsewhere, and his return is expected momentarily. After the seduction, Jean and Julie are terrified, and their first instinct is to run and hide, as Adam and Eve hid from God after tasting the forbidden fruit.

In his absence, the Count's power is exerted through objects: his gloves, his riding boots (which Jean must finish polishing before his master's return), a summoning bell, and a speaking tube. That Strindberg intended for these things to serve powerfully evocative purposes is evident in a passage from his preface, a passage usually missing from most translations: "I let inanimate objects (the Count's boots, the bell) serve as agents for *Gedankenübertragung* [thought transference]."[6] To Jean their presence is especially meaningful immediately after the seduction.

> I have only to see his gloves lying on a chair to feel myself small. I have only to hear that bell up there to jump like a skittish horse. And as I now look at his boots, standing there so grand and tall, I feel a chill go up my spine! [*kicks the boots*] Superstitions, prejudices we're taught as children (146).

Jean asserts that the superstitions could easily be forgotten if he could get to another country, perhaps a more democratic country, a republic. He claims to have "stuff" in him, "character," but then comes a false note to make us suspicious. His grand potential, only waiting to be realized, needs but one precondition: "Once I've grabbed hold of that first branch, watch me climb!"(147). The first branch again: a hollow claim. One can picture him twenty years hence, still waiting.

Jean's fear of the Count must be seen in a larger context. Strindberg says in the preface that "his inferiority is due mainly to the social milieu in which he is living at present, and he can probably shed it with his valet's livery"(107). Again, look to the tale. There is nothing circumstantial about Jean's fear; it will not evaporate in another environment because it is basic, fundamental, existential. His fear of the Count, like his fear of Kristin, is fear of life itself. This world of the play is not just set historically, a midsummer eve in late nineteenth-century Sweden, it is fixed at a particular point in mythic time and space: outside the Garden after the Fall, and the Count has the numinous power of angry Yahweh. The tragic frame Strindberg evokes is a world where man and woman are alienated not only from God but from each other and even from themselves. It is a cruel world of opposites where the law of conflict reigns: servant versus master, woman versus man, instinct to live versus instinct to die. It is a world we recognize from *The Father* and will see again in *Creditors*. Probably the most expressive portrait Strindberg rendered of its Bosch-like landscape is in a speech by the Captain in *The Father*, a speech in which one senses an atmosphere of the dreary morning after the nightmare of the loss of Eden.

> We woke up, all right, but with our feet on the pillow, and the one who woke us was himself a sleepwalker. When women grow old and stop being women, they get beards on their chins. I wonder what men get when they grow old and stop being men. And so, the dawn was sounded not by roosters, but capons, and the hens that answered didn't know the difference. When the sun should have been rising, we found ourselves in full moonlight, among the ruins, just like in the good old days. So, it wasn't an awakening after all—just a little morning nap, with wild dreams (68).

We sense, in a foreshadowing of Beckett's *Waiting for Godot* or *Endgame*, a never-quenched longing to be heroes in a world where heroism is impossible.

In *Miss Julie* the thematic armature is the swineherd and princess story, but there are references to other fairy tales and myths as well, creating a musical effect of theme and variations. Sometimes, the references are obvious and seem to serve only romantic or decorative purposes, like Jean's statement about sleeping on midsummer flowers;—here, it is hard to separate

Jean, the romantic, from Jean, the seducer. Other fairy tale resonances are implied, such as in the mysterious story of Julie's breakup with her fiancé. Jean says he witnessed the whole episode:

> They were down at the stable yard one evening and Miss Julie was "training" him, as she called it. . . . She made him leap over her riding whip, like a dog you're teaching to jump. He leaped twice, and each time she lashed him. The third time he took the whip out of her hand and broke it in small pieces; then he left (118).

In numerous fairy tales a hero has the opportunity to win a princess by performing a series of feats or by undergoing a series of trials. Not infrequently, the trials number three. In this fairy tale manqué, however, a positive resolution is foredoomed. Something is amiss on the Count's estate. A smell of death is in the air. There have been many family tragedies, and Julie is the Count's only heir; the family name will die with her. Like Blanche in *Streetcar Named Desire*, she is at the end of the line. When a suitor comes and undergoes three trials, instead of winning and accepting the princess, he rejects her. One might think that Strindberg was aiming for parody in details like this, and indeed, one critic, Milton May, has used the term "parodied fairy tale" in connection with another Strindberg play, *The Ghost Sonata*.[7] "Fairy tale manqué" seems more appropriate; it suggests something abortive and unfulfilled, which I think is the effect Strindberg intended. At one and the same time, the fairy tale manqué resonances raise hopes and dash them; promises are made that we sense cannot be kept. A bittersweet quality results, which at its worst approaches sentimentality but at its best curiously mitigates the sometimes almost unbearable harshness and pessimism that characterizes Strindberg's *Weltanschauung*.

Echoes of a number of mythic couples resound in the relationship between Jean and Julie, among them, as we have seen, Adam and Eve, and the swineherd and the princess. These are, at least potentially, positive examples, couples who are united. Echoes of other mythic pairs offer negative examples, involving confrontations that end in tragic consequences: Actaeon and Diana, and Joseph and Potiphar's wife.

Actaeon, it will be remembered, was the ill-fated hunter who surprised Diana naked in her bath and so aroused her fury by staring long and hard that she transformed him into a stag who was then hunted down and killed. In the play Diana is the name of Miss Julie's dog, and a reference to her foreshadows Julie's fate: the animal has let itself be made pregnant by the gate-keeper's pug dog. The same goddess is mentioned in another context: *A Madman's Defense*. In the novel the narrator pores through books on mythology and sculpture to find the most appropiate counterpart to the bewitching, disturbing woman with whom he has fallen in love. His conclusions become an inventory of the archetypal roles he sees women playing. He eliminates from consideration in turn Venus (the "normal woman," sure of the triumphant power of her beauty), Juno (the fecund, seductive mother), and Minerva (the flat-chested blue-stocking) and arrives at Diana: "The pale goddess, goddess of the night, afraid of the clear, terrible light of day, cruel in her involuntary chastity—a consequence of a perverted physical constitution, too much the boy, too little the girl, modest of necessity, to the point that she became furious at Actaeon when he surprised her bathing. Diana?"[8] The narrator sees the resemblance to his own love: her veiled bosom too "must be burning with clandestine desires" and when sufficiently aroused, will "crave to see blood flowing." "Ah", he says, "Diana! Yes, she is the one, the very one! . . . I wanted to rid my mind of this phantom of the chaste goddess."[9]

The similarities between this Diana image in the novel and the character of Miss Julie are striking. When Julie was a little girl, her mother, apparently a fanatical feminist bent on demon-strating the equality of the sexes, dressed her as a boy and had her learn to do everything boys did—"too much the boy, too little the girl." Julie, too, is "cruel in her involuntary chastity," as her behavior with her fiancé demonstrated. Jean tells her that as a commoner he thinks of aristocrats as hawks whose backs he cannot see because they soar so far above him. After the seduc-tion Julie says: "And now you've seen the hawk's back," to which Jean ungallantly replies: "Not exactly its *back*" (152). Actaeon caught the goddess off guard. When Jean later kills Julie's little bird, the full fury of her pent-up feelings explodes; the goddess wants to see "blood flowing": "Oh, I'd like to see your blood, your brain on a chopping block—I'd like to see your whole sex swimming in a sea of blood" (175). Finally, in the end, as dawn approaches, Julie goes off to commit suicide; like Diana, she cannot tolerate the "clear, terrible light of day."

The image of Joseph and Potiphar's wife appears when Jean refuses Julie's invitation to dance. She is both amused and offended because he seems presumptuously to believe that like the Biblical Joseph he is refusing what he regards as an improper sexual advance. The incident referred to from the period of Joseph's slavery in Egypt figures not only in the play; Strindberg found the mythic confrontation particularly expressive and used it in several contexts. In fact, Hugo von Hofmannsthal somewhat extravagantly described the Joseph theme as "the grandiose and awe-inspiring basic motif of the whole of Strindberg's work: the struggle of man's genius, of man's intensified intellectuality against the evil, the silliness of woman, against her urge to drag him down, to sap his strength."[10] In any case, like Dante, Strindberg assigned Potiphar's wife a special place in hell. In a copy of Dante's *Inferno*, purchased sometime after the turn of the century, Strindberg wrote "*Obs.*" (i.e., *nota bene*) in the margin and underscored the passage (Canto XXX: 97–100) that describes her as "she who falsely accused Joseph."[11]

Three perspectives on the Joseph story appear in works from different periods in Strindberg's life (1887–88; 1897–98; 1901): the novels *A Madman's Defense* and *Jacob Wrestles* and the play *To Damascus, III*. Here is the narrator in *A Madman's Defense* speculating on the motivations of his beloved: "Perhaps . . . she felt the extraordinary power to fascinate that she exercised over this Joseph, who was so outwardly cold, so constrained to be chaste."[12] Later, when he has tired of her provocative manner, he decides to turn the tables: "I saw it clearly. She had wanted to seduce me. It was she who gave the first kiss, who made the first advance. But from this moment on it was I who was going to play the role of seducer, for I was no 'Joseph,' despite the stubborn principles I championed concerning questions of honor."[13] Apparently, the narrator both wants and does not want to be a Joseph. He wants to resist a powerful attraction but yield to it at the same time.

In *Jacob Wrestles*, another autobiographical novel, the narrator talks about advice he would give to a son: "Do not fall for the temptations of a married woman even if she incites your masculine vanity by calling you Joseph! Honor belongs, not to Potiphar's wife, but to Joseph, whose honorable name was passed on to the man who had the courage to act as foster-father to the Savior without betraying an aversion to what was an ambiguous situation for a man to be in" (*28*, 364). More ambivalent feelings! The narrator obviously regards the role in Christ's life played by a Joseph as a dubious honor at best, and we find the same reaction to being labeled a Joseph that we found in *A Madman's Defense*. We also find another analogy drawn through the process of having one mythic figure metamorphose into another: the Joseph of the Old Testament becomes the Joseph of the New. This transformational process (about which I shall have much more to say later) was common in Strindberg's work after the Inferno period and is present in a speech made by the Tempter in *To Damascus, III*, when he relates the difficulties he found in resisting the lures of a whole "world of Potiphar's wives."

> I held my own in the battle until I was twenty-five, and didn't yield to provocation, or to. . . . Yes, I was called Joseph and I was a Joseph! I was jealous of my virtue and felt wounded by the glances of an unchaste woman . . . but I finally fell, cunningly seduced. And so I became a slave of my own passions. I was with Omphale and spun [wool]. I was degraded to the depths of degradation and suffered, suffered, suffered (*29*, 302–303).

The Joseph who falls becomes Hercules degraded. The hero instead of liberating himself becomes "a slave of his own passions." Actaeon, the fallen Joseph, Jean, and the Captain are each interpreted by Strindberg as a victim in a terrible struggle in which the enemy is not simply a woman but a mythic force that derives its power from deep roots in the hero's own unconscious. In *The Father* the force was the Great Mother; in *Miss*

Julie both Jean and Julie grapple with Eros, and all the mythic and fairy tale couples alluded to—Adam and Eve, Actaeon and Diana, Joseph and Potiphar's wife, swineherd and princess— shed light on the nature and implications of this primordial confrontation.

It is significant in the tale "The Princess in the Tree" that the heroine must be saved twice, the first time at the top of the tree, the fantastic upper world, and the second on earth, the world of ordinary human beings. Julie, too, needs saving twice. As is revealed in her dream, she needs to be saved from the repressed, prisonerlike existence she endures at the top of the pillar, and she needs to be saved from the longing to be under the earth once she reaches the ground. Jean's dream and monologue make evident that even if class differences between them could be overcome, he would not be the one to rescue her. The innocent awe he remembers feeling at the sight of the girl in the pink dress and white stockings on the rose terrace was tainted by the emotions aroused during the base journey to reach her. Spiritual longing was undermined by sexual desire, Agape corrupted by Eros, with no hope of reconciliation in sight. Even as Agape elevates the innocent girl into a saint, Eros debases her into a whore. "It pains me," says Jean after the seduction, "that what I was striving for was not something higher, more solid . . . it pains me, like seeing autumn flowers that have been whipped to pieces by the rain and transformed into mud" (*23*, 154).

The play serves almost as an ironic comment on the tale and poses a dilemma: in order to win the princess, the swineherd must liberate her from the high, airy regions, but can she descend without simultaneously becoming debased in his eyes? The swineherd aspires to transcendental truth; he wants to ascend into the light of consciousness. But in order to win his lady, he must be prepared to descend with her again to earth, to see her down from the pedestal and to accept her as a total human being, spiritual and carnal. Can they descend together without both being disillusioned? "You want to conceal the wrong," says Jean to Julie after their tryst, "by pretending to yourself that you love me. You don't, there's only physical attraction—but then your love is no better than mine—and I could never be satisfied just being an animal to you" (155). He will not be transformed by a fascination with the eternal feminine either into a beast, like Actaeon, or into an impotent object of illicit desire, like Joseph; he is in a closed circle with no way out.

In *Master Olof* and *The Father*, the hero's thrust toward higher consciousness and independence is threatened by the dark forces of the maternal unconscious. In *Miss Julie*, there are direct attacks upon the very center of consciousness, expressed in either implicit or explicit images of decapitation. Jean's stropping of his razor in full view of the audience and his beheading of Julie's bird foreshadow her suicide with his razor. There is even a macabre variation on the decapitation theme expressed in a mythic image in a scene between Jean and Kristin. As they prepare to go to church on this midsummer eve—St. John's Eve—maternal Kristin is tying his tie.

JEAN [*sleepily*]:   What's the gospel text for today?
KRISTIN: The beheading of John the Baptist, I expect.
JEAN: Oh, that's sure to be horribly long. . . .
   Hey, you're strangling me! (167).

Neither Jean nor Julie will ever reach heroic stature because they are defeated by elemental weaknesses. For Jean, it is fear, fear of true commitment to the quest. For Julie, the weakness is desire, which burns like the flames of a fire. Fear and desire, classic obstacles for the mythic hero to overcome, as the Buddha overcame them under the shade of the bo tree of enlightenment.

Late in the play Jean asks Julie if she hates men. She replies, "Yes! For the most part! But sometimes, when the weakness comes, when the passion burns—ugh! Will the fire never die down?"[14] Earlier, Jean showed that he understood her better than she understood herself, as he reacted to her coquetry.

JEAN: Are you still a child at twenty-five? Don't you know
   that it is dangerous to play with fire?
JULIE: Not for me. I'm insured (134—135).

The association of fire and passion is a tragic and humiliating legacy in Julie's family. During a period when her mother was strangely ill and sometimes gone from the house all night, a terrible fire broke out, destroying the manor house, stable, and barn. Subsequent events revealed that the mother had set the fire, and the Count, in order to rebuild the manor, was forced to borrow money from his wife's lover, a degrading situation that drove him to attempt suicide. Another linking of fire and passion appears in *Jacob Wrestles*. The narrator is describing the fatefulness of his sexual awakening. "[T]he eternal coal fire has been lit and will burn until the grave, whether it glows by itself under the ashes, or is nourished by the inflammable substances in a woman. Try to extinguish this fire through abstinence and you will see passion take perverse routes and chastity punished in strange ways. Try pouring petroleum on the ignited pyre and you will get an idea of what permissive love is like!" (*28*, 362).

For Julie, passion has taken the "perverse routes" the narrator warns of and she can no longer endure the infernal fire. In her dream the longing to get down, to yield to Eros, is followed immediately by the longing to be under the earth, to yield, in other words, to the second primal instinct for which Freud found a mythic image so useful: Thanatos. Destiny will not allow her a normal evolution or rhythm of these instincts in her life; she is doomed to see them as synonymous, synchronous. At the end of the play Eros and Thanatos have become one; the fire she has fought all her life is about to consume her. These converging images all find expression in a dreamlike speech that evokes Ragnarök, the final conflagration, and orgasmic release, and she sees Jean being transformed into the figure of death.

> JULIE [*ecstatically*]: I'm already asleep . . . the whole room is like smoke . . . and you look like an iron stove . . . that resembles a man dressed in black with a tall hat . . . and your eyes glow like coals when the fire is dying . . . and your face is a white patch like ashes. [*The sunlight is now falling on the floor and reaches Jean.*] It's so warm and good . . . [*rubbing her hands as if warming them before a fire*] . . . and so bright . . . and so peaceful! (*23*, 186).

5

Creditors

COLLECTING THE CORPSE IN THE CARGO

The sheer intense virtuosity of Strindberg's performance during his so-called naturalistic period was impressive. He was a
diligent journalist, plundering the details of his own life for
copy; a developing author, restlessly experimenting with new
forms of expression in drama and fiction; and an eloquent
mythopoeic artist, constantly searching for ways to anchor the
present more firmly in the past.

In his plays there are two progressions apparent from *The
Father* to *Creditors*. First, there is a process of distillation, Strindberg trying to present what is quintessentially dramatic and
nothing more. He scraps the elaborate intrigue apparatus of the
well-made play—with its numerous characters, complicated
subplots, and heavy exposition—in favor of a minimum of
characters presenting the heart of an action in the shortest time
possible. In *The Father* there are nine speaking roles and three
acts. In *Miss Julie* there are only three speaking roles and one act,
but there is the complication of a time change: the stage directions call for the sun to rise. *Creditors*, as well, takes place in one

act, but Strindberg took pride in the fact that it was leaner and more compact than *Miss Julie*; in a letter he boasted: "three persons, one table and two chairs, and no sunrise!"[1]

The other progression involves experimentation in a range of styles that can be seen as representing different phases in the development of dramatic form from more primitive to more sophisticated. The three plays are alike in that they all approach the boundary line of drama and ritual, even to the inclusion of sacrificial victims; in each instance the tragic fate of the protagonist has about it the quality of an offering demanded by the inexorable movement of destiny. The plays differ in that while *Miss Julie* and *Creditors* have the superbly disciplined austerity of classical tragedy, drama stripped down to the archetypal confrontation of three actors—protagonist, deuteragonist, and tritagonist—*The Father* has a rough-hewn, primitive feel, like a chunk of archaic statuary. If *Miss Julie* and *Creditors* resemble classical Greek tragedy, *The Father* seems preclassical, a throwback to an earlier time when conflict was not between two or three characters, but antiphonal, between chorus and chorus leader. At the end it is the Captain versus everyone else, the sacrificial victim versus the followers and servants of the Great Mother.

Like certain Greek tragedies, *Miss Julie* has two choruses. The first is the group of offstage midsummer celebrants who are heard mocking Julie and Jean in song before they come on stage to dance and sing while the mistress of the manor and her father's valet are making love in his room. The second chorus is Kristin. In true classic spirit she is a reminder to Jean and Julie of the larger social consequences of their actions: she warns them of the price they will have to pay for their indiscretion.

In mood and tone, *Creditors* differs sharply from its predecessors. The almost formal symmetry of its scene structure, together with the cynical, often brutal, but nevertheless elegant and witty dialogue, make the play a gem of sophisticated black comedy. The streamlined plot involves a man who comes to take vengeance against his former wife by committing a psychic murder of her current husband. Returning incognito to the same resort hotel room he once shared with his wife, Gustav

visits Adolph while Tekla is away on a trip and uses the power
of suggestion to blacken her image and to produce a fatal attack
of epilepsy in his hapless victim. The play's continuous action is
separated into three scenes: in the first, Gustav undermines
Adolph's faith in his marriage; in the second, Adolph confronts
the returning Tekla with his suspicions while Gustav eavesdrops next door; and in the third, Gustav demonstrates Tekla's
fickleness while Adolph now eavesdrops and presumably fumes
with anger until he suffers the fatal attack.

As was true of his other naturalistic plays, much of the power
of *Creditors* is due neither to its fidelity to an objective, scientific
approach, nor its elegant construction; the power is generated
by an evocation of mythic forces in conflict.

The mythic setting is the same as it was in *The Father* and the
second half of *Miss Julie*: after the Fall. In *Miss Julie* Jean and Julie
fearfully await the return of the Count, as Adam and Eve
awaited inevitable retribution from Yahweh. In *Creditors*
Yahweh has arrived in the person of Gustav. As we listen to him
pretending to speculate to the unsuspecting Adolph about how
Tekla and Adolph must have met behind his back, we can also
hear the wrathful God of the Book of Genesis describing how he
discovered that his laws had been disobeyed:

GUSTAV   [*cooly, almost jokingly*]: The husband was on a re-
           search trip and she was alone. . . . Then *he* arrived
           and gradually the emptiness was filled. By compari-
           son, the absent one began to fade, for the simple
           reason that he was at a distance—you know, fading
           in proportion to the distance. But when they felt
           passion stirring, they became uneasy—about them-
           selves, their consciences, and about him. They
           sought refuge and shielded themselves behind fig
           leaves, played brother and sister, and the more
           carnal their feelings became, the more spiritual they
           pretended their relationship to be; . . . they found
           each other in a dark corner where they were certain
           no one could see them. [*with mock severity*] But they
           felt that there was *one* who saw them through the
           darkness and they became frightened; . . . he be-
           came a nightmare who disturbed their dreams of
           love, a creditor who knocked at the door; . . . they

heard his disagreeable voice in the stillness of the
night . . . (*23*, 206–207).

There is a peculiar, omniscient quality in the speech, and this
is not the only peculiar thing about Gustav: he is uncanny, and
what makes the uncanniness particularly effective is that it
is rendered subtly. As the play unfolds, the mood is that of a
psychological thriller, and the focus of attention is primarily on
Adolph, Tekla, or their marriage; we are never encouraged to
question deeply Gustav's nature. His cynicism is entertaining
and the fact that we do not completely understand at first what
he is doing or why he is doing it only stimulates our curiosity
and adds to the suspense. When we finally discover that he is
Adolph's predecessor, was slandered by Tekla, and depicted as
an idiot in one of her novels, we can accept tentatively that his
behavior was provoked by revenge, despite the fact that he acts
"cooly, almost jokingly" and is curiously devoid of passion. Carl
Reinhold Smedmark has described Gustav as the least explained character in the play: "About him we know no more
than what his actions reveal and that he helped to shape Tekla's
personality."[2] I think we know a good deal about him, but much
of the information is mysterious.

Gustav is first presented as an unknown benefactor, whose
visit has had a salutary effect on the precarious state of Adolph's
health.

ADOLPH: In these last eight days you've given me the courage
            to face life again. It's as if your magnetism radiated
            over me. To me you've been a watchmaker, fixing
            the works in my head and rewinding the main-
            spring (197).

The numinous powers ascribed to the visitor—restoring the
"courage to face life," "magnetism," "watchmaker"—indicate
that he might be a healer of some sort. But the healer's powers
are frightening.

GUSTAV: Take my hand!
ADOLPH: What dreadful power you must have! It's like grip-
            ping an electrical machine (217–218).

Adolph is constantly startled by how much the stranger knows about his life.

GUSTAV: What did you say to annoy her?
ADOLPH   You *are* dreadful! I'm afraid of you! How can you know this?

GUSTAV: I know what it was. You said: "You ought to be ashamed of yourself. Flirting at your age, when it's too late for another lover."
ADOLPH: Did I say that? I must have said it. But how could you know? (219–220).

Tekla, too, is fascinated by Gustav's unusual powers— "You've said exactly what I was thinking," she admits to him, "you've understood me!" (251)—and she finds him disturbing, almost supernaturally so.

TEKLA: Go away! I'm afraid of you!
GUSTAV: Why?
TEKLA: You take away my soul (259–260).

Gustav's personal life is only vaguely sketched, and what he says about it himself is sometimes deliberately misleading. He tells Tekla, for example, that he is going to remarry, then later admits he lied.

TEKLA: And now you're going home to your fiancée!
GUSTAV: I have none—and never want one! I'm not going home, because I have no home and don't want any (267).

The rootlessness Gustav admits to here adds to the uncanniness. When Tekla finally discovers the destructive purpose of his visit, she asks, "Are you absolutely void of feelings?" He replies, "Absolutely" (264–265). A frightening figure without feelings and without a home. Everything we learn about Gustav tends to abstract and dehumanize him. His resemblance to the unforgiving Yahweh, who catches up with Adam and Eve, is reinforced by his occupation: a teacher of dead languages (217). What a splendidly ambivalent image! On the one hand are implied ancient tongues and ancient truths; the languages of the Bible and of religious ritual. On the other hand, obsolescence:

the languages are dead and, by implication, so is God. The character becomes an illustration of a paradox Strindberg long found fascinating, one which he would explore intensively after the Inferno. In the conscious mind of modern, skeptical man, God is dead, but in the unconscious mind a presence persists: it is we but also an Other—an awareness with awesome power. Gustav is Adolph's double and he is God, Adolph can no more escape this creditor than Adam could escape Yahweh.

As in *Miss Julie*, the aspect of the Fall theme stressed in *Creditors* is alienation. In the fear of the Count in the first play and Gustav in the second is mortal fear of alienation from the divine. A deeper implication is that, although Adam and Eve had to pay a penalty for having tasted the forbidden fruit, the punishment meted out was too severe: banishment from the harmony they shared with God.

The most eloquent expression of the alienation theme appears in the final moments of the play. Behind the dialogue between Tekla and Gustav runs another dialogue: between Eve and Yahweh, with Eve trying to fathom the meaning of alienation from the divine, and Yahweh insistent upon exercising such prerogatives as vengeance.

TEKLA: How is it that you, who regard me as innocent since I was driven by my nature and the circumstances to behave as I did . . . how can you think you have the right to vengeance?
GUSTAV: For that very reason. Because my nature and the circumstances drove me to seek vengeance!

TEKLA: Have you nothing to reproach yourself for?
TEKLA: Nothing at all! . . . Christians say that Providence governs our actions, others call it fate. So, we're guiltless, aren't we?
GUSTAV: . . . Guiltless, but responsible! Guiltless before Him, who no longer exists; responsible to yourself and to your fellow human beings.

TEKLA: I'm going to leave by the eight o'clock boat. . . .
TEKLA: Without reconciliation?
GUSTAV: Reconciliation? You use so many words that have lost their meaning (264–267).

Strindberg at one time thought of ending the play the moment Adolph reenters the room and collapses in the doorway. In the final version two additional speeches follow the collapse, resuming and concluding the sotto voce dialogue of Eve and Yahweh.

TEKLA [*throwing herself upon Adolph's body and caressing him*]:   . . .
No, God, he doesn't hear. He's dead! Oh, God in
heaven, oh my God, help us, help us!
GUSTAV: She really does love him, too! . . . Poor creature!
(269).

Something has happened to Gustav in this last speech. It is as if after disbelieving in human emotion he suddenly has cause to question the disbelief. But the gap between Tekla's cry for help and Gustav's continued detachment—between mortal aspiration and divine aloofness—is too great to bridge. Gustav resembles the God of Strindberg's creation play: the demiurge, who creates the world for his own amusement, like a game, and is oblivious to the meaning of human suffering. At the end of *Creditors* the game suddenly ends and only the gamemaster is ignorant of how high the stakes were.

Throughout the play the loss of Eden, the loss of harmony, implies a longing to restore it. This longing is what Adolph is talking about when he explains how and why he came to need Tekla: "She would be what God was for me before I became an atheist. . . . I cannot live without . . . a woman to respect and worship." Gustav replies in disgust, "Oh hell! You might as well take God back then, if you need to have something to genuflect to" (213). He is contemptuous of the lure of the eternal feminine and assumes the watchmaker role Adolph attributed to him earlier. Woman as a machine, Gustav asserts, is an inferior version of man:

GUSTAV: You see, something is wrong with the mechanism!
The watchcase is that of an expensive lever-
escapement, but the works are cheap cylinder-
escapement.

Have you ever seen a naked woman? Yes, of course!
An adolescent male with teats, an immature man, a

child that shot up but stopped developing, a chronic anemic who has regular hemorrhages thirteen times a year! Whatever can come of that? (214).

There is an outrageous objectivity in Gustav's tone, not only here but elsewhere in the play, an arrogant distancing; this is a manufacturer talking about an imperfect product, or the creator talking about an abortive creation. The effect produced is one of the secrets of the play's continuing popularity with theatre audiences: Gustav's outrageousness is amusing as well as shocking, witty as well as uncanny. "You have a way of saying rude things," Tekla tells him, "that makes it impossible to be angry with you" (260). Strindberg must have been aware that if the character came across as too portentously, too obviously God-like, the play would turn into leaden melodrama. Probably nothing is more responsible for production difficulties with his plays than the failure to understand how marvelously he could use humor both to mitigate and enrich the pessimism of his themes. "After the Fall" has comic as well as tragic aspects. The archly amusing dialogue of *Creditors* works beautifully to mute without obscuring the uncanniness. When Edward Brandes wrote in a review of the published play that he found Gustav a moralizing avenger,[3] Strindberg hastened to warn the actor who was to perform the role in the first production:

Dear Hunderup, perform the whole role playfully good-natured . . . and . . . solely as psychological demolition work— so that there is truth to Tekla's words: that she finds Gustav "so free from morality and preaching."

In other words: Gustav as the cat playing with the mouse before he bites him! Never angry, never moral, never preaching![4]

The most important clue to Gustav's mythic identity is in the last scene. While Adolph eavesdrops in the adjoining room, Tekla unknowingly allows her former husband to entice her into a compromising intimacy, and she is horrified when Gustav makes her realize the situation.

GUSTAV: Do you know where your husband is?
TEKLA: Now I think I know! . . . He's in your room next

86   CREDITORS

door! And he's heard everything! And seen everything! And he who sees his *fylgia* dies! (268).

A *fylgia* in Norse mythology is an attendant spirit, a kind of
follower or second ego, capable of assuming human form. English-speaking translators of *Creditors* have rendered fylgia as
"guardian spirit," "familiar spirit," and "ghost". In 1894, when
a French production was being prepared at Lugné-Poe's
Théâtre de l'Oeuvre and translator Georges Loiseau wrote the
author for advice, Strindberg recommended that Tekla's line
read: "*Celui qui a vu son ombre, va mourir,*" but *ombre* (ghost or
shadow) did not quite satisfy him, for he added: "In our mythology to see oneself (*Sosie?*) [double, second self] was an omen of
death."[5] The playwright's efforts at clarification went for
naught, however; the line was omitted in the published
version.[6]

Double, second self, shadow, ghost: each points up Gustav's
uncanniness. But for what purpose? Was Strindberg simply
adding a spooky quality to the play, or was he attempting to
illuminate character relationships and theme? To answer this,
we need to know more about Gustav's intentions: what has he
really come for? At the opening of the play the one thing we
know for certain is that he is interested in probing, searching,
and digging. After learning that Adolph has a serious marital
problem he asks,

> GUSTAV: "Tell me, since you've already taken me so deeply
> into your confidence, have you no other secret
> wound that torments you? It's unusual to find only
> one cause for disharmony, since life is positively
> gaudy with opportunities for things to go wrong.
> Have you no corpse in the cargo that you're keeping
> to yourself?" (203).

For English-speaking readers the phrase "corpse in the cargo"
("*lik i lasten*") is more meaningfully translated as "skeleton in the
closet," but what is lost thereby is an expressive nautical resonance. An old superstition among Scandinavian sailors holds
that a ship with a corpse on board will sink. Ibsen is usually
credited with adding a metaphoric meaning: in a letter to Georg
Brandes he used a corpse in the cargo to indicate the ghosts of

old ideas that must be dumped overboard so that new ideas can be heard. But the image has more poetic meaning than this. Peer Gynt, returning home to Norway as an old man after a wasted, unfulfilled life, is also a corpse in the cargo, and the ship he travels on goes down. In *Creditors*, the corpse is a buried mystery that perhaps should remain buried. Gustav, after first trying to get Adolph to reveal the "secret wound," seems to change his mind and indicates that it would be better to leave well enough alone:

GUSTAV: "You see, there are disharmonies in life that can never be resolved. So, you have to stuff wax in your ears and work! Work, grow old, and pile masses of new impressions on the cargo hatch—that way the corpse will remain quiet" (204).

Piling "masses of new impressions on the cargo hatch" brings to mind the passage discussed earlier in connection with *Master Olof* about the organist in *The Romantic Organist on Rånö*, whose reluctance to remember the circumstances of his mother's death caused him to "pile masses of impressions" on "the black spot" (*21*, 245). Not surprisingly, perhaps, *Creditors* and the novella were written at about the same time and provide another example of Strindberg's ability to make similar or even identical images function well in different contexts.

Adolph, like the organist, has something to hide, and Gustav is only feigning disinterest in finding out what it is; he is deadly serious about collecting the corpse, and he ferrets for it until Adolph is destroyed. If Gustav is one of the "creditors" the play is about, it is not in an ordinary sense. His uncanniness, we can now see, is similar to the uncanniness of the character in fairy tales who reappears after a long absence to collect debts that have accumulated as promises unfulfilled. Adolph owes a debt, not so much to Gustav as to himself. He has failed to pursue the quest for the lost harmony properly; there are disharmonies still to be resolved within.

In seven years of marriage Adolph has done all the giving and Tekla all the taking. The consequence is that he has become hopelessly dependent on her. He sometimes thought of being free of her, but no sooner had she gone for a time than he missed

her dreadfully. He is an Adam whose undoing was the making
of Eve:

> ADOLPH: [I] longed for her as if for my arms and legs! It's
> strange, but sometimes it seems to me as if she were
> not a separate person but a part of me, an intestine
> that carried away my will, my desire to live. It's as if
> I had deposited in her my very solar plexus that the
> anatomists talk about (23, 194).

His longing for Tekla has its roots in the same problem suffered
by the Captain in *The Father*: a difficulty in separating the need
for maternal love from the need for sexual love. And Tekla, like
Laura, no longer wants to play impossible roles:

> TEKLA: I've grown tired of being a nursemaid.
> ADOLPH: Do you hate me?
> TEKLA: No! I don't, and I don't think I can, either! But
> that's probably because you're a child (242–243).

Tekla is accused of having totally devoured Adolph—his
courage, soul, knowledge, and faith—and Gustav characterizes
the situation as an instance of "cannibalism." Yet, when Tekla
appears, she turns out not to be the terribly evil person conjured
up in the two men's conversation. The reason Adolph is so
dependent on her and has allowed his marriage to deteriorate is
that he had wanted Tekla to be his "better self," to which
Gustav responds with advice Adolph might have profited from
earlier: "Be your own better self" (209).

Gustav is not simply a bitter former husband seeking revenge, he is a force of destiny thrusting Adolph into a terrible
self-confrontation, and his uncanniness serves the purpose
Freud indicated in his essay "The Uncanny": "that class of the
terrifying which leads back to something long known to us, once
very familiar."[7] As fylgia, Gustav is Adolph's double, and a
double, says Freud, is a "ghastly harbinger of death."[8] The
terrifying and familiar thing that Adolph is led back to by
Gustav's presence is a fatal psychic weakness, a lack of will.

When Adolph speaks of a loss of will, he resembles the
protagonists in Strindberg's other naturalistic plays. The Captain says that he was an unwanted child, conceived against his

parents' will and so was born "without a will" (66). Julie says that as far as she knows she came into the world against her mother's wishes, and when she wants Jean to give her the strength to commit suicide, she says to him: "You know what I *should* do, but lack the will to. . . . Will it, Jean, order me to carry it out!" (185).

Strindberg connects faith and will in an essay, "Mysticism— For the Present," written between the time he wrote *The Father* and *Miss Julie* and *Creditors*: "Faith is nothing other than a concentration of wish and desire heightened into conscious will, and the will is the greatest manifestation of nerve movement and therefore summons for its disposal the maximum possible energy" (*22*, 186–187). Faith and will become the instruments through which psychic energy flows; when they are absent, the individual lacks the means to cope with life's problems. In the context of Strindberg's naturalistic plays, lack of will represents the incapacity to battle and conquer the destructive aspects of the unconscious. The Captain cannot overcome the challenge of the Great Mother; Julie cannot deal with the fear of Eros; and Adolph cannot resolve psychic disharmonies on his own, as an independent person, in order to become his own "better self."

Perhaps in the concept of a lack of will Strindberg was searching for a modern psychological mechanism equivalent to the tragic flaw of Greek tragedy. Both are like the concealed flaw in a piece of metal that is often invisible to the naked eye. The metal appears to be perfectly sound, until one day, under a certain kind of stress, it cracks. The concealed flaw is the corpse in the cargo Gustav is after. In this way he becomes, along with Laura in *The Father* or Jean in *Miss Julie*, not so much a villain as a catalyst who precipitates the moment of fatal stress. The Captain, Julie, and Adolph are not crucified by their adversaries; they impale themselves on their own weaknesses. The power of the unconscious arouses in them a feeling of dread, that paralyzing combination of fear and fascination. They feel a calling to fight against the power, but they are doomed soldiers in a futile war. They cannot win because of the ambivalent feelings they have about the enemy: their desire to win is undermined by a desire to surrender; the desire to live, to answer the challenge of

Eros, is canceled by a stronger allegiance to Thanatos. Gustav is the herald who reminds Adolph of the calling that went unanswered, the self that was never realized.

Gustav and Laura belong to that tribe of dramatic figures— Iago is also a member—often described as pure evil. It is difficult to find a personal motivation in them strong enough to explain the terrible destruction they bring about. Hate might explain it, but Gustav especially is not really emotionally involved enough to hate. We can understand these characters better in terms of the concept so highly valued by programmatic naturalists: survival of the fittest. Rather than forces of pure evil, they are nature's instruments for finding and eliminating weakness. In a sense, they are no more evil than any predator who searches for the one lame animal in a herd and then tracks it endlessly until it is brought down. Consequently, the sense of awe we feel in the tragic destiny of a figure like the Captain, or Othello, is not in the distance they fall but in the sovereign majesty of a nature constantly balancing the scales. "I can find the joy of life," Strindberg said in the preface to *Miss Julie*, "in its cruel and powerful battles, and my enjoyment comes from being able to know something, being able to learn something" (*23*, 101).

If Strindberg's so-called naturalistic plays survive as viable stage pieces that attract actors and audiences alike, while other specimens of the genre, even from eminences like Zola, are dead, it is because Strindberg knew how to stage the kind of confrontations that make for great drama. The intersection at which his charcters meet is only incidentally the "scientifically" fixed point of historic time and place defined by late-nineteenth-century literature, where the laws of heredity and environment reign. His people obey higher laws than deterministic naturalism. "Human society," said Joyce, "is the embodiment of changeless laws which the whimsicalities and circumstances of men and women involve and overwrap. . . . Drama has to do with the underlying laws first, in all their nakedness and divine severity, and only secondarily with the motley agents who bear them out."[9]

The real adversarial relationship between Strindberg's "motley agents" is not character versus charcter but the hero versus the Other. In *The Father* and *Miss Julie* the Other—Laura's mother in the first play, the Count in the second—is offstage, as if to indicate that its presence is so terrible that one dare not face it directly. In *Creditors* Strindberg brings the Other, Gustav, onstage, and the enemy proves as formidable as we had been led to anticipate. But whether offstage or on, the Other is both more and less than an external force; the enemy for the hero is within.

A paradox exists: because the enemy is an intimate, because the enemy is oneself, even as the Other throws down the gauntlet and challenges to mortal combat, it is a potential ally. Intimate enemy can also be intimate friend. But there is a big "if": enemy can become friend only if the hero can transcend the fear and respect that are so rightly due the Other as personification of the awesome powers of the unconscious, and learn trust. From *Master Olof* through *Creditors* we have seen that the heroes either perish, as the Captain, Julie, and Adolph do, or capitulate to a life of slavery, as do Olof and Jean. They could not learn that a calling involves the paradoxical obligation both to battle and to trust the Other.

Between 1893 and 1897 a crucial hiatus occurred in Strindberg's career as a dramatist. He not only abandoned drama but belles lettres generally. When he returned to playwriting in *To Damascus*, his hero's struggle for self-realization moved into a new phase. The hero and the Other continued to grapple, and the stakes were just as high, but the hero had acquired a measure of confidence and the contest become less one-sided. A particular mythic image now appeared and reappeared in Strindberg's fiction and drama: Jacob wrestling with the angel. The Strindbergian hero had learned that like Jacob he could wrestle all night with the Other and not only survive but earn his opponent's respect and even support. Of course, a price must be paid: Jacob walked lame for the rest of his life. And before one exults in the victory it would be well to remember, as Jung observed, that the angel emerges from the fight without a scratch.[10]

6

To Damascus, I

THE POLYPHONIC MYTHIC HERO

A decade after writing *Creditors*, six years after completing his last play and two years after surviving his agonizing Inferno ordeal, from the pen of this has-been playwright came one of the most remarkable and revolutionary plays in the history of the drama. The protagonist, known only as the Stranger, is haunted on his episodic journey through a partly realistic, partly dreamlike landscape by experiences that fit well Freud's definition of the uncanny as something both terrifying and familiar. The Stranger goes to a hotel room with a woman, the Lady, and discovers that they have both been there before separately. He meets people, seemingly totally unknown to him, who possess information about his past that he has forgotten. He visits a Doctor, who is nicknamed the Werewolf, and who may or may not be an old school friend. A man called the Beggar bears a forehead scar exactly like his own. Other characters seem to have only one purpose in life, to punish him, despite the fact that they have never met him before. In the play's eeriest setting, the asylum, the Stranger sees a group of corpselike people who, according to the stage directions, resemble figures from his past without actually being those figures. Understandably, these events often reduce the hero to a state of consternation, anxiety, and dread; typically, he asks, "What is this?"

These fantastic adventures are presented in a work that is as autobiographical as anything Strindberg ever wrote. In 1896, for example, during his Inferno Crisis, he sought help from a Dr. Eliasson in Ystad, Sweden, and elements from the scenes in the Doctor's house "clearly derive", says Gunnar Brandell, "from the milieu he found [there]."[1] Similarly, in the summer of the same year, Strindberg stayed in Austria with the family of his second wife, Frida Uhl; in the play the Stranger stays with the Lady's family, whose home is set in the same kind of stark, forbidding countryside the author visited in Austria. The list goes on and on. One might think that Strindberg was deliberately discouraging prospective interpreters from searching sources or models of meaning anywhere but in his life.

Nevertheless, *To Damascus* is not simple autobiography. Its greatness lies in a complex blending of mythic and real-life elements, so that, as Egil Törnqvist put it, "the objective and subjective viewpoints overlap."[2] Like Dante, whom he imitated in part in his novel *Inferno*, Strindberg was able to fuse personal experience and literary and mythic sources into a superbly exciting texture, at once contemporary and timeless. He wrote in an 1898 letter that the play was "a fiction with a terrifying half-reality behind it."[3] The half-reality was created from the details of his own life, but what gives the details coherence is the mythopoeic structure evoked.

A virtual gallery of famous heroes is alluded to: Christ, Saul (who was transformed into Paul on the road to Damascus), Jonah, Job, Prometheus, Hercules, and more. When the Stranger invents a name for the Lady, Eve, by implication he becomes an Adam. He is a composite portrait, now one mythic figure, now another, now both at once—and no single hero is too conspicuous. Strindberg was continuing to experiment, as he had earlier in works like *Miss Julie*, with what Brian Johnston, writing about Ibsen and Joyce, called "polyphonic mythology."[4] Each of the hero images used is like an individual melodic line, and Strindberg took advantage of the polyphonic effect produced when the lines were blended to create assonances and dissonances. If parallels between mythic figures reinforce each other, contrasts and discrepancies create ironies. The mythic journey fulfilled in one hero inspires hope; the journey aborted in another turns hope to tragedy. If autobiography is sometimes the primary melodic line, then the mythic references are independent melodies working in counterpoint.

Strindberg himself was fond of drawing analogies between musical and dramatic forms. In one of his *Open Letters to the Intimate Theatre* he describes *Hamlet* as

> a symphony, executed polyphonically with independent motifs that are woven beautifully together; it is fugued. . . . The andante of the first act initiates us into all the secrets we need to know; the second movement (act) develops the theme, which then appears in variations in the third; the largo moesto (Ophelia's madness) of the fourth movement comes to rest and finds its transition in the gravediggers' scherzo only to swell forth in the presto of the finale (*50, 69*).

That Strindberg was able to experiment more boldly and confidently in polyphonic mythology after his Inferno Crisis than he had earlier was due largely to his exposure to the various interests encompassed by the Hermetic revival in Paris in the mid-1890s: alchemy, the tarot, theosophy, the Kaballah, but especially Indic mythology (to which I shall return later in the discussion of *A Dream Play*), and Emanuel Swedenborg's theory of correspondences. Strindberg learned from Swedenborg, as did Blake, Balzac, and Yeats, how to find "in the great chaos," as Strindberg described it, an "infinite coherence."[5] But this lesson did not lead him to abandon all previous artistic commitments. "I am what I have always been:" he was quoted as saying three years after completing the play, "naturalist. . . . People have said that *To Damascus* is dreams. Certainly, but completely naturalistic."[6] The implication seems to be that if naturalism made man an integral element in nature's scheme, subject to the same laws that governed plants and other animals, correspondences made him a link in the eternal chain of being and a mirror reflecting all creation. The excitement of the creative inspiration Strindberg found in Swedenborg is evident in an aphoristic essay he wrote shortly after the turn of the century, "Poetry and the Theory of Correspondences."

The teacher spoke:
> The nature of poetry shall consist of finding counterparts on different planes (Swedenborg's correspondences); therefore the image, the metaphor, the simile are of the utmost importance. . . . If I recover in the microcosm called woman all the lines with which the cosmos is constructed—the conical sections present in a beam of light, the ellipse of a planet's orbit . . . the logarithmic spiral of the calf of the leg, the spherical triangle of the womb, the hemisphere of the breast. . . .

Then I have done more than construct similes, I have beheld Nature in our most beautiful compendium, given an equation for woman derived from the infinite universe, explained her chaos, and elevated her to dignity—although without deifying her; the Earth Spirit with reminiscences from the universe (47, 207–208).

Through metaphor, Strindberg moves from one conceptual plane to another—from microcosm to macrocosm, from autobiography to myth to art—without allowing any plane to lose its integrity. The law of metamorphosis, the fundamental basis of mythological thinking, permits anything to come from anything, because, says Ernst Cassirer, in this system "anything can stand in temporal or spatial contact with anything else."[7] Thanks to metaphor, autobiographical resemblance and mythic resonance can coexist in a character without the one contaminating the other. If the Stranger resembles Strindberg, he also resembles the Wandering Jew, for example, and it is not necessary to establish a literal identity between either the character and the author or the character and the mythic figure. And metaphor can even temper an obvious literal identification. Although the Stranger gives the Lady the name Eve, as the play progresses the resonance works so that the Lady remains *an* Eve without becoming *the* Eve.

Strindberg was keenly aware of the power of metaphor, but

he was skeptical of the relevance to drama of metaphor as *logos*, metaphor developed as dialectical discourse or exposition; in an Intimate Theatre letter he takes a critical view of Shakespeare's use of the device:

> At times there are riches that are overabundant and superfluous. One figure of speech chases another and in an important scene much is lost, because metaphor is a word-puzzle that takes its own little time to solve. Sometimes a metaphor is extended through several lines and has a didactic effect, as in Virgil or Dante. An image should illuminate a context, a correspondence, as Swedenborg would say; it should combine conceptions from two different planes: two young girls, two peaches—an image from the world of men with one from the world of plants, each just as beautiful in its own way. If this is then annotated, greater clarity may be achieved, but the elaboration diminishes the effect, as when one tries to rephrase a witticism (*50*, 224–225).[8]

Rather than the metaphor of *logos*, Strindberg used the metaphor of *mythos*, illuminating a context through the narrative, structural analogy of a mythic resonance, and in so doing, revealed the kind of commitment he made as a playwright. In choosing mythos over logos he was favoring the intuitive and even irrational over the systematically philosophical. Discussing possible revivals of Greek tragedies, he wrote: "The troubled Euripides should be tested to see if today he can move us more than the calm Sophocles"(41). Without question, Strindberg himself belongs with Euripides among the troubled rather than the calm figures in the history of the drama.

To Damascus becomes more accessible and less of a puzzle explicable only by references to Strindberg's life when we realize the enormous freedom he found in the related devices of polyphonic mythology and the metaphoric-association system of correspondences. These were means by which to keep in balance or to hold in coherent suspension such dichotomous elements as the realistic and the unrealistic, the historic and the mythic, the psychological and metaphysical. The basic conflict is still, as it was in the pre-Inferno plays, between the hero and the Other, but now Strindberg has no hesitancy about freely mixing levels of meaning: the hero versus the Other becomes simultaneously man versus himself and man versus God.

Out of the conflict comes the hope of reconciliation, a possibility that was out of the question in the pre-Inferno plays. Olof, for example, cannot reconcile his duty to accept Gert's call with his guilt for having defied his mother's authority. By contrast, reconciliation is the central thrust in *To Damascus*, and throughout there is a tension between the concept of alienation, or separation, sometimes expressed in grim images of dismemberment and death, and the concepts of atonement, reunion, and rebirth, most typically present in references, direct and indirect, to that symbol of perfection and fulfillment, the rose.

The instruments through which the Stranger is presented with possibilities of making peace with himself and with the world are doubles, or doppelgängers. If the Beggar is the Stranger's doppelgänger of the same sex, the Lady represents one of the opposite sex. Implicit in the hero's pilgrimage is the question: "Where can I be whole and complete?" The doubles—fragments of the Other—help provide the answer. The same kind of question is asked by the protagonist of the medieval drama *Everyman*, who learns that one becomes complete only in heaven. Each episode in *Everyman* carries an exhortation to accept: accept God's calling; accept the need for penance; accept the need to leave the transitory and worldly behind; accept the inevitability of death tempered by the promise of resurrection.

The answer the Stranger receives from his doubles, stated obliquely rather than directly, is also acceptance. They ask him to accept a part of himself that he has either rejected or refused to recognize. The Lady asks him to free the maiden in the tower, to free the capacity to love and become whole. The Beggar asks him to accept the humbled self and the need to have and be a friend. A more bizarre double, the madman Caesar, is by serial implication the Beggar's double, and together the two call to mind the examples in Christ's admonition: "Whoever exalts himself will be humbled; and whoever humbles himself will be exalted."[9] Caesar is one of the Doctor's patients and is permitted to putter about in the garden "regulating Creation," as the Doctor puts it (*29*, 40). The Stranger, in his vocation as writer, is also attempting to regulate Creation, and Caesar, as his double, reflects the megalomania of the artist who presumes to imitate the ultimate Creator and thus usurps divine prerogatives. At one point the Lady rebukes the Stranger: "Don't liken yourself to the Creator, because in moments like that you remind me of Caesar back home" (55). But even Caesar's answer to the Stranger is "accept." The Stranger feels guilty when he first sees the madman because he is reminded of a childhood transgression for which he was never punished. Caesar's pathetic appearance and behavior, however, suggest that the Stranger must accept, not so much past guilt, as present need to be forgiven.

In the first half of the play the Stranger resists the challenge his doubles pose, in the second half he is more amenable and consequently comes closer to understanding who he is. In effect, all the Stranger's relationships with his doubles are part of a continual intrapsychic conflict that he cannot escape, not even in solitude because, as he says, "There's always someone there. I don't know whether it's someone else or myself I sense, but in solitude one is never alone. The air gets more dense; it germinates, and beings begin to grow which are invisible but are alive and can be sensed" (9–10).

The Stranger is dimly aware that the curious beings he encounters originate within himself, that he has summoned them, unconsciously:

STRANGER: So there you are. I almost knew you'd come.
LADY: So, you did call to me. Yes, I felt it (7).

As his conscious mind strives for rational explanations of what is happening to him, his unconscious mind sends messages, now encouraging, now disapproving, couched in the evocative, but ambiguous language of mythic and symbolic images. Thus, even as the Stranger is constantly startled by frightening portents, the portents are complemented by promises of renewal. The threat of spiritual death is balanced by a wondrous, incredible opportunity for spiritual rebirth. Hence, the doubles have dual natures: they are allies when the Stranger is ready and willing to accept their help; they are enemies when he is reluctant to face the challenge of a creative self-confrontation.

The plot structure has many ingredients of a prototypal hero quest. The Stranger offers to liberate the Lady from her werewolf husband, the maiden from her captor, and he exults: "Battling trolls, liberating princesses, killing werewolves— that's what life is all about!" (30). But he takes her from her husband's home surreptitiously, not openly; they sneak off through the back gate, and he feels guilty. They flee on a pilgrimage that takes them to her family home. After a disagreement, the Stranger leaves and has an accident that puts him into a hospital, and his stay there resembles that of a Ulysses or an Aeneas in the underworld. Returning to the Lady's mother, he is reminded that he failed to settle accounts properly with the Doctor/Werewolf, which he then sets off to do. This confrontation ends inconclusively, however, and in the final scene the Lady and the Stranger are back together and seem ready to embark on another pilgrimage.

Interwoven through the plot are two mythic quest images that contribute eloquently to the thematic rhythm of alienation-reconciliation: the Ahasuerus legend and the mystical bond between the eternal feminine and the rose. Ahasuerus, the Wandering Jew, traditionally symbolizes the hero who refuses to answer the call, the Jerusalem shoemaker who taunted Christ on the road to Calvary with: "Go faster!" to which Christ replied, "I go, but you shall be waiting here for me when I return."[10] As a result, Ahasuerus is doomed to wander the earth, unable to die, until the Day of Judgment.

This legend, which first appears in literary sources in the thirteenth century, enjoyed a period of great popularity during Strindberg's lifetime, especially between 1885 and 1905. Eugène Sue's gigantic novel, *The Wandering Jew*, was typical of the vogue; Strindberg read it and admired it as a sixteen-year-old gymnasium student. During his watershed Inferno years, Strindberg identified strongly with the doomed wanderer. To Torsten Hedlund he wrote in 1896: "Doesn't it seem as if I have had an Ahasuerus judgment pronounced upon me?"[11] and in two other letters to Hedlund he talks about his "Ahasuerus path."[12] A year and a half later, just before he began *To Damascus*, he was working on a novel, *Jacob Wrestles*, in which the narrator describes trudging in Paris past stores that sell religious objects, hoping to encounter once more a Christ-like vision he had seen earlier.

> I walked the road to Calvary up the Rue Bonaparte. Never had the street seemed so vast to me as it did this evening and the shop windows gaped like abysses in which Christ appeared in a multitude of guises, now martyred, now triumphant. And while the sweat ran down in huge drops and the soles of my boots burned my feet, I walked and walked without making a single step of progress. Was I Ahasuerus, who had denied the Savior a drink of water, and now, when I wanted to follow Him and imitate Him, was incapable of approaching Him? (*28*, 348).

The narrator calls the vision he saw "*Den Okände*," "the Unknown One," the same name generally translated as "the Stranger" in *To Damascus*. In both the novel and the play the search for the Unknown One is a search for the Christ within, a symbolic inward journey to self-understanding and self-realization. Ahasuerus resists the exhortation to embark on the journey and pays with an eternal sense of desolation. An elaboration of the same theme is in a poem, published in 1903 as part of the novel *Alone*. In it, Ahasuerus, aboard a ship, resembles another wanderer: the Flying Dutchman.

> Ahasuerus stands in the bow,
> searching the gray wall before him,
> eyes moist, fists clenched,
> lips pursed in a whitened beard. . . .
>
> Out into the gray nothingness stares
> the wanderer, imprisoned on a deck,
> staring down listlessly into the deep,
> feeling as if drowned in a sack (*38*, 170).

Parallels between the plight of Ahasuerus and that of the Stranger at the beginning of the play are not hard to find: both are lonely men, separated from wife and children, despised by friends and relatives alike, and doomed to wander for an eternity. "My misfortune," says the Stranger, "is that I can't grow old" (*29*, 16). A note made for the poem and cited by Gunnar Ollén reads: "Ahasuerus: becomes young every tenth year in

order to have the strength to wander."[13] The Wandering Jew
becomes the symbol for the profoundest kind of alienation,
which is also the Stranger's state: at the opening curtain he
stands on a street corner in a city—the familiar crossroads of
myth and fairy tale—and, according to the stage directions,
"seems to wonder which way to go" (7). The buildings in the
background suggest a choice of direction in the manner of
medieval theatre settings for heaven and hell: a church and a
café, the spiritual versus the worldly. There is also a post office
and implicit in this visual image, together with auditory images
mentioned in the scene of a funeral march and church bells, is
the idea of a message, a reminder, a call. Subsequently, we learn
that a letter awaits the Stranger in the post office, but he is
reluctant to pick it up, and the march music and tolling of the
bells return again and again to make him uneasy. Like Ahasuerus, he refuses the call, and he waits.

LADY: What are you waiting for?
STRANGER: If I only knew. For forty years I have been waiting
             for something. I think it's called happiness—or
             maybe just the end of unhappiness (7–8).

But will he recognize what he has been waiting for when and if it
appears? If Ahasuerus denied Christ once, will he not do the
same thing again when the opportunity presents itself? In fact,
this is what happens in the first act of *To Damascus* where two of
the scenes contain resonances of Ahasuerus-Christ confrontations: those involving the Beggar and the funeral procession.

The Beggar is a marvelous creation, partly amusing, partly
ominous. When the Stranger is made uneasy because the Beggar's forehead scar resembles his own—they are both Cain, who
was also destined to wander—he tries to bribe the man to
disappear and look for cigar butts in another part of town.

BEGGAR: I'll go, but this is too much money. Look, I'll give
             you three quarters of it back. That way we don't
             owe each other anything more than a friendly gift.
STRANGER: Friendly gift! Am I your friend?
BEGGAR: At least I'm yours. And when you find yourself
             alone in the world, you can't be too choosy about
             people.

STRANGER: Permit me a farewell word: learn what your place is!
BEGGAR: With pleasure, with pleasure. And when we meet
             again, I'll have a greeting worthy of your farewell
             (19).

The Swedish word the Stranger uses in his farewell is the
condescending *hut*, which one says to dogs to quiet or restrain
them. There is an expression "*hut går hem*," meaning that arrogant epithets have a way of boomeranging. The Beggar's reply,
like that of Christ to Ahasuerus, has the tone of the warnings in
fairy tales that are refused by heroes, who will come to regret
their actions.

The arrival of the funeral procession is heralded several times
by the sounds of Mendelssohn's march. As was true of the
entrance of the Beggar, the procession appears immediately
after the Stranger begins drawing patterns in the sand as he sits
on a park bench. The drawing action and the response to it
suggest that the Stranger is conjuring up these apparitions
himself, that another double is emerging from his unconscious,
that he is creating his own world, and that the world is he.
Drawing in sand had a compulsive quality that Strindberg
understood well. Four years before *To Damascus* he asked in the
essay, "Ego":

> Have you never during a solitary promenade in a park or garden
> or along a boulevard sat down on a bench and with your cane
> begun to draw geometric figures in the sand? After a time you
> survey your unconscious work and see that you are enclosed in
> an infinity of concentric circles in which you yourself constitute
> the center. This is the instinct of ego expansion, the tendency to
> place oneself on the earth's axis, the inclination to fence in a plot
> of land, to trace a horizon around oneself. It is this that guides
> your cane, the radius of a circle which is always with you and
> from which you can never escape.[14]

Geometric figures like the ones Strindberg describes also
fascinated Jung, who called them *mandalas*, the Sanskrit word
for magic or sacred circles, and he wrote extensively about the
psychic need their construction satisfies, wherever they appear:
in alchemical diagrams, oriental religious art, or the drawings of
children. According to Jung, they represent the deepest kinds of

instincts toward wholeness and oneness; in them "the energy of the central point is manifested in the almost irresistible compulsion and urge to *become what one is.*"[15] To become what he is is what the Stranger has been waiting for, and part of this is symbolized in the person of the dead man whose funeral procession is approaching: both men, we learn, "could not take life seriously" and let others support their wives and children (9, 25).

The dead man also resembles someone whose identity is disguised the way facts in dreams are disguised from the dreamer. The mourners wear brown rather than black and carry unusual things: a banner with the shield of the carpenters' union, a large broadaxe, and a cushion surmounted by a speaker's gavel. When the Stranger asks who died, he is told a carpenter. The Carpenter, of course, is one of the traditional names for Christ, and the funeral procession duplicates symbolically the journey to Calvary. The Stranger does not see this, nor does he see how the earth color of the mourners' clothes— which to his mind is improper and impractical—mitigates the forbidding message of the other symbolic elements: the axe and the gavel, the latter suggesting the passing of a judgment, like the terrible judgment passed on Ahasuerus. Later, the Stranger actually says he thinks he heard a gavel fall (30).

Although the Beggar and the curiously dressed procession make a deep impression on the Stranger, he cannot answer the call they represent, and so, in effect, he denies Christ twice, and by implication denies himself. He has failed to see that behind the Beggar's caution about the necessity of friendship was the lesson of the golden rule, and that the funeral procession was a reminder of the Savior's redemptive sacrifice. The Stranger heard but refused to accept that the bells and music were tolling for him. Appropriately, even the final triumphant moments of the first scene when the Lady returns from a visit to the chapel are marred by signs of foreboding.

LADY: A candle went out on the altar and a cold wind blew
           across my face just as you cried out to me.
STRANGER: I didn't cry out; I only longed for you. . . .

LADY: Come, my liberator! [*She draws the veil down over her
             face, kisses him quickly on the mouth, and hurries out.*]
             (30–31).

The recurrence of the familiar image of the liberation of the
maiden indicates that perhaps a quest has begun, but the Lady's
action in veiling her face recalls the donning of the fig leaves and
the archetypal scene of man's first disobedience. One antici-
pates a reaction of divine wrath, and it is not long in coming:
from within the church comes the scream of women's voices, a
rose window darkens, and a heavenly sight strikes fear into the
mourners. The tree under which the Stranger sits trembles,
evoking the fate of another mythic hero with whom Strindberg
readily identified at the time he wrote the play, Buddha (see
chapter 8). Just as the Stranger sits under a tree, so Buddha sat
under the great bo tree. But while the Stranger yields to the
Lady's entreaties, Buddha steadfastly resisted the temptation of
sensual desire and went on to learn perfect enlightenment.

The Stranger experiences his sense of alienation two ways:
psychically, through a fear that he is going mad, and physically,
through a feeling that he is dismembered:

> It seems to me as if I lay chopped to pieces in Medea's cauldron
> and were being boiled slowly. I'll either turn into soap or rise up
> rejuvenated out of my own bouillon! It all depends on Medea's
> skill (23).

The cauldron is a vessel of transformation, and the Stranger
counts on the healing powers of the eternal feminine to restore
him to wholeness. Another vessel and symbol of wholeness is
the rose, and the Lady is wearing a Christmas rose when she
returns from St. Elizabeth's chapel. The Stranger sees a sign of
hope: he recalls that the Christmas rose was once used to cure
madness.

It is generally assumed by scholars that Strindberg's purpose
in the allusion to St. Elizabeth of Thuringen (1207–31) was to
draw a parallel between the saint's association with the poor and
needy and the helping role the Lady plays in the Stranger's
destiny. But St. Elizabeth's link with roses is probably more

important. The article about St. Elizabeth in the *Encyclopedia Britannica* states that

> According to the legend, much celebrated in German art, [her] husband Louis at first desired to curtail her excessive charities, and forbade her unbounded gifts to the poor. One day, returning from hunting, he met his wife descending from the Wartburg with a heavy bundle filled with bread. He sternly bade her open it; she did so, and he saw nothing but a mass of red roses. The miracle completed his conversion.[16]

Like St. Elizabeth's husband, the Stranger is in need of salvation, and the rose the Lady wears is only one of a score of references in the play to the flower that is a symbol of the means by which salvation can be attained: another maṇḍala image of unity and oneness and a classic attribute of the Great Mother. At one point in the first scene images of the rose and the Great Mother interpenetrate.

[*The sun breaks through and lights up the colored rose window above the church door, which opens and reveals the interior of the church. Organ music and the hymn* Ave Maris Stella *can be heard.*]
LADY [*exiting from the church; to the Stranger*]: Where are you? What are you doing? Why did you call to me again? Must you hang on to a woman's skirts like a child? (28).

The focus moves in sequence from the rose window and its traditional associations with Eve and the Virgin to the womb interior of Mother Church to a hymn that connects the Great Mother with another symbol of transformation and rebirth, the sea.

> Hail, thou star of ocean!
> Portal of the sky!
> Ever Virgin Mother
> Of the Lord most high!

Then comes a jarring note: the Lady is irritated because the Stranger has called to her out of his need for maternal comforting. Will he never grow up? He has a need for a confrontation in which to resolve his ambivalent relationship with the Great

Mother, and it will take place under the sign of the same flower in the rose chamber of the Lady's family home.

Christmas roses appear again at the Doctor's house, where the Stranger and the Lady pay a visit before running off together. But the Stranger senses that something is wrong: the flowers are growing in summer instead of winter, as they should; and he becomes even more anxious when he learns that the roses are being grown by a person who is, as the Doctor describes him, "somewhat mentally ill," and who broods about the "impracticality" of a nature that lets the flower stand freezing in the snow and so plants them out of season (40).

The Stranger's own fear of becoming insane has been rekindled, and when he subsequently learns that the madman is called Caesar, a nickname he himself had as a child, he finds the impression of déja vu unbearable. "I have never experienced," he confesses to the Lady, "a more painful half hour in my whole life" (42).

There is a lesson here for the Stranger if he could but read it. His double, Caesar, plants Christmas roses at the wrong time because he is incapable of understanding their message of hope and spiritual restoration: flowers that bloom at the time of the winter solstice and are thus connected with the birth of the Savior, a sign of the promise of bright rebirth emerging in the midst of icy gloom. To the Stranger, suffering in spiritual darkness, comes a sign of light, but he is not ready to understand.

The Stranger and the Lady leave the Doctor's house, but they cannot escape either roses or the Werewolf's influence. In a hotel room the wallpaper pattern is Christmas roses, but when examined more closely, the pattern is seen to contain a likeness of the Doctor. "At any moment," says the Stranger, "I expect the funeral march to start and make things complete. [*Listening*] There it is!" (50). Once more they flee, to continue their restless pilgrimage until they arrive, penniless and exhausted at the Lady's family home and the rose chamber.

[*A simple, but homelike furnished room in the forester's house. The walls are limewashed in rose red: the curtains are of thin, rose-red muslin.*

Flowers stand in the small latticed windows. . . . to the left, a couch,
above which rose-red curtains are draped in the form of a baldachin.]

[*The Lady is sitting on the couch, crocheting. The Mother is standing,*
holding a book bound in red covers.] (79).

Eve, the Mother, and the rose: a comprehensive portrait of the
eternal feminine. The moment of reconciliation seems at hand
for the Stranger, and the hopes he entertains in this setting are
similar to those of the narrator in the novel *Inferno*, in which
Strindberg used as raw material many of the same real-life
experiences contained in *To Damascus*. The narrator describes
his feelings at the threshold of the rose room in the home of his
mother-in-law's aunt:

> I stopped . . . deeply moved as if confronted by a vision. The
> walls were painted rose, as rosy as the redness of the dawns that
> had pursued me all during my journey. The curtains too were
> rose, and the windows crowded with flowers that colored the
> light filtering in. An air of infinite cleanliness reigned and the
> ancient fourposter with its canopy was fit for a virgin's repose.
> The whole room and the way it was furnished was a poem
> composed by a soul who lived only part of the time on this earth.
> The Crucified One was not there, but the blessed Virgin was,
> and a basin of holy water guarded the entrance against evil
> spirits.
>   A feeling of shame seized me. I was afraid of defiling this
> fantasy created by a pure soul who raised this temple to the Holy
> Mother (*28*, 127).

The awe and wonder pervading the scene transforms the
room into the inner sanctuary of the Great Mother, a womblike
crucible where the narrator's wounded soul can be made sound
and whole again.

In the play the Stranger's hope of finding spiritual peace and
fulfillment in the rose chamber is thwarted. The Mother lures
her daughter into doing something the Stranger had warned
against, reading his latest book. A bitter marital quarrel ensues,
and he decides to leave. The Lady, like Lot's wife, has made the
mistake of looking back, into the past, and as her husband exits,
she remains, according to the stage directions, standing for a
moment, "as if turned to stone" (*29*, 88).

Before he goes, however, the Stranger makes a portentous admission: "I am Caesar, the schoolboy, who committed a prank for which someone else was blamed. That someone was your husband—the werewolf" (84). Finally confessing that he is Caesar is the most important step yet taken, accepting a part of himself that he had previously rejected, but it is fraught with danger. By laying bare a long-buried secret, he has released energies that have been dammed up since he was a child, energies that might be difficult to harness. Significantly, over the next three scenes—the asylum, then back to the rose chamber, and the kitchen in the Mother's home—the action follows the familiar mythic route of the Greek *Nekyia*, or "night sea journey," as the Stranger traverses an underworld of nightmare memories and experiences.

The journey has a momentous beginning. The Stranger has been brought to the asylum after a curious accident which suggests Jacob's wrestling match with the angel. Found delirious on a mountain, he was shaking a crucifix threateningly at the sky, and complained of a hip pain, although no injury could be found.

The asylum is an uncommon sanctuary, an abode of shades who resemble people from the Stranger's past, and his guide through this infernal region is the Confessor, another double and messenger from the unconscious, revealing things the conscious mind would rather not face. As Scrooge was forced to watch scenes out of Christmas past and present, the Stranger is humiliated in this dreamlike sequence with reminders of neglected responsibilities.[17] The shadowy figures include: "a madman called Caesar," a Beggar, a Doctor called a Werewolf, and "two parents who worried themselves to death over a degenerate son who . . . has to answer for the fact that he did not follow his father's coffin to the cemetery and that then, while drunk, profaned his mother's grave" (92–93).

In the manner often characteristic of dreams—Strindberg would later, in the preface to *A Dream Play*, refer to *To Damascus* as his "earlier dream play"—the mention of the parents is loaded with guilt and resentment, and the effect produced is both grim and absurdly comic. Failing to follow the father's coffin is another indirect reference to Ahasuerus, but then this is coupled with a wonderfully grotesque and expressive way of showing one's hostility toward the Great Mother.

The Stranger's response to the Confessor's identification of the shades is to turn his back on them, but then he catches sight of a painting of the archangel Michael slaying the Evil One, and lowers his eyes in shame. He feels guilty when reminded of a mythic hero slaying a dragon—the metaphor for man's obligation to accept archetypal challenges and confrontations—because up to now he has only been superficially committed to this kind of responsibility. The asylum becomes a ritualistic damnation scene, with the Confessor reading over the hapless Stranger selections from the requiem mass and the curse of Deuteronomy, which as it appears in the text, is an edited and adapted version that emphasizes the Stranger's kinship with Ahasuerus:

You shall wander about in all the lands of the earth. . . .

You shall find no peace upon this earth, and your foot no rest . . . (93, 95).

In addition to the Confessor, the Stranger is attended by the Abbess, a maternal figure whom he addresses as "Mother" and who calls him, in turn, "my son." In her religious garb the Abbess evokes the presence and the message of the Virgin:

ABBESS: We take no payment here. Everything is done out of
            charity. . . .
STRANGER: I don't want charity. I don't need it.
ABBESS: It's true that it's more blessed to give than to receive,
            but it takes a generous spirit to be able to accept and
            be grateful.
STRANGER: I don't need to accept anything and ask for noth-
            ing . . . I won't be forced to be grateful.
ABBESS: Hm! Hm! hm! (90).

The woman, another double, has offered the Stranger valuable advice, but he cannot yet take it. She too urges him to accept not just charity but *caritas*, the forgiving tenderness and compassion of the eternal feminine that is most commonly idealized in maternal love.

ABBESS: If you ever need charity, you know where it can be found.
STRANGER: No, that I don't know.
ABBESS [*in a half-whisper*]: I'll tell you where. In a rose-red room, by a great flowing water.

Now, after three months of lying sick, the Stranger finds a new readiness for acceptance.

STRANGER: Yes, you're right. Only there can charity be found!

But when he returns to the rose chamber, he finds that a terrible transformation has taken place.

[*The curtains have been removed. The windows gape like black holes into the darkness outside. The furniture is covered with brown throws and pushed together downstage. The flowers are gone. A large, black iron stove is lit. The Mother stands ironing white sheets by the light of a single candle.*] (96–97).

The comforting, womblike rose chamber has turned hostile. In *Inferno* a similar metamorphosis takes place in the rose room, after which the narrator observes: "What a strange coincidence that in the good old days the torture chamber in Stockholm was called the Rose Chamber!" (*28*, 171–172).

The Stranger may think that in coming back from the asylum he has returned from hell—indeed, he says so to the Mother—but, in fact, he has only entered another region of the underworld. The Mother, like a guardian at the entrance, conducts an interrogation of sorts to ascertain whether the Stranger is ready for the next phase of the journey.

MOTHER: What do you seek here?
STRANGER: Charity.
MOTHER: At last. . . .

          Have you . . . become aware that neither you nor any other human being guides your curious destiny?
STRANGER: That's precisely what I think I have become aware of.
MOTHER: Then you've come part of the way (*29*, 99–101).

He has made real progress: he has accepted the guilt that he had kept buried since he was a child and accepted his need for caritas. But he still has far to go. Up to now, he thought his quarrels were with other people.

MOTHER: You've got it wrong. . . . It's between you and Him.
STRANGER: Whom?
MOTHER: The Unseen One who guides your destiny (102).

In the next scene the ominous sounding "Him" echoes in the Mother's farewell words as the Stranger is about to resume his quest: "But on the way, don't forget to see to him—the one you call the Werewolf" (110). The Stranger has faced many obstacles, but the greatest is still ahead: a true confrontation, which the Confessor predicted in the asylum scene. When the Stranger said he still had a fever and was "going to find a real doctor," the Confessor warned, "Be sure he is the real one; . . . he who can cure your 'beautiful pangs of conscience' " (96).

Before he leaves the Mother to go search for the Lady, the Stranger will spend the night in the attic; the Mother warns him in the manner of a fairy tale oracle: "It's good that you're not afraid of ghosts because . . . no one's ever slept through a whole night up there, for whatever reason" (104).

The mention of a strange attic brings to mind the attic in *The Father*: both places are haunted by associations with the Great Mother. In *The Father*, Bertha is alarmed because she hears singing from the room in the attic "where the cradle is"; evoked is a dark and mysterious context of mother, fear, and childhood memories. The same context is present in *To Damascus* in the scene following the one in the rose chamber, the kitchen, where we find that the curse still holds. The Stranger, like his predecessors, was unable to sleep through the night in the attic.

It is appropriate that the final scene of the night sea journey should be set in a kitchen. The place where foodstuff is modified by cooking is a vessel of transformation and transmutation and is related to Medea's cauldron and to the alchemical crucible. If the entire house is the domain of the eternal feminine, "female domination," according to Erich Neumann, "is symbolized in its center, the fireplace, the seat of warmth and food preparation, the 'hearth,' which is also the original altar."[18]

The time is that conventionally darkest part of the night, before the dawn:

[*It is dark, but the moon outside casts moving shadows of the window lattices on the floor as storm clouds pass by.*]

[*One can hear the wind murmuring. In the distance there is the roar of a waterfall; and now and then there are sounds of thumping on a wooden floor.*]
STRANGER [*entering, dressed, carrying a candle*]:
Is there someone here? . . . No one! [*crossing with the candle, which lessens somewhat the play of shadows*] What's that moving on the floor? . . .
Is there someone here? [*He crosses toward the table, but when he sees a stuffed bird of prey (on the table) he stops as though petrified.*] Jesus Christ! (105).

The moonlight and darkness, those enveloping attributes of the Great Mother, and the Stranger's anxiety suggest the presence and power of the unconscious. Only the Mother herself is needed to make the archetypal confrontation complete:

STRANGER: I couldn't sleep.
MOTHER [*gently*]:   Why not, my son?
STRANGER: Someone was walking in the room above mine.
MOTHER: That's impossible. There's no other attic above that one.

STRANGER: Who could be thumping at this time of night? Is someone locked out?
MOTHER: No, it's a horse kicking in the stable.
STRANGER: I never heard of that before.
MOTHER: Oh yes, there are horses that are tormented by the nightmare spirit (105–106).

The Swedish word Strindberg uses for the nightmare spirit, *mara*, has several meanings: either nightmare or witch or female spirit who torments humans or horses by riding or sitting on them.[19] This is the Terrible Mother as a chastising spirit, as one of the furies, the very role the Lady's Mother is fated to play in the Stranger's life. She torments him just as the mara torments the horse.

STRANGER: What is the nightmare spirit?

MOTHER: Meaning no offense, I'll tell you what [it] is: it is my
           evil conscience. Whether it is myself or someone
           who's punishing me, I don't know, and I don't
           believe I have the right to ask (106–107).

In *Master Olof* we saw how the protagonist overcame his
mother's devouring influence on a conscious level but remained
her slave on an unconscious one; and in *The Father* how the
Captain actually participated in his own destruction as an
almost willing ritual sacrifice to the Great Mother. The confrontation in *To Damascus* is different because the Mother has
another purpose: she is not trying to subjugate the Stranger to
her will; she senses a calling to prepare the hero for a decisive
confrontation with a higher power by chastising him for the sin
of hubris: "Pride must be cut down," she says (74).

As he was with many Greek mythic and religious concepts,
Strindberg was intrigued with the paradox of hubris: a sin for
which the punishment was necessary but somehow unjust. The
narrator in *Inferno* talks of "arrogance, *hubris*, the one vice that
the gods do not forgive" (*28*, 80); but the Stranger at the end of
To Damascus, II, describes pride as "the last trace of our divine
origin (*29*, 235). Unless man is presumptuous, unless he risks
hubris, he can never fulfill his destiny, but the sin must be paid
for. With hubris comes inflation and the risk of attempting to fly
too high, as Icarus did, thus incurring the wrath of the gods. In
mythic terms, whether Greek or Judeo-Christian, the committing of a hubristic act tips out of balance the scale that apportions
mortal and divine prerogatives, and we wait for the inevitable
righting of the scale to take place. Eve is tempted into the defiant
act of tasting the forbidden fruit by the Serpent's promise that
she and Adam "will be like gods knowing both good and evil."[20]
After the Stranger runs off with the Lady, he arrogantly proclaims: "I feel all the strengths of the Creator within me, for I am
He"; and "See, we are gods!" (54, 56). It has thus been certain all
along that he must pay for his arrogance; the only questions
were when and how.

The climax of the Mother's chastising has an exorcistic quality, like a ritual ceremony of purgation and purification.

MOTHER: Bend! Yield!

STRANGER:	I can't!
MOTHER:	On your knees!
STRANGER:	I won't!
MOTHER:	Christ have mercy on you! The Lord have mercy on you! . . . [*to the Stranger*] On your knees to the Crucified One! Only He can undo what has been done.
STRANGER:	No, not to Him! Not Him! And if I'm forced to do it, I'll take it back . . . later.
MOTHER:	On your knees! My son!
STRANGER:	I can't bend my knees . . . I can't . . . Help me, Eternal God!
	[*pause*]

The pause noted in the stage directions comes at an interesting place. The Stranger has been able to acknowledge and ask for help from a higher authority: the Unseen One who steers his destiny, the Unknown One, the Other, and the Mother recognizes that a turning point has been reached.

MOTHER [*hastily mumbling a prayer, then*]:	Is it better?
STRANGER [*collecting himself*]:	Yes! . . . But do you know what that was? It wasn't death. It was annihilation.
MOTHER:	The annihilation of the Divine—that which we call the death of the spirit (108–109).

The Stranger has been humbled, but without the total loss of identity that is, for example, the Captain's fate in *The Father*. He has acknowledged a higher authority without having to grovel before it. He has suffered through a long siege of hubris, and now the process of purgation and expiation has begun.

The many references in the play to the threat of madness coalesce in the concept of hubris: it is the madness of hubris that the Stranger has begun to recognize in the kitchen scene, and he goes on to a deeper understanding of it in the remaining scenes in the play. When he reacts positively to the Mother's explanation about the "annihilation of the Divine," she encourages him to pursue his quest further: "My son! You have left Jerusalem and are on the road to Damascus. Go there!" (110). The final moments of the kitchen scene are haunting and moving. The sun is rising, a proper end for a night sea journey, the movement of which is traditionally from west to east.

MOTHER: The dawn is here. It's morning and the night has
           past.
STRANGER: And what a night!

MOTHER [*looking out of the window; as though to herself*]:
           You beautiful morning star, why have you fallen so
           far from Heaven?
           [*pause*]
STRANGER: Have you noticed how—just before the sun goes
           up—we mortals shiver? Are we the children of
           darkness that we tremble before the light? (111).

The Mother's greeting to the morning star carries an echo of Lucifer. In Isaiah we find God rebuking the king of Babylon for his arrogance just as the Mother has rebuked the Stranger:

How you have fallen from Heaven, bright morning star . . .

You thought in your own mind,
    "I will scale the heavens . . .

"I will rise high above the cloud-banks
    and make myself like the Most High."
Yet you shall be brought down to Sheol,
    to the depths of the abyss.[21]

The way the mother mentions the morning star—"as if to herself"—identifies Lucifer only indirectly with the Stranger, but there are other instances in the play that reveal a more deliberate effort on the part of the author to create similar resonances in the character. When the Stranger and the Lady arrive at her family home, her grandfather observes: "Well, that was no angel," to which the Mother adds: "At least not an angel of light" (76). The Stranger himself admits that for him the sounds of church bells and the presence of holy water "are like when the Evil One sees the sign of the Cross" (14); and the Doctor's Nurse thinks he "resembles the Evil One" (34). This identification of the Stranger with the fallen angel, together with the numinous, God-like aura established about the Doctor by the Confessor's warning about finding the "real" doctor and by the Mother's admonition to be sure "to see to him"—the one called the Werewolf—all prepare us to expect that the final meeting between the two men will have a Biblical dimension: Lucifer paying a return visit to God.

After leaving the Mother's house, the Stranger has another marvelous meeting on the highway with the Beggar, who, as he promised when they first met, has a greeting worthy of the Stranger's hostile farewell, another reminder that the Stranger's hubris still needs curbing and another implied criticism of Ahasuerus's rejection of Christ: "When I once asked if you knew who I was, you replied that you weren't interested. In return I offered you my friendship, but you refused it by telling me what my place was!" The message touches a sensitive nerve:

> STRANGER [*as if to himself*]:
> Who reads my secret thoughts? Who turns my soul inside out? Who persecutes me? Why do you persecute me?
> BEGGAR: Why do you persecute me? Saul! [. . . *The sound of the funeral march is heard, as before*. . . .] (116.)

Saul, a bitter enemy of Christ's teachings before he was converted to become the apostle Paul, was struck blind by a great, dazzling light on the road to Damascus. The Beggar's "Why do you persecute me? Saul!" are the very words with which Christ rebuked his future apostle the moment after the great light flashed.[22] The Stranger, like Saul, still has some distance to travel. Fortunately for him, the Beggar holds no grudges; on the contrary, he offers to help him in his quest by advising in fairy tale fashion: "If you follow these wheel tracks in the mud, you'll come to the sea, and there the road ends! . . . just follow the tracks, follow the tracks!" (115).[23]

In the next scene, by the sea, the Stranger has found the Lady again. Later in the hotel room he tells her that he must return to the Doctor's house for the obligatory settling of accounts that he avoided before.

> STRANGER: I must see him. . . . I have a need to risk . . . everything, my freedom, my life, my well-being. I need an emotional experience so strong that the jolt will bring my true self to the surface. I long for an

agony that will restore the balance in our relationship, so that I won't have to go on feeling like a
miserable debtor (123–124).

In the two scenes at the Doctor's house, at the beginning and
the end of the play, the setting is a mélange of the ordinary and
the peculiar. The ordinary things include a courtyard enclosed
by three single-storied, wooden buildings, a rose hedge, a well,
and a basement entrance to a wine cellar. But also present are a
"woodpile in the shape of an oriental cupola" and an icebox in
which the good Doctor keeps leftovers from his surgery: bits of
arms and legs (31). The stage directions for the second scene are
the same as for the first except that the woodpile has shrunk to
half its former size and the Doctor's surgical instruments have
been assembled on a bench on the verandah where their owner
is busy polishing them.

No matter how much certain details resemble the Ystad
home of Dr. Eliasson where Strindberg visited during his
Inferno period,[24] this is no ordinary doctor and this is no ordinary doctor's house, which the Stranger understands immediately in the first scene.

STRANGER: This is certainly an original home you have here,
           Doctor; everything is very unusual. To start with,
           there's that woodpile. . . .
DOCTOR: Yes, it's been knocked down twice by lightning. . . .
STRANGER: That's terrible, and yet you still keep it there?
DOCTOR: For that very reason. And this year I've made it six
           feet higher, but also because it gives me shade in the
           summer. It's my own Jonah's gourd (39).

Jonah becomes another counterpoint theme in the play's polyphonic mythology. A Strindberg letter in 1896 to Torsten
Hedlund reveals the extent to which the author identified with
this Biblical hero, especially in a time of emotional crisis: "Have
just read the Book of Jonah; wondering if I am not a Jonah, who
resists the call, out of laziness, out of cowardice. . . . The sun
grows weary piercing my crown since the Jonah's gourds and
my humble abode have withered away."[25]

In the Book of Jonah God has the gourd grow quickly to
shield His prophet from the glaring sun. But Jonah arouses

God's displeasure by getting angry after having preached in Ninevah that the city was doomed and then seeing it spared because the people repented. In return, God has the gourd wither as quickly as it appeared. The prophet learns a painful lesson: becoming God's messenger subjects one to the arrogant temptation of assuming that one is "like the gods." If Ahasuerus is the symbol of the hero who cannot or will not answer the call, Jonah is the hero who, although finally managing to find the courage to follow God's exhortation, must still learn to pursue his calling with a properly humble sense of his own limitations.

In the second scene at the Doctor's house, an example has been set for the Stranger: the Doctor has humbly reduced the size of the woodpile, thus avoiding incurring further evidence of the Almighty's disapproval.

The house and its strange contents constitute a panorama of the world of the Stranger's unconscious, full of signs and portents. There is the danger of hubris represented by the Jonah's gourd-woodpile and by Caesar's attempting to regulate Creation. And there are signs, on the one hand, of disintegration and alienation in the images of dismemberment—the scalpels and the fragments of dead bodies—and, on the other hand, of reintegration and reconciliation in the Christmas rose and the well, symbolic source of the waters of salvation.[26] Next door lives the postmistress, who plays the funeral march on the piano, thus echoing the signs of the calls unanswered by the Stranger in the first scene: the letter not picked up and the funeral march ignored.

STRANGER: This is like Bluebeard's house.
DOCTOR [*pointedly*]: What do you mean by that? [*looking sharply at the lady*] Perhaps you think I murder my wives, eh?
STRANGER: Oh no, certainly not, it's obvious that you don't. . . . But it's as if the place were haunted (41).

Bluebeard was mentioned earlier when the Stranger tried to get the Lady to promise never again to open one of his books: "Remember Bluebeard's wife, when curiosity lured her into opening the forbidden room" (21). Then, when the Stranger was about to return to the Doctor's, he was reluctant to tell the Lady about a dream he had because

STRANGER: Then I touch the door to the closed room. . . .
LADY: The past. . . .
STRANGER: Yes.
LADY: There's always something amiss in those secret rooms (122).

The "secret rooms" where something is "amiss" are akin to the corpse in the cargo (discussed in connection with *Creditors*): all are images of long-buried sources of guilt. For the Stranger, a return to the Doctor is a return to his own past, where whatever it was that caused so much guilt and pain may be dug up and exposed. The Doctor's wine cellar functions symbolically as a repository of buried guilt. Caesar is a reminder of such secrets for the Stranger, and when the Doctor sees that his guest is upset, he locks the madman up in the cellar (45).

The ruler of this curious world is an archetypal figure but treated by the playwright ironically and with wit. He seems to have supernatural powers, for example, but one cannot be sure. In the first house scene when he tells his nurse that the Lady and the Stranger "have just come through the gate," she is surprised: "I heard nothing!" "But I," says the Doctor, "I hear!" (34). However, then we learn from the Lady that her husband is hard of hearing, and when he disappears behind the woodpile for a moment, she and the Stranger talk candidly and indiscreetly about him. The seeming contradiction creates an interestingly ambiguous effect: the Doctor is made to appear omniscient or eccentric or both at once. In the second house scene, the following exchange between the Doctor and Caesar as they await the Stranger sounds as if Lewis Carroll had written a discussion between God and one of his archangels about how they will greet an unwelcome visit from the leader of the fallen angels.

DOCTOR: Listen Caesar, if your enemy comes and lays his head on your knee, what do you do?
MADMAN: I cut it off!
DOCTOR: That's not what I taught you.
MADMAN: No, you said one should heap burning coals on it, but I think that would be a pity.

DOCTOR: O.K., we'll take his head off, and then we'll see
            (127–128).

One Biblical reference to heaping live coals is in Paul's recommendation: "If your enemy is hungry, feed him; if he is thirsty, give him a drink; by doing this you will heap live coals on his head."[27] Caesar's assertion that the Doctor said this reinforces the impression of weird, divine energy that the latter seems to project.

The deity the Doctor most closely resembles is not the terrifying Yahweh, but the demiurge from Strindberg's creation play, who has acknowledged a higher authority and is now retired from taxing divine duties: "I don't want to have thunder in my house," he says, "and I don't play with lightning bolts any more" (133). But he can still recognize the Stranger's Lucifer-like challenge: "If hell existed," the Doctor tells him, "you would be its commander" (131). The pairings of God with Lucifer and the Doctor with the Stranger suggest alienated brothers whose relationship symbolizes polar but interlocking opposites: light and dark, good and evil, the divine and the mortal. And there is the eternal problem: Which one is really good and which evil? However evil the Stranger appears to be, one wonders about the seriousness of the crime that earned him the bad reputation for which he now seeks atonement: it was not a murder, not a felony of any kind, but a childhood prank that went unpunished. It seems absurdly disproportionate for so great a sense of guilt to be the result of so insignificant a transgression. But of course this is precisely the point: the size and nature of the crime are irrelevant. One commits evil because that is the way of the world: evil and guilt are concomitant parts of the existential condition. "Why," asks the Stranger, "does one mature as a young man longing to realize noble intentions, and then go on to pursue everything that is mean and shabby, everything one despises? Why, why?" (83). Not guilty and yet guilty: it is his fate to be torn between the desire to do good and the instinct to evil. One can understand why Strindberg contemplated at one point using Merlin and Robert le Diable as models for the protagonist: each was the son of a mortal woman who was impregnated by the Devil. The Stranger must learn that even as one struggles to overcome the Evil One, there comes the realization that we are him.

If the Doctor is God, he is also the Werewolf, and the symbolic message to the Stranger once again is accept—in this case, the beast in man. It is significant that the nickname was apparently bestowed by the Lady. It is Eve, in other words, who is responsible for awakening the carnal in man. But there are other aspects to the werewolf image. Transformation is possible; he can become a man again. Like the monster in "Beauty and the Beast," he needs compassion and understanding. The Doctor thus represents an exemplary opportunity for the Stranger to reconcile opposites in his own nature, to understand that the dark side is complementary to the light.

With all the preparations set up by the mythic resonances—Ahasuerus approaching Christ, Lucifer approaching God—the confrontation between the Stranger and the Doctor leads us to expect a classic recognition and discovery scene, and we are not disappointed. The climactic moment, however, is muted and understated as the Stranger reaches for the ultimate reconciliation he has been seeking for so long.

STRANGER: Will you give me your hand?
DOCTOR: No, I can't do that. I mustn't. Besides, what good will it do for me to forgive you if you don't have the strength to forgive yourself? . . .

You challenged destiny and you were broken. There's no shame in a good fight. I did the same thing, but as you can see, I've reduced the size of my woodpile. . . .
STRANGER: One station more—and journey's end.
DOCTOR: Never journey's end, sir! . . . Farewell!
STRANGER: Farewell (132–133).

The showdown ends not on a decisive but on a curiously tentative note. In fact, the final moments of this brilliant scene have the quality of an unresolved coda. Even as the major themes of self-realization and self-acceptance are restated—in the implied references to Jacob and Jonah struggling to find a relationship with God and self that is neither abjectly servile nor hubristic—the sombre "never journey's end" takes us back to the curse upon Ahasuerus. The Stranger cannot find reconciliation outside himself because he cannot find it within.

By admitting that he was Caesar, the Stranger resurrected the child he once was; he returned to the well of being in a journey filled with guilt and pain, but also hope. He achieved what the Lady early predicted was possible: he became a child again. But the journey back is incomplete. Caesar has long been a prisoner, yearning to be freed. The first step toward liberation has been taken in the Stranger's willingness to identify himself with the madman. But he is unable to take the final step that will free Caesar and himself once and for all from the prison of the past: although he has resurrected the child, he cannot forgive him. Journey's end in the play only brings him back to where he started—the street corner.

> LADY [*entering*]:   What are you doing?
> STRANGER: Drawing in the sand—still (133).

The circular journey has returned to its origin, and the Stranger is left dissatisfied. Even the discovery he now makes that the letter he avoided fetching for so long contains good news and not bad makes him feel more ashamed than relieved. Once again the Lady tries to persuade him to search for solace in the church, but although he agrees to accompany her there, he says he will not stay. The mood is almost as uncertain as the opening moments of the play when we first saw him standing and wondering which way to turn. But this is not the opening, it is the end.

Some critics have argued that the implication of the equivocal final curtain is that the meaning of *To Damascus* is revealed only in the totality of the trilogy. Others have maintained that Strindberg meant for the first part to stand on its own, as an independent entity, and that there is no evidence that he intended from the start to write two additional plays on the same theme.[28] Both viewpoints are valid, I think. The play is complete even if the ending seems to lack a sense of finality. One does not need to read parts two and three to understand the

Stranger's plight. He will continue his wandering in search of peace of mind and soul until he finds it in the grave. Ironically, he is back where he started from at the end of part one not because he completes a circle but because he is unable to break one: the circle of evil, guilt, and repentance. The Stranger may have learned that he can become a child again, but he cannot truly be reborn spiritually until he has resealed the exposed wound of the past and closed the circle with a bond of forgiveness.

7

Easter

PERSEPHONE'S RETURN

One might argue that *Easter* only narrowly deserves to be included among Strindberg's major plays. Although audiences have been attracted to what was for Strindberg an unusually serene and reconciliatory tone, there is an awkwardness about the play. The playwright's effort to inform his drama with the solemnity of religious ritual observance by hanging the act structure on the temporal divisions of the Easter Passion—Maundy Thursday, Good Friday, and Easter Eve—led to uneven results. References to Christ are so numerous, analogies to the Passion so obviously drawn, that the effect produced is embarrassingly close to religiosity. Despite these weaknesses, however, the play is redeemed by an elemental power centered around one of Strindberg's most captivating and mythopoeically expressive characters: Eleonora.

The setting is realistic-naturalistic, at least on the surface: the Heyst home, located in a university town identified by scholars as Lund in southern Sweden.[1] The family is a troubled one. Mr. Heyst is away in prison serving time for embezzling trust funds, and his wife stubbornly says she believes him innocent, hoping his sentence will be overturned on a technicality. The present breadwinner is Elis, her son, a young teacher of Latin, who, like the Stranger in *To Damascus*, is profoundly alienated from the world and from himself. For a number of reasons he has become bitter and frustrated: because his mother refuses to accept that his father was guilty; because his friend and pupil/disciple Petrus has not only stolen ideas from his unfinished dissertation but appears to be trying to steal his fiancée Kristina as well; because Kristina offers him help and love, which he cannot accept; because he is obliged to provide a home and tutoring for a young orphan, Benjamin, whose trust funds were among those embezzled by Mr. Heyst; because another of his father's victims, Mr. Lindkvist, seems to have moved to town as a creditor come to claim his due; and finally, because he was compelled to have his mentally disturbed sister Eleonora institutionalized. Elis sees himself suffering as Christ did, and among the more blatant references to the Passion in the play is his reaction to the news that Petrus has befriended someone whose politics Elis abhors, the local governor: "and [Petrus] denied his teacher and said: 'I know not the man.' And the cock crowed again! Wasn't there a governor once called Pontius, surnamed Pilate?" (*33*, 85). This and lines like Mrs. Heyst's exclamation: "Oh God, why hast Thou forsaken me?" turn the family ordeal into perhaps too direct a parallel to the Passion (86). Because the Imitation of Christ becomes too palpable, its ability to set off poetic resonances is blunted, and other, perhaps more important mythic images are obscured in the process.

As in *The Father*, with which *Easter* seems at first to have nothing in common, the energy core is a group of characters who constitute an archetypal configuration: the eternal feminine. It is the task of the respective protagonists to integrate this configuration into their lives, but whereas the Captain succumbs in this effort and is lost, Elis is reborn and saved. The reason for the difference is a shift in focus; each play is dominated by a different phase of the archetype. In the first the phase is the maternal, that of the Great Goddess, who knows nothing but the secret of her womb. In the second it is a reunion of mother and daughter—*heuresis*[2]—a context of enormous creative potential for spiritual transformation. Whether consciously or unconsciously, Strindberg drew attention to one of the most eloquent examples in myth of heuresis: the story of Demeter, goddess of agriculture, and her daughter Persephone.

Persephone—or Prosperine as she is known in Ovid's *Metamorphoses*, a Strindberg favorite—while picking flowers is tricked by Hades, lord of the underworld, into reaching for a particularly lovely narcissus. The moment she touches the flower, the earth opens up and Hades spirits her away to his realm. Demeter becomes distraught over her daughter's disappearance. The result of her anguish is that all vegetation ceases to grow, and mankind is threatened with famine. Zeus is forced to intervene and negotiates an agreement with his brother Hades: Persephone may return for eight months of every year to her mother, but she must spend the winter with her husband in the underworld. And so, once a year, after mother and daughter are reunited, the earth becomes green again.

In *Easter*, details of the myth have been changed and the sequence of events has been rearranged, but the essential elements are present. The time is spring and Eleonora/Persephone returns from the mental institution. The vague but evocative outlines of her description of the place put one in mind of the sterile home of anguished shades in the dark regions of the underworld.

ELEONORA: . . . there, where I came from, where the sun never shines, where the walls are white and bare as in a bathroom, where only weeping and wailing is heard, where I sat away a year of my life!

BENJAMIN: What do you mean?

ELEONORA: Where people are tortured, worse than in a prison, where the damned live, where unrest has its home, where despair keeps watch night and day. A place from which no one ever returns.

BENJAMIN: Do you mean worse than a prison?

ELEONORA: In prison you are condemned, but there, you are damned! In prison they question you and listen to you. There, no one hears you! (102–103).

Like Persephone, Eleonora is a blend of innocence, sadness, and joy. In Greek mythology Persephone was referred to as "the

maiden whose name may not be spoken."³ When Eleonora
appears and announces that she is a member of the family,
Benjamin is surprised.

BENJAMIN: How strange that no one has ever talked about you.
ELEONORA: People don't talk about the dead! (59).

Both Persephone and Eleonora suffer terribly as the consequence of a momentary, pitifully innocent temptation: the
desire to possess a flower. Eleonora, on her way home from the
institution, takes a daffodil from an unattended florist's shop.
Although she leaves payment for it, she later comes to fear that
the money may go astray and that she will be accused of theft.
Strindberg could not have chosen a more appropriate flower,
and, with his deep interest in botany, could not have been
ignorant of the various meanings associated with it. The daffodil's genus is *Narcissus*, Persephone's flower. The Swedish name
for it is *påsklilja*, which translated literally would be "Easter
lily," and the lily, like the rose, is a traditional attribute of the
Virgin Mary. As he did in *To Damascus*, Strindberg uses a flower
as an ambivalent symbol of both the bond that joins and the
tension that divides mother from daughter in the eternal-femi-
nine configuration.

The basic rhythm of the play as of the myth—separation and
reunion—is the counterbalancing movement of life itself, the
diastole and the systole. For most of the play Mrs. Heyst does
not fully and warmly acknowledge her daughter and in fact has
been distant with her for some time. When Eleonora presses her
mother's hand to her lips, Mrs. Heyst "restrains her emotion,"
according to the stage directions (80). But then comes Easter
Eve and the end of alienation:

ELEONORA: You kissed me, Mother. You haven't done that
               for years (110).

Mrs. Heyst has come to understand the sacrificial role her
daughter plays as the messenger of vernal hope:

MRS. HEYST: This child of sorrow has come with joy, though
               not of this world. Her troubled feelings have
               been transformed into peace, and she shares it
               with everyone. Sane or not, for me she is wise

> because she understands how to bear life's bur-
> dens better than I do, than we do (105).

A complication interrupts. The arrival of the newspaper con-
firms Mrs. Heyst's fear that Eleonora will be charged with theft
of the flower and once again incarcerated. Like Demeter, she
laments that her daughter must return to the darkness.

> MRS. HEYST: She's lost . . . found again and lost (108).

But like the final emergence of a spring whose return has been
prolonged, the eventual establishment of Eleonora's innocence
is certain. The triumph of Persephone is as inexorable as was
her tragedy in the lengthening shadows of the preceding
autumn. The florist finds the money the girl left behind; mother
and daughter can once again be reunited.

The realization of the significance of her daughter's redemptive suffering has an enormously liberating effect upon Mrs.
Heyst. She can now see through the veil of self-deception that
clouded her vision. "Was I sane, Elis, was I sane when I believed
your father was innocent? I was certainly aware that he was
convicted on tangible, material evidence and that he had confessed!" She is free of the suffocating power of the past and can
see that Elis is still trapped in delusion, that he cannot yet accept
one of life's most demanding, but vital challenges.

> MRS. HEYST: And you, Elis, are you in your right mind when
>   you can't see that Kristina loves you . . . and
>   believe instead that she hates you?
> ELIS: It's a strange way to love!
> MRS. HEYST: No! Inwardly, she's been frozen by your cold-
>   ness, and you're the one who hates. But you're
>   unjust, and so you have to suffer (105).

The reunion of mother and daughter is not the climax of the
play. Elis has more lessons to learn before the lost harmony he
misses, both in himself and in his family, can be completely
restored. What the heuresis, the vernal miracle, does is to set the
stage for this restoration, and Strindberg enhances and amplifies the reunion by enveloping it in vegetation imagery.

Scholars have speculated that the source for the family name was a Belgian spa Strindberg visited for a fortnight in 1898: Heist-op-den-Berg.[4] This may be, but *heister* is the German word for sapling or young tree. And there are other surnames in the play associated with trees. Petrus' last name is Holmblad, or Islet-leaf, and Benjamin's feared tutor is Algren, or Alder-branch. The creditor Lindkvist's name could be translated as Linden-switch, and switch reinforces the recurrent theme in the play of chastisement and punishment. Elis receives an anonymous gift of a bundle of birch twigs, which leads to the idea that he is in need of a "birching." But he senses that there may be a positive side to the gift: chastisement can lead to repentance, and repentance to reconciliation. Elis himself says the twig might carry the promise of an Aaron's rod, the stave of Moses's brother, which bloomed miraculously as a sign that God had chosen him (51).

In addition to the surnames and numerous mentions of Eleonora's daffodil, there are other tree, flower, plant, herb, and fruit references scattered throughout the play. A bird dropped a twig at Elis's feet as he walked past the cathedral, and he wishes it had been an olive branch; he remembers the willows and linden trees in bloom by the family's summer cottage as well as a student song in which birches and lindens were mentioned. Mrs. Heyst peels apples for applesauce. Eleonora says she heard starlings talking in a walnut tree, and she speaks with authority about the psychic effects produced by consuming henbane and belladonna; furthermore, she is conversant in "the silent language of the flowers"(67). As Elis reads the painful proceedings of his father's trial, a word catches like a thorn in his eye (77). A rumor says that a tulip was stolen and not a daffodil (84). Eleonora identifies with flowers that have blossomed prematurely and must endure a late spring frost—anemones and snowdrops—and she looks forward to the coming of violets.

The repetition of vegetation images is as pervasive as similar details in the background of a medieval tapestry, and the cumulative effect reinforces the Demeter-Persephone leitmotif. Even the order of associations has a natural rhythm: Eleonora and the daffodil, Mrs. Heyst and the apple—virgin with flower, mother with fruit.[5]

There are other mythic resonances in the play in addition to those connected with vegetation. The bird that dropped the twig at Elis's feet was a dove, and although the twig was not an olive branch, Elis took it as a token of peace. The Heysts await the coming of spring as Noah awaited the waters of the Deluge to recede. The day before *Easter* was to premiere, Strindberg wrote to Harriet Bosse, who was playing Eleonora: "I . . . thank God He sent you, the little dove with olive branch, not the birch. The Deluge has ended, the old has drowned, and the earth shall again be green."[6]

Elis complains that everything is obscured by a "black veil," which suggests the material, earthly prison of profane space and concrete time. To penetrate this veil, according to Mircea Eliade, it is necessary to return to a decisive cosmic moment in which profane space is transformed into transcendent space, and concrete time into mythic time.[7] Eleonora is the catalyst of this transformation. Her very presence turns the realistic moment into the magic of "once upon a time." "For me," she tells Benjamin, "time and space do not exist"(61). Her mission is to bring important messages, as Mrs. Heyst says, which cannot be adequately defined in terms like *rational* or *irrational*. Benjamin admits to Eleonora, "I really don't understand the words you're saying, but I think I understand what you mean"(62); and "It seems that everything you say, I've already thought myself" (69).

The feeling of "once upon a time" is established quickly in the moments immediately prior to and following Eleonora's first entrance. A solemn mood is set as objects are handled almost ceremoniously, and allusions are made to punishment, spring, and hope.

> ELIS [*taking the birch bough from the dining room table and placing it behind the mirror*]:
>> It wasn't an olive branch the dove brought . . . it was a birch! [*He exits. Eleonora enters from upstage, a sixteen-year-old girl who wears a pigtail down her back. She is carrying a yellow daffodil in a pot. Without seeing, or seeming to see Benjamin, she takes the water carafe from the sideboard, waters the flower, and places it on the table,*

*where she then sits opposite Benjamin, watching him and
imitating his gestures. Benjamin reacts in surprise.*]
ELEONORA [*pointing at the daffodil*]:
    Do you know what *this* is?
BENJAMIN [*childishly, simply*]:
    Of course I know—it's a daffodil! . . . But who are
    you?
ELEONORA [*friendly, but sadly*]:
    Yes, who are you? (58).

What a splendid entrance! Our attention is riveted upon the
girl and the flower through a sweep of scenic action that is at
once simple and concrete, strange and evocative. When Eleonora imitates Benjamin's gestures and repeats his question, an
interesting effect is achieved: on the one hand, we are witness-
ing a meeting between troubled adolescents—an insecure boy
and an emotionally disturbed girl; on the other hand, we are
watching Benjamin on the brink of an archetypal confrontation,
face to face with a counterpart, or double, whose purpose, at
least in part, is to introduce him to the mystery of the eternal
feminine, to bring warmth and encouragement to someone who
up till now has seen the world as cold and inhospitable.

But if Eleonora brings a hopeful message of vernal renewal
and rebirth to the Heyst home, the message is tinged with
melancholy. The return of spring can only partly mitigate the
painful knowledge that the earthly passage remains a vale of
tears. If Eleonora is Persephone, she is also, in the manner of
Strindberg's polyphonic mythology, Sophia, the Gnostic figure
of divine wisdom, fated to "suffer every possible kind of
suffering."[8] Eleonora even suffers with distant loved ones: with
her father in prison and her sister in America. Her illness, she
says, is "not a sickness unto death, but to the glory of God." In
her brother's life she is not just his mentally ill sister, she is also,
as Strindberg himself described her in a letter, "Christ in
Man."[9] Elis, in his reluctance to deal with her, becomes a
variation of the Ahasuerus motif: the man who tries to deny the
calling from the Christ within.

Elis's name is close to Elisa, the Swedish name for the
Biblical Elisha, to whom Elijah passed his mantle, the symbol of

the prophet's calling and mission, but also, in the language of
Gnosticism, of the body, the earthly garment of flesh and blood,
which must some day be exchanged and transcended. That
Strindberg was aware of this twofold meaning is attested in a
letter he wrote to Torsten Hedlund in 1896: "Cf.: Elijah's
mantle! Nessus's shirt!"[10] In *Easter* the symbolic values of the
mantle as calling and the garment as burden are made manifest
in Elis's overcoat. In the opening scene he is seen removing the
coat and hanging it up. "You know", says Elis to Kristina, "it's
so heavy—[*hefting the coat with his hand*]—as if it had soaked up
all the troubles of winter, the sweat of anguish and the dust of
school"(39). When Eleonora passes the coat, she pats it sympathetically, and says "Poor Elis!"(70). Mrs. Heyst points to it and
scolds her son: "I told you, that coat is not to hang there!"(71).
For her, it represents unpleasant truths she would rather not be
reminded of.

If Elis's name leads one to think of Elisha and Elijah, Helios,
the Greek god of the sun also comes to mind. And if the coming
of spring suggests the return of Persephone, it also suggests the
return of Helios.

ELIS: Look, the sun has come back again . . . He went
           away in November. I remember the day he dis-
           appeared behind the brewery across the street. Oh,
           this winter! This long winter!(40).

Later, the presence of the moon is felt.

ELEONORA: Go and draw the curtain, Benjamin. I want God to
           see us.
           [*Benjamin rises and obeys. Moonlight falls into the room.*]
ELEONORA: Do you see the full moon? It's the Easter moon!
           And now you know that the sun is still there,
           though it's the moon that gives us the light!(97).

In some mythologies a brother-sister kinship exists between
the sun and moon, and in alchemy, the arcane science with
which Strindberg was so preoccupied during and after the
Inferno years, there is the androgyne, or "Rebis," a being
signifying the merging of opposites and the end of the agony
resulting from the separation of the sexes. Strindberg's attitude

toward the concept of the androgyne is revealed implicitly and explicitly in letters in which he identified two of the models he used for Eleonora. The real-life model was his mentally ill sister, Elisabeth, whose life seemed mystically bound with his own. "She was like my twin," he wrote in a letter to Harriet Bosse in December 1904.[11] The fictional model for the Easter girl was the androgynous central character of Balzac's *Séraphita*, whose parents were disciples of Swedenborg. Explaining *Easter* to Harriet in a letter in 1901, he refers to "Eleonora's kin, Balzac's Séraphita-Séraphitus, the Angel, for whom earthly love does not exist because he-she is *l'époux et l'épouse de l'humanité*. Symbol of the highest, most perfect type of human being, which haunts much of the very latest modern literature and which some people feel is on its way down to us."[12]

The androgynous aspect of the relationship between Elis and Eleonora helps to explain the different ways the characters complement each other. Beyond the balancings of male-female, brother-sister, sun-moon we have Elis, as a teacher, associated with the life of the intellect, and Eleonora, poor, mad Eleonora, associated with the irrational and the dark world of the unconscious. Elis dreads her return from the institution, but she is a part of him that he cannot repudiate. Their closeness is revealed in the girl's description of her brother as her "only friend on earth"(69).

Mother, beloved, and sister/androgyne: Elis must settle accounts with each of the faces of the eternal feminine, but, as in *To Damascus*, the ultimate, superior creditor, the one to whom the hero must eventually answer is a masculine, paternal force. Just as the Stranger and the Lady are haunted on their pilgrimage by reminders of the Doctor, so the Heysts are constantly made aware that Lindkvist is approaching, frighteningly: in act two he stands by the street lamp outside, and his shadow on the curtains expands enormously—expressionistically—as he starts toward the house.

Again, as in *To Damascus*, it is the maternal confrontation that prepares the protagonist for the paternal confrontation. Mrs. Heyst serves two functions in this regard. First, by finally accepting the fact of her husband's guilt and reuniting with her

134 34 EASTER

daughter, she dissipates much of the tension in the house. Second, she provides an important answer to Elis's question of whether the family ordeal has come to an end.

ELIS:	Now can we throw the birch on the fire?
MRS. HEYST:	Not yet! There's something else.
ELIS:	Lindkvist?
MRS. HEYST:	He's standing outside.
ELIS:	Now that I've seen a ray of sunshine I'm not afraid to meet the giant. Let him come!

Elis is confident to the point of cockiness, and Mrs. Heyst warns him, "You know what happens to those who are proud"(111). We are reminded of the Mother's warning in *To Damascus*: "Pride must be cut down"(29, 74).

Lindkvist, a wonderfully grotesque invention, is a bogeyman out of Dickens, and his entrance is a combination of the terrifying and the absurd. Strindberg realized that the character would present problems, that his presence could spill a performance over into farce; Lindkvist, he insisted, must not be played by a comic actor.[13]

> [*Lindkvist enters from the right. He is an earnest, elderly man of weird appearance. His gray hair is arranged in an upswept forelock and trimmed at the temples in the manner of a hussar. Big, black bushy eyebrows. Short, close-clipped black sideburns. Round, black horn-rimmed eyeglasses. Large carnelian charms on his watchchain; a Spanish cane in his hand. He is dressed in black with a fur coat; top boots with leather galoshes that squeak. When he enters, his eyes are riveted probingly on Elis . . . .*] (33, 112).

The "upswept forelock" and earnest mien are reminiscent of the stern God of Strindberg's creation play, who has "horns like the Moses of Michelangelo." But as with the Doctor in *To Damascus*, this godlike figure has given up throwing thunderbolts. Much of his bite has gone, and even his bark is more jovial than frightening: "Do you know who I am? . . . [*disguising his voice*] I am the giant of Skinflint Mountain, who scares little children!" (124–125). And as in many fairy tales, the protagonist's fear of the confrontation is worse than the confrontation itself. Lindkvist has good reason to want vengeance, but he does not seek it. On the contrary, he points a way for the hero to break out of the circle of guilt and anguish that torments him. To be sure, Elis still has a hard lesson to learn: he must recognize that he needs the saving grace of love, which he has lost, and that he has tendencies toward hubris that must be curbed.

ELIS: Why don't we just hand his paper over to the
            hangman? That way we can at least be spared this
            lengthy and painful execution.
LINDKVIST: I see.
ELIS: Young or not, I ask for no mercy, only justice!
LINDKVIST: Is that right? No mercy, no mercy!(113).

Elis sounds like the Stranger refusing charity from the Abbess. But Lindkvist's arguments—now persuasive, now coercive—melt Elis's defiance and cause him to agree to resolve his differences with Petrus and Kristina. Lindkvist points out that his own family has suffered much because of Heyst's embezzlement and that Elis in his stubborness risks sacrificing his mother and sister on the altar of pride. What finally wins the day is the fact that Lindkvist has come not with a destructive claim but a healing gift. Although he has been wronged by Heyst, forty years earlier Elis's father was the only one in town to befriend him in a time of trouble. Because of that act of generosity, Lindkvist can now cancel his claim; the gift he brings is forgiveness, and with it, reconciliation. "You see," he says, "there is a charity which goes against justice and transcends it! . . . That is mercy!"(115).

If the analogies in *Easter* to the Passion seem too obvious or facile, one cannot deny the naive power of the ending effected by the gifts brought by the two angels, Eleonora and Lindkvist. As Lindkvist brings forgiveness, Eleonora brings an infinite capacity for bearing suffering so as to lighten the burdens of others; she is Sophia: victim and redeemer in one. Strindberg indicated the archetypal dimension of the reconciliation in a letter to Harriet Bosse on the day *Easter* was premiered (April 4, 1901): "The Lost Father wants to be introduced to his children—you have been given the honor of reestablishing the relationship."[14]

The message of the Passion, the return of Persephone, the

wisdom of the melancholy Sophia, the creditor's forgiveness, and Elis's new-found capacity to accept love and mercy all coincide with the vernal promise of the Easter season. However forced some of the details in the play may seem, the resolution is no moment of simplistic mawkishness. The Heysts, all of them, have earned the right to turn their backs on the darkness and walk toward the light.

8

A Dream Play

THE GREAT DREAM OF LIFE AND THE VEIL OF *MĀYĀ*

Strindberg knew he had created something important in *A Dream Play*, but perhaps something too innovative for theatregoers to accept. As he had on an earlier occasion, for *Miss Julie*, he added a preface, explaining that his intention in the new play was "to imitate the disconnected but apparently logical form of the dream. Anything can happen; everything is possible and probable. Time and space do not exist. . . . The characters split, double, multiply, evaporate, condense, thin out, and converge" (*36*, 215). It was as if the author was aware that his work might give the impression of an amorphous, incoherent mass and he wanted to make clear that the kaleidoscopic effect produced was deliberate and not accidental. Perhaps with the same concern for clarity and coherence, five years after completing the play he added a prologue, the most openly mythological scene he ever wrote with the exception of his creation play. Like the prologue to *Faust*, it takes place on a heavenly plane and serves as a structural guide or frame of reference for the entire play. The Indic god Indra sends his daughter to earth to discover whether the conspicuous lamentations he hears from the inhabitants there are justified. In the scenes on earth that follow, the Daughter, also called Agnes, becomes intimately involved with three men—the Officer, the Lawyer, and the Poet—and sees and experiences enough to convince her that the earthlings' lamentations are indeed justified. "Human beings," she observes again and again, "are to be pitied" (229). Thus educated, she leaves with her knowledge to return to heaven.

Unfortunately, the prologue simplifies as much as it clarifies, and not surprisingly many productions of the play have turned out like decorative pageants: instead of a drama with tension and conflict, we have a series of exempla illustrating Agnes's journey and the theme "human beings are to be pitied" until the message becomes blatant and redundant. Some directors have tried to avoid creating the exemplum effect by altering the text and focusing the action more sharply and clearly. Ingmar Bergman, for example, in his memorable 1970 production abridged the prologue and placed it at the end of the third scene, setting the action on a small raised stage, and thus creating a very theatrical play-within-a-play episode. Bergman also adopted a novel solution to a question that has puzzled many: If this is a dream, who is the dreamer? The author's preface says that "one consciousness is superior to all the others—the dreamer's," but the identity of this consciousness is a matter of dispute. Bergman made the Poet the dreamer. Although the character does not appear in the text until half way through, the director had him enter at the opening and sit down at a small table downstage, there to remain for much of the action as a kind of prompter or conductor. There were a number of fine things about this production (in particular the simplified, suggestive setting in place of the cumbersome, illusionistic scenery that is often devised) but theatricalizing the Prologue so completely, and making the Poet the dreamer, were not among them. The first change was part of a program of demythologization that was carried out throughout the production, and I believe it was a mistake. In richness, complexity, and inventiveness, Strindberg's polyphonic mythology reaches a special kind of intensity in *A Dream Play*: a

superb blend of elements drawn from a variety of sources—
Hindu, Greek, and Biblical mythology, Mahayana Buddhism,
Gnosticism, the chivalric tradition of the quest of the knight
errant, and tales from the Arabian Nights. To strip the play
almost entirely of these resonances, as Bergman did, is not to
destroy the work, but to leave out an important dimension, like
reproducing a color painting in a black and white photograph.

The second change, making the Poet so obviously the
dreamer, tends to reduce the importance of Agnes's role: she
becomes less a partner of the Poet in the action and more a
figment of his imagination. Nevertheless, if the play in Bergman's production was less evocative and ambiguous than it
might have been, and should be, it was infinitely more dramatic
and exciting than it has appeared in more pedestrian interpretations. Furthermore, his adaptation was important in the history
of the play, compelling us to reexamine it from a different
perspective and to reevaluate two of its most important features:
the ways in which the action is focused and the mythic themes
developed.

Singling out the Poet as the dreamer obscures the fact that
the focus throughout is not single but dual. In each of the
separate scenes between Agnes and the three most important
men she meets, what we observe are two dreamers at once, each
dreaming an action in which the other person plays a part. In
other words, there is not one major dreamer but four, and three
pairs of reciprocal dreams: Agnes-Officer, Agnes-Lawyer,
Agnes-Poet. Each dream evolves both as a separate entity and as
a part of the other dreams, producing a fuguelike effect, not
unlike that which Strindberg said he admired in Shakespeare's
Hamlet.

The chief source of inspiration for the use of the device of
reciprocal dreams was probably Rudyard Kipling's story "The
Brushwood Boy," in which two people discover that they have
shared common dreams. Strindberg first read the story in February 1899 and praised it highly in letters to Harriet Bosse only
a half-year before he wrote *A Dream Play*.[1] But he might also
have been influenced by an old idol, Schopenhauer, who had
much to say about the nature of dreams and their relation to

reality. A passage such as the following from *Transcendente Spekulation* could pass as both an explanation of and a justification for the approach to characterization in *A Dream Play* because it defines so sharply the basic subject, which is not the nature of dreams or a dream life dramatized, but the dreamlike quality of life, reality as a dream. In dreams, says Schopenhauer,

> only *one* ego actually wills and experiences while the others are nothing but phantoms, whereas in the great dream of life there exists a reciprocal relationship: each not only appears in the other's dream precisely as there required, but also experiences the other in a similar way in his own dream; . . . each dreams only what is appropriate to his own metaphysical guidance, and yet all the life dreams are interwoven so artfully that, while each experiences only what redounds to his own increase, he performs what the others require. . . .

Hence, everything interlocks and harmonizes with everything else.[2]

To speculate, as some critics have, about whether Strindberg faithfully imitates actual dreams or dream processes is to miss the point. *A Dream Play* is a variation on the old theme Schopenhauer describes as "the great dream of life." In notes for the preface that were never published with the play, Strindberg cites his predecessors: Calderon (*Life Is a Dream*) and Shakespeare, who "in *The Tempest* has Prospero say that 'we are such stuff / As dreams are made on.' "[3] Schopenhauer's use of words such as *interwoven* and *interlock* emphasizes the whole of life as a fabric, and this too is in keeping with Strindberg's central theme. In another passage intended for the preface but never included, he advises: "Whoever follows the author during the brief hours of his sleepwalker route will perhaps find a certain similarity between the apparent jumble of a dream and life's motley, unmanageable canvas, woven by the 'World Weaver'— she who sets up the 'warp' of human destinies and then constructs the 'woof' from our intersecting interests and our variable passions."[4]

The "canvas woven by the 'World Weaver' " calls to mind the complex Indic image of the "web" or "veil of *māyā*," *māyā* meaning not only the dream of life—the tissue of objects, things, and people that constitute what men believe to be reality—but also the seductive, fecund image of woman as Earth Mother. In the play itself, Agnes talks about Māyā as Earth Mother as she tries to answer the Poet's questions about the riddle of existence.

> At the dawn of time before the sun shone, Brahmā, the divine primordial force, went forth and let himself be seduced by Māyā, the mother of the world, in order to propagate himself. This contact between divine primeval matter and earthly matter was heaven's original sin. Thus, the world, life, and human beings are only a phantom, a semblance, a dream image (324).

The speech was borrowed almost verbatim from one of Strindberg's favorite reference books, a survey history of world literature by Arvid Ahnfelt, and inserted when the play was almost finished.[5] Because the Māyā story was added late, several scholars have concluded that the influence of Indic mythology on *A Dream Play* is negligible and inconsistent. The god Indra, for example, had no daughter, and so Agnes must be assumed to be Strindberg's own invention. But this is to confuse a poet's responsibilities with those of a theologian, logician, or philosopher. A poet is obliged only to be sensitive to the energies that glow in mythic metaphors. Aeschylus, Sophocles, and Euripides—and later Eugene O'Neill—were sensitive to the poetic energies of the Orestes myth, and each departed from or embellished the original in his own way. Similarly, Strindberg was attracted to the metaphor of māyā and turned it to his own purposes. It is not an isolated image dropped into the text at the last minute, but a concept fundamental to an understanding of the meaning of the play.

It is difficult to pinpoint exactly when Strindberg became familiar with māyā or a māyā-like concept, but it might have been as early as the 1870s, the time he first became impressed by Schopenhauer. Māyā is a basic and recurrent expression in *The World As Will*, where we find scores of passages like the following: "The eyes of the uncultured individual are clouded, as the Indians say, by the veil of māyā. To him is revealed not the thing-in-itself, but only the phenomenon in time and space. . .

In this form of his limited knowledge he sees not the inner nature of things, which is one, but its phenomena as separated, detached, innumerable, very different, indeed opposed."[6] Part of Agnes's mission in A Dream Play is to try to help mortals understand that they see not "the inner nature of things, which is one," but the multiplicity, the misleading, illusory veil of māyā, "phenomena as separated, detached, innumerable, very different, indeed opposed."

The fabric image of earthly existence as a veil connects with the many references in myth to woman as the archetypal weaver, or, as Eric Neumann puts it, "the Great Mother who weaves the web of life and spins the threads of fate, regardless whether she appears as one Great Spinstress or, as so frequently, in a lunar triad."[7] In Greek mythology the triad consists of the Fates and in Norse mythology of the Norns. The simple act of a woman knitting or sewing or crocheting suggests the primal rhythm of creation/destruction: even as one of the Norns spins the thread of life, another waits to cut it.

Women working with fabrics figure prominently in many of Strindberg's plays. In *Master Olof* Kristina knits (2, 115) and in *The Father* Bertha embroiders (23, 51). In *To Damascus, I*, and *A Dream Play* we find several interesting parallels. In each case there is a woman who crochets (the Lady and the Stage Doorkeeper, respectively) and a mother who tends to domestic chores involving fabrics: in the first play the Lady's mother irons curtains; and in the second the Officer's mother puts identification marks in newly sewn shirts. Strindberg's motivation for specifying these activities was surely not simply to provide actresses with something to do. It is evident throughout his works that he regarded sewing and weaving as quintessential feminine concerns, both in a positive and negative sense. "What is it you're always crocheting?" asks the Stranger of the Lady.

> STRANGER: You sit there like one of the Fates, drawing the threads between your fingers . . . But don't stop. The most beautiful thing I know is a woman bending over her work or her child. What are you crocheting?
>
> LADY: It's nothing. Just some needlework (29, 54).

There is a tone of awe in the exchange: man admiring woman's instinct to create without conscious intention. But the creator is potentially a destroyer. The Captain in *The Father* feels secure wrapped in Laura's shawl only until he remembers that the fabric of feminine allure is also a snare. Bertha's embroidery, Laura's shawl, the straitjacket: all are strands in a gigantic web that is enveloping the Captain.

The seduction of Brahmā by Māyā is also mentioned in Strindberg's novel *Black Banners* (1904/07) by the character Kilo, who then concludes:

> Plato is right when he regards our concepts of things to be the true realities and the things themselves only schematic shadow images. Schopenhauer said it best: matter lacks reality. That's why the materialists of our day are so far from the truth that they are on the other side. You see these desperate people drifting about with nothing to guide them; they walk in darkness and bump into things; they nose in the earth like swine hunting truffles; they turn their backs on the original images and see only the reflected images. That's why they worship Māyā, the earth spirit, woman, and when they don't want to serve God in love, they have to serve Omphale in hate (*41*, 185–186).

Omphale, we remember from *The Father*, is the Terrible Mother figure who enslaves Hercules. As we shall see, the Officer in *A Dream Play* is another Hercules who has trouble with the Great Mother.

For Strindberg, Māyā is one woman and all women: temptress and sister, Good as well as Terrible Mother. But even more, she becomes the prime symbol of the sensual lure of life itself. She is the source of deepest joy but also deepest sorrow, for the victory signified in her power to seduce implies the triumph of matter over spirit. In Strindberg's copy of Ahnfelt's survey text, the description of Brahmā's fall is followed by a section in which Strindberg underscored a portion: "It is the ascetic's mission to annihilate [the dream image or phantom which men perceive as reality]. However, this mission comes into conflict with the love instinct, and the result is an endless vacillation between *a battle with sensual pleasure and the tortures of penitence*."[8] The inner division between the sensualist and the

ascetic was an old story in Strindberg's works as well as his life
and was especially trying for him during the Inferno years. As
he confessed in an 1895 letter (see chap. 1), "I am . . . a woman-
hater, for I hate the earth because it binds my spirit and because
I love it. Woman to me is the earth with all its splendors, the tie
that binds. . . ."⁹ In *A Dream Play* the Quarantine Master asks
to be introduced to Agnes.

> OFFICER: No, that wouldn't be proper! [*sotto voce*] That's
>   Indra's own daughter, you know!
> QUARANTINE MASTER:
>   Indra's? I thought it was Varuṇa in person (*36, 265*).

Varuṇa is the Indic god who binds and ensnares, and his
attribute is a rope, cord, or noose.

Māyā is also life in the mundane world, the prison of history
where man suffers under the tyranny of the fixed locus of time
and space. In *A Dream Play* a mythic woman attempts to explain
this prison. Like Eleanora in *Easter*, Agnes is able to stand
outside time and space to view the truth from a perspective
denied ordinary mortals. But she too becomes one of the prisoners and learns that the primary task of liberation is to seek release
from māyā. In a March 1907 letter to his German translator,
written only days before *A Dream Play* was to premiere, Strindberg discussed a character in *The Ghost Sonata*: "The Colonel plays
out his auto comedy to its end; for him illusion (māyā) has
become reality. . . . [It is my] conviction that we live in a world
of madness and confusion (illusion) out of which we must battle
our way."¹⁰

THE FOUR DREAMS

The structure I have suggested in the play of four dreamers
experiencing three sets of reciprocal dreams—Agnes and the
Officer, Agnes and the Lawyer, Agnes and the Poet—might
also be viewed as two dreamers—the woman and the man—
sharing one dream. Evert Sprinchorn suggests that Strindberg
"intended that all the men coalesce into one male and all the

women into one female."[11] I prefer to think of the three men as separate but interrelated characters with a progression indicated in the order in which they appear, like the stages in the development of a man's life from least mature to most mature: Officer, Lawyer, Poet. Moreover, this progression is directly related to the purpose Agnes has in their lives: she plays the role their individual dreams demand. For the Officer she evokes memories of his mother; for the Lawyer she becomes a sexual partner; and for the Poet she becomes soul mate with whom communion is possible on the highest spiritual level. For purposes of discussion, the scenes in the play are grouped as follows:

Agnes's dream, part one
   1. prologue
   2. outside the castle
Officer's dream
   3. inside the castle
   4. Officer's childhood home
   5. theatre alley
Lawyer's dream
   6. Lawyer's office
   7. church
   8. Fingal's Grotto
   9. kitchen-bedroom
Agnes's dream, part two
   10. Foulport
   11. Fairhaven
   12. Riviera
Poet's dream
   13. Fingal's Grotto
   14. theatre alley
   15. outside the castle

Several things should be noted. First, although I spoke of reciprocal dreams, for the sake of clarity they have been isolated into separate units: three reciprocal dreams dealt with by halves, if you will. Second, I have broken Agnes's dream into two parts. For reasons that should become apparent, the Agnes who comes to the Officer and the Lawyer is quite a different person than the one who goes off to Fairhaven and Foulport and then becomes involved with the Poet. Third, the dream units designated are not mutually exclusive compartments. Although there is a definite structure of beginning, middle, and end for each man's dream, the Officer and the Lawyer both reappear several times after their individual dreams with Agnes are complete, and the Poet appears for the first time long before his dream with Agnes actually gets under way.

Agnes's Dream, Part One
The Dream of the Incarnation

Critics and scholars have advanced several figures from myth as models for Agnes. Ejnar Thomsen, for example, mentions Agni, the Indic god of fire; agnus dei, the lamb of God; and St. Agnes, the martyr condemned to a brothel.[12]

The case for the resemblance between Agnes and Agni is strong. One of Strindberg's favorite reference sources during the Inferno period was Viktor Rydberg's *Teutonic Mythology*, in which the *RgVeda* is quoted liberally in the subject of Agni's qualities and characteristics as the fire god and special messenger or mediator between the worlds of the gods and of men: "Agni's father . . . arranged it so that Agni came to our fathers"; [Agni] "knows all wisdom and all lore; . . . he was 'the husband to wives'"; "Agni is 'the listening one,' who perceives everything"; "I praise with song the Friend of man whom the gods sent down to be herald and messenger."[13] Except that Agnes is female, her resemblance to Agni is striking.

There are at least two other important pieces of evidence that attest to Strindberg's interest not only in Agni but in Indic mythology generally. The first is in a letter he wrote to Torsten Hedlund in 1896:

> Today I finished reading a book about India and I no longer know where I belong. It seems . . . [that the author of my books has been] someone other than me and that this alter ego was a Hindu. . . . Consider [this quotation from *Dans l'Inde* by André Chevrillon]: "Indra, Varuṇa, Agni, Sūrya are elemental spirits, not frozen or fixed in definite attributes, not comprehended as separate persons and unalterable, but floating, billowing, transforming themselves one into the other— The rosey dawn is also the sun; the sun is fire as well; fire is lightning, which is storm and rain."[14]

A similar quotation from the *RgVeda* is marked in a book Strindberg owned, *Le Buddhisme*, by G. de Lafont, published the year before the letter to Hedlund was written: "The divine spirit that moves in the heavens is called Indra, Mitra, Varuṇa, Agni; the sages give to this unique Being more than one name: it is Agni, Yama, Mātariśvan."[15]

The Indic gods are virtually interchangeable, not fixed personalities but dynamic forces: now individual, now plural; now palpable, now evanescent; now anthropomorphic, now the five elements—ether (or space), wind (or air), fire, water, and earth.[16] Strindberg responded strongly, as he did to Swedenborg's theory of correspondences, to the vast artistic potential in the pantheism of Indic mythology: the possibility of creating within a single work of art an almost infinite series of coherent patterns, one melding into another and all joined in a unified one.

From the lists of gods cited, three are important in connection with *A Dream Play*: Indra, Varuṇa, and Agni. Indra, the warrior king of the gods, had as attribute the lightning bolt and was giver of rain; Varuṇa, Indra's predecessor as king, controlled the rhythmic order of the universe, regulating the motions of the heavens and the circulation of waters; and Agni, the envoy and host of sacrifical fire, initiated men in the art of poetry. In the prologue of *A Dream Play* Indra sends his daughter, later called Agnes (read: Agni) to earth as a mediator. The Quarantine Master, as noted, mistakes her for Varuṇa. In the second Fingal's Grotto sequence, Agnes/Agni and the Poet discuss what poetry is and seem to conclude that poetry, dream, and life are one. They also sing hymns to heaven on the interrelatedness of the elements wind, water, fire, and earth, and Agnes decides to return to the fifth element, the ineffable ether. At the end of the play, she agrees to carry a message to Indra from the Poet, and before she leaves, throws her shoes, symbols of her earthbound existence, onto a special fire, used also in similar ritual fashion by other characters to rid themselves of earthly illusions. In summary, it seems likely that in the writing of *A Dream Play* Strindberg was strongly influenced by the various descriptions he read of Indic deities. As a young artist, he had been under the sway of his native Norse mythology, and one result, the poem "Loki's Blasphemies" (1883), concerned the ruthless mischief-maker of the gods. Now, Eastern mythology beckoned more powerfully. The Swedish critic Oscar Levertin found a more apt metaphor than he probably knew when he described Strindberg's return to Sweden after long exile at the turn of the century: "Loki has come home an Indian fakir."[17]

Another possible model for Agnes, as for Eleonora in *Easter*, is the Gnostic figure of divine wisdom: Pistis Sophia. Thomsen recommended something that supports this view: that Agnes's recurrent line "Life is evil" be regarded not as a moral but as a metaphysical observation.[18] To illustrate his point Thomsen cites an exchange between Agnes and the Officer in which the latter complains about the onerous chores he has to perform.

OFFICER: Why do I have to look after horses? Clean stables
            and spread sawdust?
DAUGHTER: So that you'll long to get away (224).

Here in a nutshell is both the basic movement of the play and a brief summary of Gnostic metaphysics. Out of an increasing awareness that earthly life is a prison in which the bright light of spirit is trapped in the dark gloom of matter comes, for those who possess this knowledge (gnosis), a longing of the spirit to be liberated. When the play is viewed in this way, each scene, instead of ending on a conclusive note—an either implicit or explicit chorus of "life is evil"/"Human beings are to be pitied"—focuses attention on a continuity of process and transformation. A tension builds as the darker the truths revealed about the suffocating power of matter, the greater the longing of spirit to be free. Just as Agnes tries to help mortals to understand māyā, she tries to get them to turn away from the darkness toward the light.

Evidence of Strindberg's interest in Gnosticism can be found in his *Occult Diary*, where passages from *Pistis Sophia* were quoted in 1898,[19] and in his own copy of the work,[20] where marginal notations appear next to some of the following passages.

It is related in *Pistis Sophia* that she "was one of the twenty-four superior emanations" and that she was forced to flee her "Aeon," or special place in the cosmos, and "fell into the depths of the dark chaos and was exposed there to attacks from the Archons [rulers] of this chaos and from those above." But if Sophia's "trials were great, her courage was even greater," and she turned toward the light and addressed to it a series of hymns. Finally, she was drawn upward from her fallen state and redeemed from the chaos.

Agnes, too, falls into a "dark chaos" whose rulers—the Chancellor and deans of the university—attack her when she attempts to bring them the message of the meaning of existence. Like Sophia, her "trials" are great, and she addresses hymns to a higher authority and finally escapes the chaos. She is a child of light and wisdom; she is one woman and all women. "You know everything," the Billposter tells her, "and that's why everyone comes to you with their troubles" (240). And although the Blind Man cannot see her, he recognizes her voice: "Every time life smiled, I heard that voice, like the murmur of a wind from the south, like a chord of harp music from above" (240).

The sequence of resonances in the character, first one mythic figure and then another, creates the kind of freedom of movement and expression paralleled in music by the device of modulation. The character retains an integrity of identity through several changes, but is transformed nevertheless, like a musical theme that suddenly shifts into a new key. We have continuity and change at one and the same time. *A Dream Play* becomes a variation on yet another theme: the Ovidian *Metamorphoses*.

One element of continuity in this modulating flow is the image of the godhead incarnate. Agnes is even likened, indirectly, to an implied incarnation, a character out of the *Thousand and One Nights*: Harun al-Rashid, the legendary caliph of Baghdad (c. 764–809), who dressed as a commoner and walked among his people to discover how law and order were kept. When Agnes is asked by the Poet to explain the injustices they see on their journey, she replies:

DAUGHTER: Your questions are so difficult to answer because . . . there are so many unforeseen problems . . .

POET: That's what Caliph Harun the Just also real-
              ized. . . . He just sat calmly on his throne and from
              up there he never saw how others had it down
              below. Finally, their complaints reached his exalted
              ear. So one fine day he stepped down, disguised
              himself, and walked unnoticed among the masses to
              see the workings of justice.
DAUGHTER: Surely you don't think that I am Harun the Just?

The discussion is interrupted by the Officer, who, as usual,
seeks to avoid any confrontation that could lead to disturbing
truths.

OFFICER: Let's talk about something else (271).

There is a tone of rebuke in the Poet's reference to Harun,
and Agnes reacts to it defensively. He disapproves of the condescending authority who sits aloof and removed from those he
rules, issuing orders from on high like Yahweh or like the
demiurge of the creation play, a hubristic figure in need of a
lesson in humility. The Indra of the prologue has some of this
same quality. Like the demiurge, he has little sympathy for the
earth's inhabitants and calls them an "ungrateful race" (219).
Agnes, like the Lucifer of the earlier play, who disagrees with
God, thinks Indra judges mankind too harshly, and whereas she
agrees to descend to them, he declines her invitation to follow
along.

The Yahweh of the pre-Inferno plays becomes the incar-
nated deity of the post-Inferno plays. "Yahweh," Strindberg
writes in an essay, "In the Cemetery," "is the God of vengeance" (27, 598). The narrator of *Jacob Wrestles* talks much more
sympathetically about a different kind of deity: "The God who
heard for so long the lamentations of mankind about the
wretchedness of earthly life that He finally resolved to descend,
to let Himself be born and live in order to test the difficulties
involved in being human. Him I can comprehend!" (28, 384–
385). "Just as man must suffer from God," says Jung, "so God
must suffer from man. Otherwise there can be no reconciliation
between the two."[21]

Agnes's mission is to be a messenger in both directions: to
bring the truth about the nature of mortality to God and the

truth about the nature of the divine to man. When the Christ-like vision or apparition in *Jacob Wrestles* speaks, the narrator describes it "as if within me I heard a voice resound" (342). The transcendent Yahweh has become the immanent Christ. *"Est deus in nobis,"* says Ovid ("There is a god within us"). In Strindberg's copy of a biography of Swedenborg there is a marginal notation marking a quotation taken from the writings of Dr. Pordage, the seventeenth-century English mystic:

> I did not succeed in discovering the primal principle of divine wisdom as long as I searched for it outside and above me; but when I turned my glances within my own *self*, I was surprised to see that He was settled there . . . and that He constituted the root of my life. I thus found God when I descended into myself, He, whom I had in vain and for so long sought outside myself by trying to ascend to Him.[22]

What the Officer, the Lawyer, and the Poet face in Agnes is not only the godhead incarnate but the spark of the divine within themselves. "You are a child of heaven," the Officer says admiringly to her. "So are you," she replies (36, 223). God, by assuming the life of man, enables man to realize the God within himself.

There are two important implications in Strindberg's selection of a female rather than a male incarnation. First, in terms of correspondences, Indra's thunderbolt and Agni's fire are part of the same elemental substance, the first on a heavenly plane, the second on an earthly one, and some mythographers maintain that the two gods symbolize a relationship that long captivated the Indo-European imagination: that of Father Heaven and Mother Earth.[23] Second, when the Poet reminds Agnes that Indra once sent his son on the same mission she has undertaken, she asks:

DAUGHTER: Wasn't the condition of mankind improved as a result of his visit to earth? Answer truthfully!
POET: Improved? . . . Yes, a little. Very little! (324).

Instead of a male, Christ-like figure as the instrument for reconciliation with the divine, reconciliation with existence, Strindberg chose an older symbol: the eternal feminine, or the triple goddess, the "White Goddess," as Robert Graves has referred to the figure.[24] The White Goddess is a lunar deity, queen of the night, and when Indra first draws his daughter's attention to the planet beneath them, she responds: "You mentioned the earth—is it that dark / and heavy world that is lit up by the moon?" (218).

The triple role Agnes subsequently plays—mother to the Officer, lover to the Laywer, and sister to the Poet—is another of the several mythic triads in Strindberg's plays. In *Master Olof*, there are three women who appear with the hero in the tavern scene: the prostitute, Olof's mother, and his future wife, the last two sharing the same name, Kristina (which underscores the unity underlying the triad). In *The Father* three women hover over the Captain's deathbed: his wife, his old nurse, and his daughter. In *Easter*, Elis's mother and sister are reconciled in an important scene that helps prepare his own reconciliation with his beloved, another Kristina. In *A Dream Play*, there is a Kristina and a Kristine, and they too have archetypal roles to play, especially, the first, the Officer's mother, who has a vital place in his dream.

The Officer and the Dream of the Child Man

The Officer's dream is intimately bound up with a physical setting, which as symbol vies with māyā as the controlling image in the play: the castle. It is the first thing Agnes sees on her earthly journey, and she rushes inside to find the Officer. References to the castle reappear throughout the play, and at the end the building is the subject of a bizarre stage direction: a giant flower blooms from its roof.

In fact, castles, or variants thereof, actual and symbolic—towers, prisons, fortresses—appear regularly in Strindberg's work from his earliest days. We have already discussed, for example, the references to maiden and tower, an association cluster in which the building is an obstacle that separates a pair of potential lovers: a maiden is imprisoned in a tower by a magician or a dragon or some other evil force and is finally rescued by a shining knight. Maiden and tower—*jungfru* and *tornet* in Swedish—are also mentioned in *Son of a Servant Woman*. While describing the books that had a powerful effect on his imagination, the narrator singles out a novel by a popular mid-nineteenth-century Swedish authoress, Emilie Flygare-Carlén, *Jungfrutornet*, or *The Maiden's Tower*.

> [The stories of] unhappy love moved him. But the most important thing was that he felt like an adult with these adult characters. He understood what they said and he realized that he was no longer a child. These grown people were his equals. He too had been unhappy in love, had suffered and fought, but he continued to be detained in the prison of childhood. And now he became fully aware that his soul was in prison. It had been ready to fly for a long time, but its wings had been clipped and it had been put in a cage (*18*, 100).

The feelings described are conventionally romantic, but the poetic resonances and implications are important for the light they cast on Strindberg's way of handling three interrelated images. In his symbolic language the tower/prison often means childhood, the maiden the soul, and the liberator adult love, spiritual and carnal. The maiden knows that the liberator may bring pain along with the joy of freedom, but unless she is willing to face the pain, true liberation will never take place, and the soul will forever remain a captive in childhood.

The title of Flygare-Carlén's novel was probably inspired by a tower called Jungfrutornet in the city of Wisby on Gotland, an island off the southeast coast of Sweden. Part of a wall built in the late 1200s, when Wisby was the prosperous commercial center of northern Europe, the structure has long been a popular symbol in Sweden for the tragedy of unhappy love. Legend has it that a young maiden unwittingly betrayed Wisby and caused it to be plundered when she gave the keys of the city gate to her lover, who turned out to be the marauding king of Denmark, Waldemar Atterdag. As punishment, the citizens cruelly sealed her alive in Jungfrutornet, which still stands today, partly in ruins, as does most of ancient Wisby.[25]

Scholars have established that the probable, immediate inspiration for the castle in *A Dream Play* was a cavalry barracks in Stockholm, built in the mid-1890s; Strindberg could see it from his apartment window nearby, and supposedly it also provided him with the subject for a poem, "My Magic Castle."[26] Frida Uhl, Strindberg's second wife, contended, however, that the playwright used the term "magic castle" as early as 1893, in Berlin, when referring to an impressive building she and Strindberg passed regularly on promenades: the ill-fated Reichstag.[27] Although we have reason to be skeptical about the accuracy of details in Frida Uhl's story—for example, Strindberg is quoted as saying things in Berlin which make it sound as if he was ready at any moment to begin the first draft of *A Dream Play*—it is not surprising to learn that he was preoccupied with images of castles and towers, for this was one of his oldest habits. In his autobiography he records that one of the most memorable events in his childhood was a visit to Drottningholm, the charming royal pleasure castle outside Stockholm. And his final home, which today houses a museum to his memory, is in a Stockholm apartment building he nicknamed the Blue Tower.

In *A Dream Play*, a working title for which was *The Growing Castle*,[28] the castle/tower image is pervasive and its meaning complex. I said that Agnes is confronted by the castle immediately upon her arrival on earth, but there is an earlier reference as well. The stage directions for the prologue describe the heavenly backdrop as representing "cloud caps resembling shattered slate mountains with ruins of castles and fortresses" (*36*, 217). Then we have the description in the stage directions of the scene that follows, where the backdrop is a forest of giant hollyhocks over the top of which is visible

[. . . *The gilded roof of a castle topped by a flower bud resembling a crown. Below the foundation walls of the castle are piles of straw, spread out to cover manure from the stables.*]

DAUGHTER: The castle is still growing out of the earth . . . Do you see how much it's grown since last year?

GLAZIER [*to himself*]: I've never seen the castle before . . . have never heard of a castle growing . . . but [*to the Daughter, with firm conviction*] yes, it's grown eight feet . . . (221)

In description and dialogue, simultaneously economical and rich, matter-of-fact and evocative, logical and absurd, a fairy talelike mood is set and then almost immediatey undermined and mocked. As he did in *Miss Julie* and would do again in *The Ghost Sonata*, Strindberg was working with a special form: the fairy tale manqué.

Agnes is drawn toward adventure. In castles there are mysteries and treasures, but this one seems more mysterious than most: it appears to be a living thing. No wonder the Glazier—Agnes's earthly father, as we subsequently learn—is surprised. Who has ever heard of a castle growing? But then the Glazier reverses himself and says that it has indeed grown and he can see by how much. It is as if Agnes can sense instantly strange truths that the Glazier, mere earthling that he is, either fails to see or has forgotten. This phenomenon is even more evident in the following exchange:

DAUGHTER: Do you know who lives in that castle?
GLAZIER: I used to know, but I can't remember.
DAUGHTER: I think there's a prisoner inside . . . and I'm sure he's sitting there waiting for me to free him.
GLAZIER: But at what cost?
DAUGHTER: One doesn't bargain over what one has to do. Let's go into the castle! . . .
GLAZIER: Yes, let's go! (222).

A castle and a captive: the spirit of adventure continues to evolve, but in an uncommon way: the rescuer is a maiden, and the captive is not exactly overjoyed to see her.

DAUGHTER: You're a prisoner in your own rooms. I've come to free you!
OFFICER: I guess I've been waiting for this, but I wasn't sure you'd want to (223).

The Officer's ambiguous response is reminiscent of the opening line of *To Damascus*, where the Stranger greets the Lady with "So there you are. I was almost sure you'd come" (29, 7). Agnes, like the Lady, has been summoned by the dreamer; she has been called up out of the depths of his being to bring him the challenge of liberation.

DAUGHTER: The castle is strong—it has seven walls—but it can be done. Do you want to or not?
OFFICER: To be honest, I don't know, for either way it'll be painful. Every joy in life is paid for with twice its worth in sorrow. It's hard to have to sit here, but the price I'd have to pay for the sweetness of freedom would be threefold pain. . . . Agnes, I'd just as soon put up with it, if only I can see you (36, 223).

The Officer's prison is the same as that of the narrator in *Son of a Servant Woman*, childhood. The difference is that the latter wants to be liberated and the former does not. It is not that the Officer does not recognize Agnes in her symbolic role as love come to free the soul.

DAUGHTER: What do you see in me?
OFFICER: The beauty that gives harmony to the universe. . . . There are lines in your form that I find only in the orbits of the solar system, in a lovely chord of music, in the vibrations of light . . . You are a child of heaven (223).

The Officer is also a child, but in a negative sense. Although his military vocation gives him the conventional credentials of a hero, he is captive in his own house. To be a hero, especially in fairy tales, entails accepting the responsibilities of growing up, and this the Officer cannot do. When Agnes first enters she finds him rocking in a chair and striking his saber on a table.

DAUGHTER [*crossing to the Officer and gently taking the saber from his hand*]: No, no, you mustn't do that!
OFFICER: Please, Agnes, let me keep my saber.
DAUGHTER: No, you're chopping the table to pieces! (222–223).

The tone of the scene is that of a mother scolding a child, or as Evert Sprinchorn observes with a strong Freudian bias: "A good nineteenth-century mother . . . telling her son, rocking in his cradle, not to masturbate."[29] Later, the Officer complains like an irresponsible boy about having to do unpleasant chores in the stable, and although he would like to get away, he says

OFFICER: It's so hard to find one's way out.

DAUGHTER: But everyone has a duty to seek freedom in the
            light! (224)

The texture of mythic resonances is rich and dense, despite the
leanness of the dialogue, and the dominant tone is Gnostic. The
castle/tower is the prison of the world, the prison of matter
(*Prisoners* was another working title for the play which Strindberg discarded).[30] Agnes is the Alien One, the stranger from the
realm of light, who at this point plays the role of the messenger
bringing the promise of liberation to a spark of the divine
trapped in matter. The Officer too is a child of heaven. Agnes's
earlier reference to seven walls picks up a resonance from the
prologue where Indra talks of the season in which he and Agnes
have arrived in the region of the earth; "the seventh house of the
sun," Libra, autumn. In Gnostic symbolism, according to Hans
Jonas,

> as in the macrocosm man is enclosed by the seven spheres, so in
> the human microcosm again [the divine spark or] pneuma is
> enclosed by the seven soul-vestments originating from them. In
> its unredeemed state the pneuma thus immersed in soul and flesh
> is unconscious of itself, benumbed, asleep or intoxicated by the
> poison of the world: in brief, it is "ignorant." Its awakening and
> liberation is effected through "knowledge."[31]

If the Officer is a slumbering spark reluctant to be liberated,
he is also a variant of Hercules, the prototypal hero. The play's
opening stage directions mention that straw has been spread out
over manure, part of the chore the Officer objects to having to
perform. What is implied is the fifth of Hercules's twelve labors:
the cleansing of King Augeas's filthy stables, a feat that the
demigod, in contrast to the Officer who toils endlessly, accomplished in one day. Strindberg was quite familiar with the fifth
labor: in 1883 he used it as the subject of an amusing, satirical,
short story.[32] In fact, he was familiar with and fascinated by the
entire Hercules myth. Conspicuous references to it appear, in
addition to the short story, in *The Father* (1887); the novels *By the
Open Sea* (1890),[33] *Inferno* (1897), and *Black Banners* (1904); *To
Damascus, II*, (1898); the essay collection *A Blue Book* (1907); and
the poetry collection *Word Play and Minor Art* (1903). At one
point, sometime after 1903, to judge from the watermark in the

manuscript, Strindberg planned, but never executed, a full-length play entitled *Omphale*. Moreover, so sophisticated was he about the demigod's legend that he was careful to distinguish between the Greek Heracles and the Roman Hercules. In an 1895 letter to Torsten Hedlund he wrote: "The Romans did indeed make an athlete of Heracles, but the Hellenes retained theirs as symbol, because they could see beneath the surface."[34] Some indication of what this ambivalent symbol meant to Strindberg is in the final passages of the novel *By the Open Sea*, in which the central character, Axel Borg, muses in dreamlike fashion about the significance of Hercules as he sails out to sea in a small boat, presumably to kill himself. As far as I know, this is the only place in his published works where Strindberg used both the Greek and Roman spellings of the name. As Borg sets sail, he takes his bearings on the beta star in the constellation Hercules! "Hercules . . . the god of strength and wisdom, who killed the Lernean hydra with its hundred heads, who cleansed the Augean stables, captured the man-eating mare of Diomedes, tore the girdle from the Amazon queen, brought Cerberus back from hell, and finally fell because of the stupidity of a woman who poisoned him out of sheer love after he had in madness served the nymph Omphale for three years . . . " At this point there is a subtle change in the narrative style, like a shifting of gears. The Roman Hercules is left behind as a new course is set, metaphorically.

> Out toward the one who had at least been given a place in heaven, who had never let himself be whipped or his face spat upon without striking or spitting back like a man, out toward the self-immolator, who could fall only by his own strong hand without begging for the mercy of the chalice, out towards Heracles, who liberated Prometheus, the bringer of light, himself the son of a god and a mortal woman (*24*, 243).

In Strindberg's view, it would seem, the Hercules who is the simple strong man, who dies after his wife, Deianeira, sends the shirt poisoned with Nessus's blood, is to be remembered chiefly for having been Omphale's slave. Heracles, by contrast, is independent and in control of his fate, free of Omphale, a self-immolator whose courage Zeus so admired that he raised the demigod to the status of one of the Olympian immortals. Hercules is a would-be hero; Heracles is a true one. We are reminded of Kilo's speech from *Black Banners*, in which he condemns the unenlightened men who "worship Māyā, the earth spirit, woman, and when they don't want to serve God in love, they have to serve Omphale in hate" (*41*, 185–186). This is precisely the Officer's destiny in *A Dream Play*: he too worships woman (māyā) and fails to liberate himself from Omphale in her archetypal role as Great Mother, a failure that becomes clear in the next scene of the Officer's dream.

When the Officer complains to Agnes about how unjustly life has treated him, the castle setting dissolves and the pair are transported, as if by means of a cinematic flashback, into the past, to the Officer's family home. Agnes's role as triple goddess brings to mind that one of the goddess's identities was that of muse, and the first muse of the ancient Greek triad was Mnemosyne (Memory). The mere fact of Agnes's presence helps to trigger the flashback: a new woman in the Officer's life jars loose a memory of the first one.

[*Voices are now heard from behind the dividing screen, which is drawn aside. The Officer and Daughter turn to look in that direction, then stop, their movements and expressions frozen.*]

[*At a table sits the Mother, sickly. Before her burns a tallow candle, which she trims from time to time with a pair of candle scissors. On the table lie piles of newly sewn shirts, which she marks with marking ink and a quill pen. To the left stands a brown wardrobe.*]

FATHER [*offering her a silk lace shawl, gently*]:   Don't you want it?
MOTHER: A silk lace shawl for me? My dear, what use would that be?

FATHER: And you're thinking of your children, first and last.
MOTHER: But they've been my life: my justification . . . my joy and my sorrow (*36*, 224–225).

Strindberg had returned to a favorite theme, a dying mother, the Great Mother at the moment of her greatest power, able to enforce her authority over her son, as we saw earlier in *Master Olof*, through the weapon of guilt. Abruptly, the mother shat-

ters the unity of time and space: past and present become one as
she calls her son to her side.

MOTHER: Who is that girl?
OFFICER [*whispering*]:   That's Agnes!
MOTHER: Oh, is that Agnes? Do you know what they're
           saying? . . . That she's the daughter of the god
           Indra, who begged to be able to come down to earth
           in order to feel what it really means to be a human
           being . . . But don't say anything!

There is a mischievous quality in the Mother's probing, "Who is
that girl?," as if the old woman is jealous of Agnes. She puts one
in mind of Olof's mother, who wanted her son to leave his wife
and return to the life of a celibate churchman. Further echoes of
the earlier play can be detected as the scene continues.

MOTHER [*aloud*]:   Alfred, dear, I'll soon be leaving you and your
                     brothers and sisters . . . I want to tell you
                     something you must never forget.
OFFICER [*sadly*]:   What is it, mother?:
MOTHER: Just one thing: never quarrel with God! (226).

Behind her words ring the words of Olof's mother on her
deathbed: "Take up again the faith I gave you, and I'll forgive
you. . . . I see Him, I see God staring angrily!" (2, 145). In
both instances the deity invoked is the transcendent God of the
Book of Genesis, Yahweh, and both women, as noted earlier,
are named Kristina. As in the case of Master Olof, a mother's
power over her son continues even after her death. When Alfred
complains that a childhood injustice he suffered ruined his life,
his mother rebukes him by exposing an old cause for guilt.

MOTHER: Go to that wardrobe . . .
OFFICER [*ashamed*]:   So you know about it. That's . . .
MOTHER: *The Swiss Family Robinson* . . . Which . . .
OFFICER: Don't say any more! . . .
MOTHER: Which your brother was punished for . . .
           and which *you* had torn up and hidden!
OFFICER: Just think—that wardrobe can still be there
           after twenty years . . . We moved so many
           times, and my mother died ten years ago!
MOTHER: Well, what of it? You always have to ques-
           tion everything and that way you spoil the
           best things life has to offer you! (36, 227).

The action moves on two planes at once and illuminates each brilliantly. At one moment we are in the past and the next in the present as the Officer breaks off contact with this painful memory at a very appropriate place, psychologically: the instant when his awareness of the burden of guilt and of his mother's power is most intense. And her reaction to this awareness is also appropriate, but in another context. When she criticizes with "you always have to question everything," she could be a witch out of a fairy tale who fears that her victim is getting close to discovering the secret of the spell she has over him. She need not fear, however: her Alfred does not have the heroic will necessary to break the spell. Despite that, Agnes now proceeds to instruct him: "Yes, life is difficult, but love conquers everything! Come and see!" (229). She and the Officer go off for a fresh adventure in another unusual setting:

[*An old, dirty, free-standing fire wall. In the middle of the wall a gate opens on an alley, which leads to a brightly-lit green area where a giant blue monkshood (aconitum) can be seen. To the left of the gate sits the Stage Doorkeeper with a shawl over her head and shoulders. She is crocheting a star-patterned comforter. To the right is a billboard, which the Billposter is cleaning. Beside him stands a fishing net with a green handle. Farther to the right is a door with an air hole in the shape of a four-leafed clover. To the left of the gate stands a small linden tree with a pitch-black trunk and several pale green leaves. Next to it is a cellar air hole.*]

DAUGHTER: Isn't the star comforter finished yet?
DOORKEEPER: No, my dear. Twenty-six years is no time for
               such a task! (229–230).

Once again we are confronted with a profusion of mythic resonances, primary among which are the kinds of fabric images (comforter, shawl, net) which symbolize the great web of life (māyā) and the Stage Doorkeeper herself (a World Weaver figure) is, as Guy Vogelweith has indicated, Māyā personified.[35] The fact that the item she is crocheting is star-patterned emphasizes her role as the goddess of night, which also makes her the goddess of time, since the moon, as Erich Neumann observes, "is the true chronometer of the primordial era. From menstruation, with its supposed relation to the moon, pregnancy, and beyond, the woman is regulated by and dependent on time, so it is she who determines time."[36] Later in the scene, Agnes puts on the Doorkeeper's shawl and takes over the woman's guardian duties. She too becomes Māyā and the goddess of time. In fact, at one point stage time becomes mythic time as lights flash on and off rapidly to indicate the passage of many days and nights; the action startles Alfred:

> OFFICER: What is this? [*in time to the changing lights*] Light and dark; light and dark?
> DAUGHTER: Day and night; day and night! . . . A merciful providence wants to shorten your waiting. That's why the days fly by, chasing the nights (238).

What the Officer is waiting for is his beloved, Victoria, and we learn that he has been waiting for years. Where he has been waiting, apparently, is an alley leading to a theatre where Victoria is a performer. I say apparently because some of the elements of the place—the fire wall, the monkshood, the cellar air hole, and the Doorkeeper—have an infernal quality, suggesting the entrance to the underworld: that threshold of adventure with which mythic heroes have been traditionally confronted. According to Robert Graves, some mythographers hold that the witch-flower, aconite (monkshood), rose up from the spot near the entrance of the underworld where saliva dropped from the mouth of the great watchdog, Cerberus.[37] Thresholds, whether to the underworld or to towers, are generally guarded by such animals or dragons or doorkeepers of one kind or another. These guardians test the hero's mettle, for he must overcome their refusal to allow him to enter.

If the stage alley suggests the entrance to the underworld, it also suggests the approach to a tower. When Alfred enters, the stage directions indicate that he looks upward to call, "Victoria!" and then a woman's voice responds from above with, "I'm here!" (232). Thus, where the first scene presents an actual castle prison with a knight whom a maiden comes to rescue, now, by implication, we have a tower containing a maiden and a knight errant who has come for her.

Agnes, in the meantime, continuing to test what it is like to be human, has taken the Doorkeeper's place, wearing the shawl that has soaked up so many years of suffering it stings like

nettles. The Officer, no longer recognizing her, approaches
with a request that shows he has the proper instinct for a knight
errant: to enter the tower as a liberator.

OFFICER [*to the Daughter*]:
          Listen, madam, let me go up and fetch my bride! - - -
DOORKEEPER [*standing behind the Daughter*]:
          No one's allowed on to the stage!
OFFICER: For seven years I've been pacing here! (233).

Another brief passage that yields far more meaning than is
apparent at first glance. The Doorkeeper swiftly and firmly
denies Alfred's request; the guardian at the threshold refuses the
hero access. Symbolically, the theatre setting is a place of
illusion (māyā) as well as the familiar image: "all the world's a
stage." The line "No one's allowed on to the stage" can be taken
to mean that opportunities to perform in this world are not
given, like presents, they must be taken by individuals who are
prepared to assert themselves, by heroes who are ready to use
force if necessary to get the dragon to back down. As we have
already observed, the Officer is no hero; all it takes is one roar of
the dragon to get him to give up the quest. He will continue to
wait. The stage directions call for him to exit and reenter several
times during the alley scene, and each time he has grown
perceptibly older and the bouquet of roses he carries has withered until at last it is only a bunch of dried twigs. He grows older
but he never grows up, and he never wins Victoria because he
never really wants to. Later, in the Foulport scene, when the
Quarantine Master indicates that a girl passing in a boat and
identified as Victoria might be the girl the Officer has been
waiting for, Alfred denies it. "I have my own," he says, "and
mine no one will ever see" (272).

The three scenes that begin in the castle and end in the
theatre alley encompass the full development of the Officer's
dream. Alfred has had three chances to understand Agnes's
message—first, to accept the maiden as liberator, then to break
free of the power of the Great Mother, and finally to free the
maiden in the tower in his own right—but he has failed each
time. He reappears in other scenes, returning like a leitmotif

representing the irresponsible life with his shout of "Victoria!" but he never develops a higher level of awareness. In a sense, his dream is recapitulated later in the play in the touching and amusing, nightmarish schoolroom scene, where he is forced to relive some of the most humiliating experiences of his childhood as a grown man sitting in the midst of young boys. When Alfred protests at the indignity of being treated like a school child, the Schoolmaster points out to him the lesson he has never learned: "We have to mature!" (282).

The transition from the Officer's dream to the Lawyer's dream is effected through an ingenious device. Throughout the theatre alley scene the Officer speculates about the strange door he has observed every day of the seven years he has waited for Victoria.

> OFFICER: And this door I've seen two thousand five hundred and fifty-five times without finding out where it leads to! And that clover-leaf opening that's supposed to let in light—for whom does it let in light? Is someone in there? Does someone live there? (233).

His curiosity at last grows strong enough for him to send for someone to open it. The Glazier arrives to find a crowd of people waiting, but before he can open the door, he is stopped by a policeman who appears suddenly and unexpectedly to announce, "In the name of the law I forbid the opening of this door!" Alfred is upset and decides to seek legal advice. "To the Lawyer's!" (244), he proclaims, and exits with Agnes. When they reappear, the theatre alley has been transformed into the Lawyer's office.

The door is a splendidly multivalent symbol, serving different vital purposes in all the reciprocal dreams. In Alfred's, it is another indication of his ambivalent approach to life: wanting to be liberated and not wanting to at the same time. The Policeman who prevents the opening of the door is a censor figure from the Officer's unconscious, barring the revelation of a buried secret. Later, in the Lawyer's office, when Alfred has an opportunity to tell about the door, he says instead, "I only wanted to ask if Miss Victoria has left!" to which the Lawyer, despite apparently meeting his prospective client for the first time, responds in the marvelously absurd fashion typical of dreams: "No, she hasn't, you can rest assured" (247).

The door resembles the entrance to the mysterious room in Bluebeard's castle, another rich symbol of the unknown, the forbidden, and the unconscious. And it reminds Alfred of doors from his childhood:

> It looks like a pantry door I saw when I was four years old and one Sunday afternoon went off with the maid—off, to other houses, other maids. But I never got beyond the kitchen. . . . I've seen so many kitchens in my day and the pantries were always in the entry halls, with bored round holes and a clover leaf (233–234).

Conjured up in the description is a vision of a man remaining eternally that small boy who felt comfortable but was in awe as he sat in kitchens, those bastions of feminine authority, where there was both sustenance and mystery. In his entire life Alfred never gets beyond the kitchen.

The Lawyer and the Dream of Material Man

The clover-leaf door from the theatre alley reappears in the Lawyer's office, but altered, like everything else.

> [*The scene changes in full view of the audience . . . Thus: the gate remains and functions as the gate in an office railing. . . . The Door-keeper's hut turns to open toward the audience and becomes the niche for the Lawyer's desk. The linden tree, leafless, is a coat-and-hat stand. The billboard is hung with royal proclamations and court decisions. The door with the four-leafed clover opening now belongs to a storage cabinet for documents.*] (244).

The transformation of the setting reveals a critical continuity of identity between the two scenes. Objects have changed, but somehow remain the same. One implication is that no matter how the two locations may seem to differ from each other, underneath they are fundamentally alike: we are still in a world of illusion and pain, the world of māyā.

There is also a continuity of identity between the Officer and the Lawyer. Alfred, we will remember, reacted defensively when his mother pointed to the wardrobe. Now it is his turn to point, in this instance to the intriguing clover-leaf door, and his host becomes as upset as he was earlier:

LAWYER: Why are you pointing at my cabinet?
OFFICER: I was thinking that that door resembled . . .
LAWYER: Not at all. Oh no. No, no, no! (247).

The cabinet, like the wardrobe and the theatre alley door, carries implications of buried guilt and corpses in the cargo.

In other respects the Officer and Lawyer seem very different from each other, but, in fact, their very dissimilarity creates a kind of bond between them: they are polar opposites. If Alfred symbolizes the irresponsible man, the Lawyer (whose name we learn later is Axel) symbolizes the responsible one. The law practice he pursues is dedicated to the difficult job of righting injustices, and his clients are mostly poor people. In short, Axel has the heroic qualities Alfred only dreams about. Agnes senses these qualities the moment she enters, and between her and the Lawyer there develops a rapport and intimacy she never found with the Officer. But there is great pain in his face, symbol of the burden of his calling: "*His face bears witness to extraordinary suffering; it is chalk-white, lined and with corpselike purple shadows; it is ugly and reflects all the crime and vice with which his profession has compelled him to come into contact.*" (244). The anguish he bears is the price he must pay as a special kind of hero: the Promethean or Christ figure, who performs heroic deeds and suffers terribly as a result. Axel has challenged the canons of his society, as the Stranger did in *To Damascus*, and he too must expect ingratitude in return.

Church bells are heard pealing in the distance, time for the Lawyer to receive the doctorate in law he has earned. Another scene and another transformation: the objects in the office become objects in a church where the awards ceremony is to take place. But the authorities refuse to grant Axel his doctorate; he receives no laurel wreath of triumph. As if in recompense, Agnes tries to awaken in him a realization of the basic nature of this world of lies; standing by the church organ, she points to the mirror used by the organist to see the congregation behind him.

DAUGHTER:	Do you know what I see in this mirror? . . . The true image of the world . . . before it got turned around!
LAWYER:	How did it get turned around?
DAUGHTER:	When the copy was made . . .
LAWYER:	That's it—you're right! The copy . . . I always suspected this was a false copy . . . and when I began to remember the original, I became dissatisfied with everything . . . People called me malcontent . . . (249).

The truth about the world of māyā merges into the lesson of Plato's cave, where men believe they are seeing things in themselves but are only observing the shadow images of the things projected on the wall of the cave. The same lesson was expressed slightly differently in the theatre alley scene. The Billposter tells the Officer that he has dreamt for fifty years about getting a fishing net and now that he finally has it, he is disappointed.

BILLPOSTER:	The net was good, all right, but not *quite* as I had imagined.
OFFICER [*stressing the words*]:	Not quite as I had imagined! . . . That's very well put! Nothing is as I had imagined! ˙. . . It's always greater in my imagination, better than it turns out to be (239–240).

The Officer has found a reason for his waiting: better to wait for rather than fetch the girl of his dreams; that way he will never be disappointed. A real woman is a phantom, a pale copy of the original image, the ideal woman, the "thing in itself." But at the same time Alfred will never free the maiden and so will never advance to a higher level of self-realization. In contrast, the Lawyer is cast in a heroic mold: he must pursue the quest, which necessitates accepting the challenge of liberating the soul image even if it means yielding to māyā. Agnes has made a similar choice. She showed her heroic mettle in her dream with the Officer by attempting to free the prisoner. When she found him to be a boy, she turned to a man, the Lawyer, and when she sees that he is not awarded the wreath of academic honor, she crowns him instead with the cruelest of hero's mantles: a wreath of thorns.

Axel is a hero who is ready to evolve further; he is ready to be transformed. And the setting, a church interior, is, as it was in *Master Olof* and *To Damascus*, an appropriate vessel of transformation. Other such vessels include cauldrons—recall the reference to Medea's cauldron in *To Damascus*—and caves. And a cave is what the church organ in *A Dream Play* now changes into: specifically, Fingal's Grotto on Staffa Island in the Hebrides, in the nineteenth century a popular setting for legends and celebrated, for example, by Mendelssohn in an overture.

There are a number of references to Fingal's Grotto in Strindberg's works, and cumulatively they constitute an image of a primal place, an archetypal setting where sound and music originate and where the elements have their home—in mythic terms the underworld as center of the earth. Organs are also mentioned several times, and they too have a primordial quality. The narrator of *Jacob Wrestles* speaks of the power of the organ to play "notes and harmonies I have never heard before but which seem familiar—like memories from the days of my forefathers or even earlier" (*28*, 385). The sounds never heard but yet familiar are primal sounds, antedating even human memory, the elemental sounds of the winds and the sea. The stage directions for the grotto scene specify that "*the sea swells in under the basalt pillars and produces a sound ensemble effect of wind and wave*" (*36*, 251).

A *Blue Book* essay (1907) mentions the grotto's resemblance to the same instrument, "Fingal's Organ" (*46*, 310), and in the novella *The Romantic Organist on Rånö* (1888) the organist of the title, who has seen a picture of the cavern in a reference book, dreams of his own instrument as "a great basalt grotto and the treader of the bellows was Aeolus, who made the tempest" (*21*, 232). In another essay (1896), the grotto is mentioned in a discussion of the origins of various biological and geological structures and the author concludes

> I leave . . . [the regions of] the bowels of the earth, which for the sterile disbeliever seem still to conceal its greatest secrets, but not for the fearless skeptic who explores everything and remains watchful, receptive.
> Great Pan is certainly not dead, although he has been sick, but

sometime or other an Orpheus must descend into the underworld to sing life into stones that are not dead, but only asleep! (27, 234–235).

Resonances of Pan, the nature god, and Orpheus, the mortal associated with music and poetry, are important not only in *A Dream Play* but in much of Strindberg's later work. Having identified in the 1880s with the scientific objectivity of naturalism as it was championed by Zola, Strindberg turned in the mid- and late-1890s to what he saw as a new naturalism: a pantheistic naturism. An explanation for this new approach can be found in a passage from the Swedish version of the novel *Inferno*:

> Why spit upon Naturalism when it . . . inaugurates a new period and is endowed with the possibility of growing and developing? The gods are returning to us and the battle cry sounded by writers and artists—Back to Pan!—has reverberated so manifoldly that Nature has awakened again after her centuries-long slumber! . . . So let there be Naturalism; let there be a rebirth of the harmony between matter and spirit! (28, 58–60).

Later in the same novel the narrator says that in his research in alchemy and the occult he was "rival to Orpheus" and had been given the task of "bringing back to life Nature, which had died in the hands of scholars and scientists" (81). And in a letter about *Inferno*, Strindberg said he felt he had a calling to be the "Zola of the Occult."[38] *A Dream Play* is the richest example of how faithfully he fulfilled this calling.

Of the two scenes in Fingal's Grotto, the second is more complex and important, and in it the Poet carries resonances of the traditional first poet, Orpheus. But the first scene, although brief, is also important for the mood established by the location.

LAWYER: Where are we, sister?
DAUGHTER: What do you hear?
LAWYER: I hear drops falling. . . .
DAUGHTER: Those are tears, the tears of mankind . . . What
             else do you hear?
LAWYER: A sighing . . . a moaning . . . a wailing. . . .
DAUGHTER: Why this eternal complaining? Is there nothing
             in life to be happy about?

LAWYER:	Yes, the sweetest which is also the bitterest—
	love! A wife and a home; the best things and the
	worst.
DAUGHTER:	I must try it!
LAWYER:	With me?
DAUGHTER:	With you! You know where the pitfalls are, so
	we can avoid them (36, 251–252).

The sounds of the sea and winds coalesce with human tears and cries of pain in a nuptial scene at the bottom of the sea in the center of the world. It is another dawn of creation. In Fingal's Grotto, as at the union of Dido and Aeneas, turbulent elemental forces are in motion, and as that earlier union was doomed, so is the marriage of Agnes and the Lawyer.

Transformation again—to a kitchen-bedroom setting within the Lawyer's office, where the soft poetry of love has turned to the harsh prose of domestic life. Agnes and the Lawyer have a home and a child, but their marriage is breaking up: each likes what the other hates, and trivial annoyances have destroyed the rapport they once shared. To make matters worse, a maid is busy pasting cracks around the window.

KRISTINE:	I'm pasting, I'm pasting!
DAUGHTER [*pale and gaunt, sitting by the stove*]:	
	You're shutting out the air! I'm suffocating! (254).

The maid's name, Kristine, echoes the name of the Officer's mother, Kristina, and her action suggests another image of the stultifying Terrible Mother. Agnes's journey to the underworld in Fingal's Grotto has led her to the lowest ring of hell. It is little wonder that she is glad to see the Officer when he suddenly turns up as gay and carefree as ever.

OFFICER:	Are you coming with me now?
DAUGHTER:	Right away! But where?
OFFICER:	To Fairhaven! There it's summer and the sun is
	shining and there are young people, children,
	and flowers! There's singing and dancing, par-
	ties and feasting!
DAUGHTER:	Then that's where I want to go!

The reciprocal dream of Agnes and the Lawyer is over, even though he, like the Officer, will turn up again. The impossibility of their dream—the dream of marriage making one out of two, of restoring unity and harmony in a world of multiplicity—is expressed by Axel in a metaphor drawn appropriately from the matter-of-fact domesticity of conjugal life: a hairpin Agnes has dropped.

LAWYER: Look at this! Two prongs, but one pin! It's two but it's one! If I bend it, it becomes two, without ceasing to be one! It means: these two are one. But if I break it—like this—then the two are two. . . . And if they're parallel—they'll never never meet each other—[and then it's like ice] that neither bears nor breaks.

As the Lawyer uses the hairpin as a symbol of the hopelessness of his dream, the Officer interprets it all as a mathematical game.

OFFICER: The hairpin is the most perfect thing in all creation! A straight line which is identical with two parallel lines.

LAWYER: A lock that fastens when it is open!

OFFICER: Fastening open a braid of hair which remains open when it is fastened . . .

LAWYER: Like this door! When I close it, I open the way out, for you, Agnes! [*He withdraws and closes the door.*] (263–264).

Axel's dream is the dream of man trapped in matter. Where Alfred symbolized man with his head in the clouds, uncommitted man, Axel is man with his feet planted firmly on the ground, and his watchword is commitment to responsibility. In fact, the Lawyer is attached too firmly to the earth. Where Alfred is blind to the necessity of earthly duty, Axel is blind in a different way: he cannot see that sometimes spiritual duties must take precedence over material ones. When Alfred reappears in the play's remaining scenes he reintroduces, as he does now in the Lawyer's dream, the leitmotif of the uncommitted, self-indulgent life. When Axel reappears, he brings a reminder of the call to duty, to life's responsibilities. He tells Agnes, for example, that her child needs her, and she is torn between duty to others and duty to self.

Agnes has seen two extremes of the implications of earthly love—the Officer who cannot commit himself and the Lawyer who can—and she has found neither satisfactory. She is like a princess in a fairy tale who has met two princes, each with serious failings. Our expectations regarding fairy tales lead us to await the appearance of a third prince.

Agnes's Dream, Part Two
The Journey Toward Enlightenment

The Officer's return to fetch Agnes and to take her to the curious islands of Fairhaven and Foulport does not indicate any change in his character in the direction of the heroic.[39] He is still irresponsible Alfred, and his relationship with Agnes is strictly that of a guide for a traveler moving through an unfamiliar landscape. What Strindberg probably intended with the Officer's return was an element of continuity sorely needed in the scenes that follow. Up to this point the focus has been relatively stable and firm. Either Agnes or the Officer or the Lawyer or a combination of two of the three were in the foreground as active participants, as initiators of action, as generators of forward movement: Agnes comes as liberator; the Officer waits for Victoria; Agnes and the Lawyer get married. In the Foulport/Fairhaven section, however, except for the schoolroom scene in which Alfred is humiliated for having failed to grow up, the Officer and Agnes are reduced to spectators or interested observers, and the focus diffuses. Two important new characters are introduced, the Quarantine Master and the Poet, but they do not move the action forward in the way Agnes, Alfred, and Axel did in the first half of the play. In what I have designated as part two of Agnes's dream, the Quarantine Master at the weird resort he runs is like a ringmaster at a circus, and the Poet is a chorus figure, commenting on the absurdity and injustice of it all.

The Quarantine Master, a marvelously bizarre figure dressed like a Moor and wearing a black mask, is so fully rendered a character that several critics and scholars are inclined to rank him in importance with the Officer, Lawyer, and Poet. Maurice Valency, for example, interprets the quartet of men biographically as the "four aspects of the author, the dreamer, and in their composite life is indicated his manifold nature."[40] But the Quarantine Master is outside the main line of action for a simple reason: he has no direct and personal relationship with Agnes. Nevertheless, he is a fascinating figure, and the mythic resonances he evokes are significant. One model for the character that comes to mind is the demiurge of the creation play. Like that figure, the Quarantine Master is the manager of an infernal world where people are tortured and tormented. The mythic dimension of this torture is more clearly communicated in the French word *quarantaine*, which can mean either a quarantine period or the number forty, a number closely associated, especially by medieval Christianity, with suffering, penance, and the hope of atonement.[41] As O. B. Hardison points out, forty is the number of days of Lent and of the

> deluge that destroyed all men except Noah, it is the number of years that the Hebrew people were condemned to spend in the wilderness, and it is the number of days of the fasts of Moses and Elias before they approached the Lord on Mount Sinai and Mount Horeb. Finally, it is the number of days spent by Christ in the desert and the number of hours between the Crucifixion and the Resurrection.[42]

Explicit or implicit references to the number are recurrent in Strindberg's works, and they generally point to a period of trial and tribulation that precedes an important confrontation or reconciliation. Elias fasting before proceeding to Horeb, the Mount of God, brings to mind Elis, in *Easter*, whose moment of reconciliation coincides with the end of the forty days of Lent. The Stranger in *To Damascus* has waited forty years for something that turns out to be the self-confrontation he so long resisted. References to quarantine masters appear both in the short story collection *Fairhaven and Foulport* and the play *The Dance of Death*. In *A Dream Play* one of the involuntary clients who arrives in Foulport asks how long he will be required to stay and is told forty days and nights. And Strindberg in his *Occult Diary* described the play as having been written "after 40 days of suffering (Aug., Sept. 1901), when Harriet was carrying my unborn last child."[43]

Despite the stimulating presence of the Quarantine Master,

the scenes that constitute the second part of Agnes's dream tend in production to be the most didactic, reduced to tableaux illustrating the thesis that "life is evil" and "Human beings are to be pitied." This is especially true of the third scene in the section, the Riviera, in which Agnes observes the plight of coal bearers, who are surrounded by affluence and luxury but must themselves struggle just to survive.

The Quarantine Master is most important for the theme he represents, penitential suffering, because it is associated with a structure of action that ties together the scenes in which he appears and prepares the way for the final reciprocal dream between Agnes and the Poet: the story of Śākyamuni, the sage of the Śākya clan, who was to become the Buddha, the Enlightened One.

Scholars date the beginning of the period when Strindberg became really interested in Buddhism as 1894,[44] when, according to Frida Uhl, he found a book on the subject in her grandfather's house.[45] Certainly, after this time many references to Buddha and Buddhism appear in his letters and works, but the interest was probably stimulated earlier. In 1886, for example, he wrote knowingly of Buddhism in his autobiography (*19*, 60), and it is likely, as I noted in the first chapter, that he absorbed even earlier some of Schopenhauer's enthusiasm for the subject: "[I] have to concede to Buddhism," the German philosopher wrote, "pre-eminence over [other religions]."[46] Śākyamuni is the name Buddha received when he left his wife and child to pursue an ascetic life, and in 1894 Strindberg, separated as he was from Frida and their child, identified strongly with this phase of Buddha's life. The interest developed into a passion; a half-dozen well-marked books on Buddhism can be found in his final library. It should be noted, though, that his reasons for studying the subject, however personal, were at least partly, perhaps even primarily artistic: another source of resonances for his polyphonic mythology. A passage from a 1907 letter to his German translator is illuminating in this regard. He had just finished reading *Karma*, a play by the German author Carl Bleibtreu, and he quoted the prologue to the play in the letter:

" 'Everything that exists in the world has its prototype (ethereal) in the transcendental.' (Swedenborg's Theory of Correspondences, Plato's Reminiscences). . . . Bleibtreu, who is a Buddhist, should write in a Buddhist spirit, with subjects taken from reality, not *about* Buddha's teachings!"[47] Two principles are evident that are applicable to Strindberg's own use of mythic resonances: first, it is the spirit, and not the letter of the mythic source, to which one must be faithful; and second, the spirit must be firmly grounded in reality. Whatever mythic energies are present must glow behind a facade of real-life details. "First physics, then metaphysics," as Strindberg put it in a letter.[48] But this does not mean that he ranked the elements drawn from life higher in importance than the spirit behind them. In the preface to *A Dream Play*, he says that "the imagination spins out and weaves new patterns" upon "an insignificant foundation of reality" (*36*, 215).

Buddha's Sermon in the Deer Park of Benares—a statement of precepts resembling Christ's Sermon on the Mount—contains an important doctrine on moderation, and in a book on Buddhism owned by Strindberg a portion of the following passage concerning the doctrine is marked: "It is in the equilibrium of the faculties and inner harmony that truth is found. . . . [Buddha said], 'There are two extremes which he who leads a spiritual life must repudiate. What are these two extremes? The first is a life of pleasure, devoted to pleasure and entertainment: this is base, ignoble, contrary to the spirit, unworthy, vain. The other is a life of self-denial; this is sorrowful, unworthy, vain.' "[49] The two extremes rejected—the sensual life devoted to pleasure and the ascetic life leading to emaciation—resemble the descriptions of life on the two islands in *A Dream Play*, Fairhaven and Foulport, respectively. Agnes and the Officer reach the second island first, despite Alfred's intention to go directly to Fairhaven, and they find the Quarantine Master's domain to be a kind of infernal health spa:

[*Visible in the foreground to the right are charred hills covered with red heather and black and white stumps of trees left after a forest fire; red pigsties and outhouses. Below is an open, medical-gymnastic treatment center, where people are exercising on machines resembling instruments of torture. In the foreground to the left a section of the quarantine complex: open sheds with furnaces, boilers, and pipes.]* (264).

Across a channel of water is the much more inviting view of Fairhaven.

[A beautiful beach with trees and flag-decorated piers where white boats are moored, some with raised sails, some without. Small Italian villas, pavilions, kiosks, marble statues are visible on the beach between the trees.] (265).

Things turn out to be pretty grim on Foulport, but they are not much better on Fairhaven, outward appearances notwithstanding. Life in both places is a parade of human misery and unhappiness, and some of Agnes's experiences recall those attributed to Gautama Siddhartha, the prince who was to become Buddha. In Strindberg's book on Buddhism passages are marked which describe how Gautama's father raised his son to be ignorant of the evil and wretchedness of the world and how the prince discovered these things for himself on four different outings with his retinue. On the first, he was shocked at the sight of an old man and was told that he too would age one day and become infirm. The second time he saw a sick man, crippled by disease, and was apprised that this was an evil common to all. On the third outing, he saw a dead man being borne in a funeral procession, and "this time," according to the version of the legend in Strindberg's book, "his meditations were profound, for he knew that nothing can escape death. . . ; he had seen and understood the fragility and nothingness of life."[50]

Agnes and the Officer on their journey also learn about "the fragility and the nothingness of life," especially old age, disease, and death. An old man in a wheelchair, who is called Don Juan, is accompanied by a gaunt, ugly, sixty-year-old woman and her forty-year-old male lover. "Don Juan," the Quarantine Master says mockingly. "Look at him—he's still in love with that spook at his side. He doesn't notice that she's grown old—that she's ugly, unfaithful, cruel" (267). On Fairhaven there is a vacation atmosphere, as the Officer had promised, but also the tragedy of physical affliction: the man who owns the island and everything on it is blind, so he cannot see his beautiful beaches and villas. And there is unrequited love. A girl, Edith, is in love with the Blind Man's son, the Lieutenant, but he is in love with another girl, Alice. But Alice too is destined to suffer: the lieutenant dies when his ship goes down at sea.

In the legend of Buddha the fourth sign Prince Gautama receives alters his entire life: he encounters an ascetic mendicant who convinces the prince to abandon his family and turn his back on everything that is an obstacle to the meditative life. In Strindberg's book on Buddhism the margin is marked next to the description of what happens next: "The news was delivered to him of the birth of his son Rahula and . . . [he saw that the birth was only a] chain that threatened to attach him to the life he wanted to flee."[51]

Late in *A Dream Play*, after Agnes has decided to withdraw from the world and journey into the wilderness with the Poet, she is stopped by the Lawyer.

LAWYER [*crossing to her and grasping her arm*]:
Have you forgotten your duties?
DAUGHTER: Oh God, no! But I have higher duties.
LAWYER: And your child?
DAUGHTER: My child! What of it?
LAWYER: Your child is calling for you.
DAUGHTER: My child! Alas, I am earthbound . . . .

You look like a demon when you say that word *duty*! . . . But what if one has two duties to fulfill, as I have?
LAWYER: Then fulfill first one, and then the other!
DAUGHTER: The highest first . . . and so, dearest, look after my child while I fulfill my duty (319–321).[52]

Agnes's duty involves pursuing the same goal pursued by Prince Gautama: to become an enlightened being, a Bodhisattva, and Joseph Campbell tells us that "Bodhisattvas, the Future Buddhas, after knowing the flavor of the world, have always, following the birth of a son, departed to the forest."[53] It is significant that the essence of the Bodhisattva is defined by the word *karuṇā*, which means "compassion for all beings." It calls to mind Agnes's repeated observation: "Human beings are to be pitied." How she proceeds toward this higher level of awareness, the Bodisattvahood, is intricately bound up with her relationship with the Poet, and with the unfolding of their reciprocal dream.

The Poet and the Dream of the Androgyne

The typical fairy tale of the princess choosing among suitors has an interesting application to *A Dream Play*. This princess finds the first two aspirants wanting: Alfred demands too little of the maiden, and Axel too much. An implicit question arises: Where can she find the man who will make demands but still leave her the opportunity to be spiritually free and complete? The Poet turns up as the next candidate. Like other characters in the play, his first appearance is sudden and unexpected, but he fits easily and seamlessly into the texture of the action. He and Agnes immediately talk familiarly with each other, developing the kind of personal communication we have come to expect between the suitors and the princess.

The Poet also establishes a connection between himself and one of his predecessors: he champions the cause of poor mistreated Lina, the downtrodden servant girl who appears earlier in the Officer's family home. In fact, all three men in Agnes's life are related, and together they resemble the Indic divine trinity, or trimūrti: Śiva the destroyer, Viṣṇu the preserver, and Brahmā the creator. The Officer is part of the military, the chief purpose of which is to be ready to make war, that most efficient of all engines of destruction. The Lawyer's vocation is the maintenance of social order, the defining and preserving of the contracts between men that hold together the social fabric. And the Poet as artistic creator emulates the original creator.

Strindberg was fascinated by the concept of the trimūrti, especially when he was in Paris in the mid-1890s, as he was fascinated by Indic religion and mythology generally. In a *Blue Book* essay he explains that "when Buddhism (mixed with Vedāntism) became the fashion in 1890 . . . the new trinity, Brahmā-Viṣṇu-Śiva, met no objections" (*46*, 179). In his letters from 1894 and 1895 there are a score of trimūrti references, many illustrated with drawings of triangles; they appear to have been parts of an elaborate game he concocted with his old college friend Leopold Littmansson, in which he poked fun at friends and enemies through rhymes, puns, and private allusions. A number of the trimūrtis were meant to symbolize unpleasant truths about Sweden, and the author, down and out in France, used black humor to give vent to the hostility he felt toward his native land. One such trimūrti was labeled "*Split— Kredit—Skit*," which translated literally would be "Discord— Credit—Shit."[54] But Strindberg took more than a joking attitude toward the trimūrti, which through correspondences, became analgous to the Christian Trinity. Recall his letter cited in the first chapter in which he rendered an esoteric interpretation of one of his own paintings: "The three masts [of a ship] with three top cross bars look like Golgotha or three crosses on graves and might be a trimūrti, but this is a matter of taste (subjective)."

The trimūrti of men suggested in *A Dream Play* is handled structurally like other examples of ternary symbolism: the introduction of a third factor either resolves a tension and/or climaxes a progression established by the first two factors. The Poet serves both functions: where the Officer is the irresponsible man and the Lawyer the overly responsible one, the Poet concerns himself with higher responsibilities. Where the Officer and the Lawyer are both blinded by māyā—Alfred, a prisoner of his own past and slave to the Great Mother, and Axel, a prisoner of the present and enmeshed in matter—the Poet's perspective is not limited to the past or the present; he is free to soar higher and see farther than his predecessors. In an 1896 essay published in a Parisian occult journal, Strindberg wrote that before the resurgence of interest in Swedenborg's correspondences, "The psychic ability to 'see similarities everywhere' was permissible only for the *skalds*, those harmless image makers" (27, 358). The Stranger in *To Damascus*, also a writer, a skald, says "Life—which before was a great nonsense—has taken on purpose and now I see a design where once I saw only mere chance" (29, 10). The Poet and the Stranger stand for the artist as prophet, as soothsayer; each is Orpheus, who, as

Strindberg said, must "descend into the underworld to sing life into stones that are not dead, but only asleep!" (27, 234–235). But if the three men in A Dream Play resemble collectively a trimūrti, the variety they constitute is a strange one. The Officer may be a warrior, but he is a rather puny one; this is Śiva as a schoolboy. The Lawyer, although dedicated to preserving justice and strengthening the bonds between men, finds himself involved first professionally and then personally in divorce. "Do you know what's the worst of all?", he asks. "To separate husbands and wives!" (36, 245). As for the Poet, he mocks the very act of creation in an entrance speech that is a kind of parody of Swedenborg's theory of correspondences: an inventory of the aborted works of creators from the creator god in Egyptian mythology down to the lowliest artisan:

POET [ecstatically]:
Out of clay the god Ptah created man on a potter's wheel, a lathe,—[skeptically]—or some other damned thing! . . . [ecstatically] Out of clay the sculptor creates his more or less immortal masterpieces—[skeptically]—which mostly are only junk! [ecstatically] Out of clay are manufactured these containers so necessary in the pantry and called by the common names of jars and plates—[skeptically]— although I don't give a damn what they're called. [ecstatically] This is clay! When clay is liquid it's called mud—C'est mon affaire! (269).

This is the Indic trimūrti treated ironically with a vengeance: the Poet as a cynical creator, the Officer as an ineffectual destroyer, and the Lawyer as a destructive preserver. Yet all is consistent with Strindberg's handling of the mythic theme: in this prison world of matter, of clay and mud, the tripartite god, who is one god and who has sinned against himself, is himself a prisoner of māyā.

Together, like their Indic counterparts, the Poet, Lawyer, and Officer are symbolic of the rhythmic movement of the life force: the cycle of birth, life, and death that the Hindus epitomized as the Great Round of saṁsāra, a round reminiscent of the familiar alchemical sign: the Ouroboros, the great earth serpent devouring its own tail. The three men also collectively symbolize masculine force, as Agnes symbolizes feminine force, and the basic thrust in the play, as we have seen, is toward a synthesis, a reconciliation of the feminine and the masculine. Agnes as agent of this synthesis has failed twice—with the Officer and with the Lawyer. Now she tries again with the Poet. At stake is ultimate atonement: the reconciliation of all the great opposites: man and woman, heaven and earth, good and evil, man and God.

A passage marked in the margin in Strindberg's book on Buddhism describes how the opposites came into being. The Vedāntic system of Hindu philosophy,

> taking as point of departure the metaphysical unity of the Supreme Being . . . conceived of *Brahman*, the neutral being, absolute, invariable, eternal, without attribute, and consequently, having no relation to individual beings. . . ; in order to create the world, *Brahman* is obliged to create itself in order to become manifest, and thus it became *Brahmā*, the great creator of the worlds, issuing forth from the infinite substance. But how is *Brahmā*, the active masculine principle, able to emerge from *Brahman*, the neutral principle? The Vedāntic school resolved the problem through means of the principle called māyā, illusion, otherwise described as matter, the significance of which is that of measurement and space. Much later, Plato must have developed this same theory, to which he gave the name . . . the universal mother . . .[55]

Brahman's act of becoming Brahmā sets in motion a world of duality and multiplicity, and the concept of the masculine thus derives from an original asexual force, an original oneness. Similarly, a number of mythologies conceive of a creator god as an androgynous being, half male, half female, and the concept of a return to original wholeness implies a fusion of two into one. In *A Dream Play* the Lawyer discovers, as he describes in his metaphor of the hairpin, that for him at any rate, the possibility of a fusion taking place is a tantalizing, frustrating dream. One will remain two. The closest he and Agnes can approach each other is the closeness of parallel lines, a disappointing condition like that of ice that "neither bears nor breaks."

But now Agnes has found another candidate suitor, and she takes him to the same place she took the Lawyer: Fingal's

Grotto. The second grotto scene, like the Fairhaven/Foulport scenes, presents difficulties in production. In the island scenes the problem is the episodic structure and diffused focus that threaten to dissipate dramatic tension. In the grotto Strindberg, the lyricist, threatens to drown the dramatist under the various hymns of the elements addressed to Indra, and some of the imagery is so fleeting and seemingly obscure that scholars like Martin Lamm have warned against "fruitless attempts at interpretation."[56] The scene has a potential for ritualistic power, however, that has never been adequately explored, and the clue to this potential lies in the mythic dimension Strindberg has given to the setting and in the archetypal presence suggested in the intimacy between Agnes and the Poet: the androgyne.

Just as with Hercules and Heracles, the first, the bully boy hero of outward action, the second, the searcher hero of inward realization, so with mythic images of half-men, half-women. Strindberg makes clear his preference for the subtly symbolic over the blatantly concrete, for the androgyne over the hermaphrodite. In his 1887 polemical essay, "The Last Word on the Woman Question," he writes that "the most famous of feminist agitators are hermaphrodites" (54, 286); and in the novel written the same year, A Madman's Defense, the narrator complains about the woman he calls "the hermaphrodite who robbed me of my wife."[57] In contrast, Strindberg wrote admiringly in a letter in 1901 of the androgynous central character of Balzac's Séraphita as "the Angel, for whom earthly love does not exist because he-she is l'époux et l'épouse de l'humanité."

The expressive handling of the androgyne theme in Easter (Elis and Eleonora) and A Dream Play (the Poet and Agnes) is markedly different from the often gross exploitation and degrading of the symbol in the works of the French and English fin de siècle decadents, who perceived the androgyne, according to Mircea Eliade, "simply as a hermaphrodite in whom both sexes exist anatomically and physiologically. They are conceived not with a wholeness resulting from the fusion of the sexes but with a superabundance of erotic possibilities."[58] Where the hermaphrodite is a biological synthesis, the androgyne, especially under the influence of alchemy, is a symbolic synthesis; where the first is an unnatural freak of nature, the second is a spiritual ideal, an image of the harmony that existed before the Fall. "Androgeneity," says Gaston Bachelard, "is not buried away in some indistinct bestiality at the obscure origins of life. It is a dialectic at the summit."[59]

The androgyne theme implicit in the second Fingal's Grotto scene explains why Agnes's relationship with the Poet, unlike her relationship with the Lawyer, is asexual with a suggestion of the spiritual affinity between a brother and sister. "Spirit sublime," says Faust,

> Then to the cave secure thou leadest me,
> Then show'st me mine own self, and in my breast
> The deep, mysterious miracles unfold . . .[60]

As in the first grotto scene, the presence of ocean waters dominates the mood.

> [*Long green waves break slowly into the grotto; in the foregound a red bell buoy rocks on the waves. . . ; the music of the winds, the music of the waves. . . .*]
> POET: Where have you led me?
> DAUGHTER: Far from the murmur and groaning of the children of man to the end of the ocean and into this grotto, which we call *Indra's Ear* since they say the king of heaven listens here to the lamentations of mortals (*36*, 297).

In Agnes's explanation there is a naive, childlike quality that belies the coherent mythic pattern Strindberg was following. Hearing and sound are associated with the first in the hierarchy of elements in Indic mythology: ether or space. A verse cited by Joseph Campbell from the *Taittirīya Upanishad* records that

> From the Self (*ātman*) space arose;
> From space, wind;
> From wind, fire;
> From fire, water;
> From water, earth;
> And from the earth, herbs, food . . .[61]

What Agnes signals, therefore, is a new beginning, a new creation. "Sound and ether," according to Heinrich Zimmer, "signify the first, truth-pregnant moment of creation, the productive energy of the Absolute, in its pristine, cosmogenetic strength."[62] As Agnes proceeds to recite the songs of the winds and the waves, we have simultaneously an account of the ordering and developing of the elements in creation and a recapitulation of her entire journey from the ether to earth. One might argue that Strindberg failed to integrate the songs properly into the action, but they are not static or gratuitous. They must not be examined separately, like a suite of individual poems—that way we lose sight of how they participate in the dynamic, transformational quality of the scene. There is a continuous sequence of thematic development present, which melds each element with every other element in an endless chain of correspondences. Agnes sets the sequence in motion when she responds to the Poet's question of how and why the place came to be called Indra's Ear.

> DAUGHTER: Don't you see how the grotto is shaped like a snail shell? Yes, of course you do. Don't you know that your own ear is shaped like a snail shell? You know, but you haven't thought about it. [*picking up a snail shell from the beach*] Didn't you ever as a child hold a snail shell to your ear and listen . . . listen to the buzz of your heart's blood, the murmur of thoughts in your brain, the bursting of thousands of small, worn-out threads in the fabric of your body . . . If you can hear things like this in a little shell, imagine what may be heard in one this big! (297).

Threads bursting in the fabric of the body bring to mind the greater fabric of life, the veil of māyā, as the microcosm that is man is made to reflect the macrocosm of the universe, just as the cochlea of the human inner ear reflects the snail shell, which in turn reflects the cavern and Indra's ear. But the Poet is at first deaf to this symphony of transformations and correspondences; all he hears is the sound of the second element, wind and air, so Agnes tries to interpret for him the origin of the winds and their connection to other elements.

> Born under heaven's skies
> we were chased by the flames of Indra's lightning
> down onto dusty earth . . .

Like Agnes, the winds suffered from earth's pollution.

> Out over the wide ocean we stretched
> to cleanse our lungs,
> shake our wings,
> and wash our feet (298).

The "Song of the Winds" is followed by the "Song of the Waves." In keeping with the spirit of Indic mythology, Strindberg has the waters intimately related to the other elements. In the book he owned on Buddhism the note, "*Obs.*" (i.e., *nota bene*), is marked next to a passage describing the elements: "Each of the elements acquired the quality of those that preceded it, so that the more advanced an element is in the series, the more qualities it has."[63] In the "Song of the Waves" the waves speak of rocking the winds to rest and are

> like fire's flames;
> wet flames are we.
> Quenching, burning,
> cleansing, bathing,
> begetting, conceiving (300).

The churning action of the elements is the churning movement of life itself, and all is interconnected. The winds, for example, moving through human lungs, become the very lamentations that Agnes came to earth to scrutinize. And the sequence from "quenching" to "conceiving" recalls the rhythm of the trimūrti, which has destruction prepare the way for new creation.

After the songs, Agnes and the Poet spot in the grotto waters the wreckage of the ship that sailed away from Fairhaven with the Blind Man's son. It is now part of the flotsam and jetsam that symbolize mankind's futile effort to seek permanence and meaning in life.

DAUGHTER: Look what the sea has plundered and smashed...
All that remains of these sunken ships are their figureheads . . . and the names: Justice, Friendship, Golden Peace, Hope—this is all that's left of hope—deceitful hope!

The reminder of Fairhaven triggers for Agnes memories of everything she has been through on her journey.

DAUGHTER:	These things I have dreamed.
POET:	These things I once wrote.
DAUGHTER:	Then you know what poetry is . . .
POET:	Then I know what dreaming is . . . What is poetry?
DAUGHTER:	Not reality, but more than reality . . . not dreaming, but waking dreams (301).

Nowhere in the play is the dual focus of the reciprocal dreams used more expressively and poetically. We have arrived at a crossroad of crossroads where many things meet at once, where poetry, dream, life, and myth intersect. Agnes and the Poet almost seem to exchange characters, so that one moment she is his mirror image or creation and the next moment he is hers. The symbolic, ultimate reconciliation of the androgyne seems about to take place. But then the spell is broken. Agnes suddenly realizes all the implications of her incarnation.

| DAUGHTER: | I have stayed too long down here, bathing in mud, like you . . . My thoughts can no longer fly—clay on their wings, earth on their feet. . . . And I myself . . . [lifting her arms] I'm sinking, sinking . . . Help me, Father, God of Heaven! [silence] I can no longer hear his answer! The ether no longer carries the sound from his lips to the shell of my ear . . . the silver thread has snapped . . . Alas! I am earthbound (302). |

Agnes has once again reached the nadir that was symbolized earlier by her imprisonment in the domestic hell of the Lawyer's home. The sacred sound contact with the ether has been broken, and she is out of touch with the Eternal One, who is both transcendent and immanent. And with the snapping of the silver thread she also loses contact with the deepest part of herself. The thread, or *sūtrātman* in Vedic teaching, says J. E. Cirlot, "expresses the sacred inner path which binds the outer consciousness of man (his intellect) with his spiritual essence (the 'centre' or 'silver palace')."[64] At the realization of this interruption in communication with higher regions, Agnes knows that she must return to her origin. But she has other tasks to perform before she leaves. She and the Poet see a strange ship.

POET:	I think it's the ghost ship.
DAUGHTER:	What's that?
POET:	The Flying Dutchman.
DAUGHTER:	Him? Why is he punished so severely, and why does he never come ashore?
POET:	Because he had seven unfaithful wives.

Strindberg was more than a little fascinated by the Flying Dutchman. He worked on a dramatic fragment dealing with the theme less than a year after *A Dream Play*. The reference introduced here in the grotto scene initiates a new phase in Agnes's relationship with the Poet, and the dream of ultimate reconciliation begins to dissolve in all planes. Agnes asks if the Dutchman cannot be liberated from his curse.

POET:	Liberated? One should be careful about liberating . . .
DAUGHTER:	Why?
POET:	Because . . . No, it's not the Dutchman! It's an ordinary ship in distress! . . . Why doesn't the buoy sound now? . . . Look—the sea is rising; the waves are getting higher. We'll soon be shut up in this cave! Now the ship's bell is ringing!— Soon we'll have another figurehead. . . . The crew is waving to us . . . but we ourselves are lost!
DAUGHTER:	Don't you want to be liberated?
POET:	Yes, of course, of course I do, but not now . . . and not by water! (305–306).

Another passage that, despite its brevity, is crowded with mythic resonances. As at the very opening of the play, Agnes approaches a man with the challenge of liberation, and again her offer is refused. But this time Agnes is playing a different role: before she was the maiden as soul-liberating image; now she is the goddess of the sea in a cavern that has become a dangerous place, a burial vault for ships. On the one hand, she is *Stella Maris*, the sea goddess as Good Mother, and on the other, the monstrous Scylla, the Terrible Mother of Greek mythology who lies in her sea cave waiting to devour victims, such as the six sailors she snatched off Ulysses's ship. In Agnes's cave are battered remains of ships' figureheads; in Scylla's lair are helms of lost ships. Little wonder, then, that the Poet is reluctant to be liberated by water. A dark side of Agnes's character has been evoked, and the Poet retreats from it.

Another transformation takes place. The Poet sees that the ship is really a house with a telephone tower—another tower image—that

> POET: . . . reaches up in the clouds . . . It's a modern Tower of Babel, sending wires upward—to notify those above. . . .
>
> DAUGHTER: Child, human thought needs no wire to transmit it. . . . The prayers of the devout penetrate all worlds . . . It's surely not the Tower of Babel. If you want to storm heaven, then storm it with your prayers.

Man and the goddess—the mortal and the divine—in a crucial impasse. In reaching to heaven to demand ultimate reconciliation, man risks hubris, and the deity responds with the admonition to storm heaven with prayers, not demands. The Poet rebuts the admonition in a passage of unusual but elusive beauty, containing an image that parallels the Lawyer's image of the hairpin, an image that illuminates the impossibility of multileveled reconciliation, either between man or woman, or, through the extension of correspondences, between man and God, man and existence. What the Poet saw first as a ship, then a house and telephone tower, has been transformed again into another kind of tower:

> POET: I see a snow-covered heath, a drill field . . . The winter sun is shining behind a church on the hill, and the tower casts its long shadow on the snow . . . Now a group of soldiers comes marching on the heath. They're marching on the tower, upward, toward the spire. Now they're on the cross, and I sense that the first person to step on the weathercock must die . . . Now they're nearing it—the corporal is in the lead . . . Aha! A cloud is moving over the heath—blotting out the sun . . . Now everything is gone—the water of the cloud has quenched the fire of the sun! . . . The light of the sun created the dark image of the tower, but the dark image of the cloud smothered the dark image of the tower (308–309).

Marching on the church tower carries the same risk as building
the Tower of Babel: hubris and consequently the arousing of the
wrath of god. But then the tower vanishes; it was only an
illusion, māyā, perhaps implying that even reconciliation itself
was only an illusion. And how appropriate that the scene should
end as it began, in a flow of the elements in action: "The water of
the cloud has quenched the fire of the sun."

Fingal's Grotto itself vanishes during the poet's last speech,
returning us to the theatre alley where people gather for the
clover-leaf door to be opened. "The suspicion is," says Agnes,
"that deposited within is the key to the riddle of the world"
(310). This is precisely what is contained there, but no one is
pleased when the door is opened and the answer to the riddle
turns out to be: "Nothing." The University Chancellor demands an explanation.

CHANCELLOR: Will you kindly tell us what your purpose was in
               having the door opened?
DAUGHTER: No, my friends! If I told you, you wouldn't
               believe it.
DEAN OF MEDICINE:
               But there's nothing there.
DAUGHTER: You've expressed it exactly . . . But you haven't
               understood it! (318).

Agnes has reached another level of awareness as a Bodhisattva,
an enlightened one. First came karuṇā—"Human beings are to
be pitied"—the compassion for all beings; now she understands
that the universe is śūnyatā, the void, nothingness. But only the
Poet will listen; the others are ready to stone Agnes for her
presumptuousness. "The unenlightened," wrote Heinrich
Zimmer, "behold only māyā, the differentiated realm of delu-
sory forms and notions, but by the enlightened ones all is
experienced as the Void beyond differentiation."[65]

The scene now changes to the castle exterior, where it all
began. Agnes/Agni, with the help of fire, is about to ascend into
the ether. She relates to the Poet the story of Brahmā's seduction
by Māyā, explaining

DAUGHTER: Thus, the world, life, and human beings are only a
          phantom, a semblance, a dream image . . .

POET: My dream!
DAUGHTER: A dream come true! . . . But to be liberated from
          earthly substance, Brahmā's descendents seek self-
          denial and suffering. There you have suffering as
          liberator. But this yearning for suffering comes in
          conflict with the desire for pleasure or love (324).

And the result, she concludes, is a world of irreconcilable
opposites: a conflict between "the pain of pleasure and the
pleasure of suffering"; a world of multiplicity expressed in the
movement of elemental forces: "conflict between opposites generates power, as fire and water generate the power of steam"
(325).

Agnes's first step in ascension to the ether is to throw her
shoes into the fire in which earthly delusions are burned: the
Doorkeeper's shawl, the shabby remnants of the Officer's bouquet of roses, the Billposter's bills (but not his net—that he will
not give up), and so forth. And when Agnes now exits into the
castle, the chrysanthemum bud bursts into flower. In Indic
religious doctrine the most important sacred end is *mokṣa*
("release from delusion"). As Joseph Campbell describes it:
"Sitting at the world navel, pressing back through the welling
creative force that was surging into and through his own being,
the Buddha actually broke back into the void beyond, and—
ironically—the universe immediately burst into bloom."[66]

9

The Ghost Sonata

LIBERATOR IN THE HOUSE OF *MĀYĀ*

Two men stare up at the facade of an upper-middle-class apartment house in a city resembling turn-of-the-century Stockholm, and both have missions to accomplish inside. An old, crippled man in a wheelchair, Jacob Hummel wants to settle ancient grudges with the house's occupants. A young student, Arkenholz, wants to meet a beautiful girl who has enchanted him. He imagines a marvelous life there with a wife, happy children, and a handsome income. Herein the main action of the play: the three scenes—the street, the round drawing room, and the hyacinth room—constitute a multidirectional journey in time, into the painful legacy of the past and into what appears to be the bright promise of the future.[1]

The house that figures so prominently in this journey is a place of many mythic mansions. As it represents for the Student his hopes and dreams, it is the house of life; while for eighty-year-old Hummel, it is the house of memory and death. In notes Strindberg made for the play, the working title, *Kāma-Loka: A*

Buddhist Drama, appears (45, 342). In Buddhism the term refers to the realm (Loka) of desire (Kāma), an appropriate name for a house where the lives of its occupants are linked in a network of desire and deceit.

The Consul, at the opening of the play recently deceased and now wandering the house as a ghost, long before had had an affair with the Superintendent's Wife. The result was a daughter currently having an affair with and probably pregnant by the Consul's son-in-law, the Baron. In the past the Baron was the lover of another tenant, the Colonel's wife. This woman, whose name is Amalia, but who is called the Mummy because she sits all the time in a deathlike pose in a closet, had an affair with Jacob Hummel as well, which produced Adèle, the lovely Young Lady who fascinates the Student. Hummel says that he seduced Amalia in revenge for the fact that his old fiancèe, Beate von Holsteinkrona, still another tenant in the house, had been seduced by Amalia's husband, the Colonel. The totals: five illicit love affairs and three pregnancies out of wedlock. The Mummy accurately observes: "Crimes and secrets and guilt bind us to each other" (183). *Binding* underscores the image of a web or net of emotional entanglements, and this in turn recalls the Indic metaphor for the illusory fabric of life: the house is also the world of māyā.[2]

Strindberg's absorption with the metaphor of a house as the world of māyā is especially apparent in the play *The Burned Site*, another in the suite of Chamber Plays, as Strindberg called them, to which *The Ghost Sonata* belongs. In *The Burned Site*, two brothers stand over the scorched ruins of their family home.

> STRANGER: How interwoven it all is—our fates and those of others.
> THE DYER: Surely it's the same everywhere . . .
> STRANGER: Exactly, yes, the same everywhere . . . When you're young you see the web set up on the loom: parents, relatives, friends, acquaintances, and servants—they make up the warp. Later on in life you see the woof, and the shuttle of destiny moves the threads back and forth. Sometimes it breaks, but is tied together again and so continues. The beam drives; the yarn is forced into flourishes and curli-

cues and the fabric emerges. In later years, when you have really learned to see, you discover that all the curlicues form a pattern, a monogram, an ornament, hieroglyphics, which only now can be deciphered: this is life! The World Weaver has woven it! (96–97).

Another of the house's mythic identities is Norse, revealed indirectly through a song, excerpts from which the Student sings at the ends of scenes two and three: "*Sólarljod* " ("The Song of the Sun"), a thirteenth-century Icelandic hymn. A mixture of pagan Viking and Christian elements, "The Song of the Sun" describes a journey beyond the land of the living to the House of Torment (*Kvalheim*), an infernal place of punishment, resembling purgatory.

House of life, death, torment, and desire: the home of troubled shades, a place familiar in quest myths as the underworld, the perils of which a hero must face and overcome. All these associations and more envelop the house in *The Ghost Sonata*. As in many myths and fairy tales, one must enter such a region very cautiously. Hummel has waited long for the proper instrument to help him gain access: a Sunday child, symbol of happiness and success and possessor of the gift of second sight. Opportunity knocks with the appearance of the Student, who was born on a Sunday and has suddenly won renown because he assisted in rescue operations after a house collapsed. He too turns out to be enmeshed in the web of intrigue that connects all the characters: his father apparently was once cheated by the Old Man in a business venture. A pact is contrived by Hummel: young Arkenholz will get to meet the girl, and the Old Man will be admitted to the house. Hummel knows that the Colonel and the Young Lady are accustomed to attending the opera, and so he arranges for the Student to sit next to them at a performance of the *Valkyrie* in order to meet and get acquainted.

The allusion to Wagner's romantic world of mythic heroes and damsels in distress makes a fitting background for the Student's relationship with the Young Lady, and is another example of an old Strindberg theme, maiden and tower, a theme evoked in a simple action near the end of the first scene.

[The Young Lady has dropped her bracelet through the open window. The Student crosses slowly, picks up the bracelet and hands it to her. She thanks him stiffly.] (169–170).

Like a signal for help sent by a captive princess, the bracelet the Student retrieves sets up conventional fairy tale expectations of rescue, love, and a happy ending. But *The Ghost Sonata*, like *Miss Julie*, is a fairy tale manqué, and Strindberg undermines expectations even as he raises them. The Young Lady does not seem particularly grateful to Arkenholz—she "thanks him stiffly." Later in the play we learn that she never intended the bracelet as a romantic signal: it fell from her wrist by accident. Moreover, the potential liberator's credentials become suspect as he describes the dreamlike incident the night before which earned him his quick reputation as a heroic rescuer.

> STUDENT: Yesterday . . . I was drawn to that secluded street where the house later collapsed . . . I arrived there and stopped in front of a building I'd never seen before . . . Then I noticed a crack in the wall and heard the floorboards breaking. I ran forward and snatched up a child who was walking beneath the wall . . . The next moment the house collapsed . . . I was rescued, but in my arms, where I thought I held the child, there was nothing (160).

The elements of the fairy tale manqué are in place and cast shadows of foreboding over the couple's future: the Young Lady is either indifferent to or ignorant of the need to be rescued, and the Student seems incapable of setting anyone free.

Fairy tale manqué gives the house setting still another identity: a tower prison where a captive attracts the attention of a knight errant. But it is something more: it is also the landscape of Hummel's unconscious mind. He believes he has come to reveal unpleasant truths about the people who live there, to strip away the sham and pretense and to disclose the corruption beneath. He is a creditor come to collect the corpse in the cargo and, like Gustav in *Creditors*, he has a predator's instinct for locating hidden weaknesses. But Hummel has actually embarked, as has the Stranger in *To Damascus*, on a journey toward self-confrontation. His return to the house is a return to his own past, where he too has left buried secrets and unpaid debts.

The Old Man faces a formidable adversary: an archetypal configuration of women, all of whom he has betrayed in one way or another. There is Beate, his former fiancée, whom he abandoned after she was seduced by the Colonel; Amalia, whom he left pregnant with his child; and the child herself, the beautiful Adèle. Each of the women's lives is blighted. Beate never married and is a lonely recluse; Amalia sits in a closet as if under a curse; and Adèle is mortally ill. As the Student learns, she is sick "at the source of life" (209). In notes for the play Strindberg wrote: "The Daughter has Cancer";[3] he found a literal explanation for something which, as we shall see, carries symbolic weight as well. In the play proper the exact nature of the disease is left ambiguous.

There is another woman Hummel betrayed, the mysterious Milkmaid; and she plays a very important role in his fate. In her character reality, myth, and dream overlap. At the opening of the play Hummel sits reading a newspaper in the street in front of the house.

[*The Milkmaid enters from around the corner carrying bottles in a wire basket. She is wearing summer clothes, with brown shoes, black stockings, and a white cap. She takes off the cap and hangs it on the fountain, wipes the sweat from her forehead, takes a drink from the dipper, washes her hands, and arranges her hair, using the water as a mirror.*]

[*When the Milkmaid has finished her toilet, the Student enters from the left, sleepless and unshaven. He goes directly to the fountain.*

[*pause*]

STUDENT: May I borrow the dipper? [*The Milkmaid hugs the dipper closely.*] Aren't you through using it? [*The Milkmaid stares at him in terror.*]
OLD MAN [*to himself*]:
          Who is he talking to . . . I don't see anyone . . . Is he crazy? (150).

Later, Hummel's curiosity about what the Student was doing leads him to ask:

OLD MAN: Explain something to me: why were you gesturing just now by the fountain? And why were you talking to yourself?

STUDENT: Didn't you see the milkmaid I was talking to?
OLD MAN [*terrified*]:
            Milkmaid?
STUDENT: Yes, certainly. She handed me the dipper.
OLD MAN: Is that right? So that's what it was (160–161).

After this, Hummel is able to see the girl. The first time, at the end of the street scene, he is frightened; the second time, in the scene in the round drawing room, he is terrified and not long afterward dies.

The terror Hummel feels when haunted by a reminder of the Milkmaid is justified realistically. In the round drawing room, Bengtsson, the Colonel's servant, says he recalls that many years earlier in Hamburg the Old Man was accused of luring "a girl out onto ice in order to drown her, because she had witnessed a crime he was afraid would be discovered" (193).

Bengtsson's revelation has led some scholars to assume that the apparition of the Milkmaid simply represents Hummel's guilty conscience, but she is much more than that: she is the personification of an image that has roots in the profoundest depths of his being. Even as her youth suggests a virginal quality, her occupation connects her with the maternal; she is maiden and mother, both at the same time, a symbol of two important aspects of the eternal feminine. The Old Man has long and carefully repressed his memory of her, and when it forces its way into his consciousness once too often, it destroys him.

Hummel's death after he sees the Milkmaid is the climax of the scene in the round drawing room, but another female figure, the Mummy, actually presides authoritatively over this ritualistic moment, and her presence is felt strongly in several ways. As she sits for most of the first half of the play in the closet, behind a wallpapered door, squawking like a parrot, a statue of her as a beautiful young woman stands in the room, surrounded by potted palms. The complex of images—mummy, closet, wallpapered door, parrot, statue—is broadly evocative. Realistically, it is perhaps understandable that a respectable bourgeois household would prefer to keep the family eccentric—Bengtsson calls her "dotty" (175)—out of sight, and what could be more effective than behind a door that is virtually invisible? On the level of myth, we have in the contrast between the statue and the mummy portraits of Eve before and after the Fall. In fairy tale terms, Amalia is like a pitiful monster of some kind, waiting to be released from a terrible spell placed upon her by some wicked magician. Metaphorically, as the Mummy, she is almost too literally a corpse in the cargo, a skeleton in the closet, one of Bluebeard's dreadful secrets. Psychologically, she and the Milkmaid are linked, representing elements that Hummel has fled or rejected all his life: love and compassion. They are aspects of himself that were never released and assimilated, and like the Furies, sooner or later they will have their revenge. "You see," Hummel tells the Student, "I've been taking all my life; now I have a yearning to be able to give! to give!" (164). Even if he means what he says, however, the realization has come too late. In the persons of the Milkmaid, Beate, the Mummy, and Adèle, Hummel has betrayed the eternal feminine in all its aspects: mother, beloved, and daughter. Now the Mummy sits waiting for him, like a sibyl of Nemesis, and, according to Bengtsson, the length of time she has been waiting is that fateful mythic number: forty years, signifying the period of preparation that precedes an important event. At Hummel's arrival in the round drawing room, he is more accurate than he knows when he says "my visit is almost expected, if not looked forward to" (179).

As vital and imaginative as are the archetypal figures of the Mummy and the Milkmaid, Strindberg's polyphonic mythology in the play is nowhere more richly developed than in the character of Jacob Hummel, who shares with Gustav in *Creditors* a godlike presence and terrible powers. When at one point he grabs hold of the Student, the latter complains: "Let go of my hand, you're draining my strength, you're freezing me" (163). Adolph, we recall, reacts in a similar way when touched by Gustav: "What dreadful power you must have! It's like gripping an electrical machine" (23, 218). Hummel presents himself to the Student as a potential benefactor, but the young man is suspicious. When the Old Man leaves for a time, the Student questions his servant, Johansson.

STUDENT: Who is your employer?
JOHANSSON: Well! He's a lot of things, and he's been
              everything.

STUDENT: Is he sane?
JOHANSSON: Yes, and what is *that*? . . . he wants
            power . . . All day long he rides around in his
            chariot like the god Thor. He looks through
            houses, collapses them, opens up streets,
            reconstructs city squares. But he also breaks
            into houses, creeps in through windows, rav-
            ages people's destinies, kills his enemies, and
            forgives nothing. . . . Can you imagine that
            that little cripple was once a Don Juan?(*45*,
            168–169).

Another Strindbergian medley of polyphonic mythic resonances enriches a character. Hummel is Don Juan, that slave of
desire, and Thor,[4] the thunderer, ready to level anything with
his mighty hammer. In Johansson's remark that his master has
"been everything" and a later observation that the Old Man is a
"magician"(178), are indications that Hummel is also the Norse
king of gods, Odin, whose magic, according to Mircea Eliade,
consisted of "ubiquity, power of assuming different forms,
ability to paralyse his adversary with fear, 'binding' him."[5] The
Mummy accuses Hummel: "You murdered the Consul they
buried today, you strangled him with debts. You stole the
Student by binding him with a fake debt of his father, who
never owed you a penny"(192).

The Old Man's first name, Jacob, and the difficulty he has
walking—in the first scene he is confined to a wheelchair and in
the second he hobbles about on crutches—calls to mind the
Biblical patriarch and points up Hummel's resemblance to
another Jacob figure, the alienated Stranger in *To Damascus*. "No
one knows me," Hummel says, "not really" (158).

The Biblical allusions to Jacob have been noted by Stephen
C. Bandy, who points out, for example, that the name Leah
(Jacob's first wife), is similar to Amalia (Hummel's old love).[6] A
reference to the New Testament is contained in an early scene
between the Student and the Milkmaid:

STUDENT [*slowly*]:
            Would you do me a big favor? [*pause*] The thing
            is, my eyes are inflamed, as you can see, and my
            hands have been touching wounds and dead
            bodies, so I don't dare bring my hands near my

eyes . . . Will you take this clean handkerchief,
moisten it in fresh water, and bathe my poor
eyes? . . . Will you do that? . . . Will you be the
Good Samaritan? [*She hesitates but does as he asks.*]
(151).

Bandy cites as parallel the incident described in John 4:7–14
when Jesus meets a Samaritan woman at the spring called
"Jacob's well," asks her for water, and tells her that he is the
Messiah. But there is another Biblical incident involving Jacob
and a well: the meeting with his first love, Rachel: "Rachel came
up with her father's flock, for she was a shepherdess. When
Jacob saw Rachel, the daughter of Laban his mother's brother,
with Laban's flock, he stepped forward, rolled the stone off the
mouth of the well, and watered Laban's sheep. He kissed
Rachel and was moved to tears."[7]

Some of the same quiet tenderness, mystery, and wonder
lingering over this Biblical episode is present in the Milkmaid
scene. Shepherdess and Milkmaid suggest pastoral, idyllic
innocence, and the presence of the well/fountain implies the
waters of salvation and the water of life. Writing of Rachel,
Joseph Campbell observes that "the sense of such a female by a
spring is of an apparition of the abyss: psychologically, the
unconscious; mythologically, the Land below Waves, Hell,
Purgatory, or Heaven. She is a portion of oneself, one's destiny,
or, as Schopenhauer states in his meditation on Fate, one's
secret intention for oneself."[8] One reason Hummel is terrified
when he finally allows himself to see the Milkmaid is that he
cannot handle the guilt he feels for having so long neglected a
"secret intention" he had for himself.

Another Strindberg character confronted by a frightening
female vision is the Captain in *The Dance of Death*, who lies asleep
on a couch after suffering one of his periodic comalike attacks.

[*The wind can be heard blowing outside. The upstage door blows open,
and an Old Woman, looking poor and disagreeable, peeks in.*]
CAPTAIN [*seeing the Old Woman and becoming afraid*]:
Who are you? What do you want?
OLD WOMAN: Oh, sir, I only wanted to close the door.
Good night, sir; sleep well [*closes the door and
exits*].

[*Alice enters from the left with pillows and a blanket.*]

CAPTAIN: Who was that at the door? Was it anyone?
ALICE: Yes, it was old Maia from the poorhouse who
              passed by.
CAPTAIN: Are you sure?
ALICE: Are you afraid?
CAPTAIN: I, afraid? Of course not! (*34*, 63–64).

Another Maia—Queen Māyā, Earth Mother—frightening the
Captain, despite his denial to the contrary, because she has
come as an eternal creditor, the Great Mother come to reclaim
her own. In part this is the same fear that Hummel has of the
Milkmaid. In Norse mythology female figures who come to
fetch dead warriors are Valkyries, another echo of the Wagner
opera the Student attends; Pavel Fraenkl is one of several critics
who identify the Milkmaid as a Valkyrie.[9]

The house in *The Ghost Sonata* is like a separate world ruled
over by Hummel; it is certainly his property. He has been
buying up promissory notes signed by the Colonel; he
"strangled" the Consul with debts; and he has intimate knowledge of the house's occupants.

STUDENT: Do you know the people who live there?
OLD MAN: All of them. At my age you know everybody,
              their fathers, and their forefathers before
              them, and you're always related to them in
              some way. . . . I take an interest in people's
              destinies (*45*, 157–158).
              I have an infinitely long life behind me—infi-
              nitely(163).

The Student senses in his relationship with the Old Man the
presence of an unworldly dimension.

STUDENT: I don't understand any of this, but it is like a
              fairy tale . . .
OLD MAN: My whole life is like a book of fairy tales, young
              man, and although the tales are different, a
              single thread joins them together and the
              leitmotif returns like clockwork (158).

If Hummel's life is a book of fairy tales, the single thread that
joins them is his resemblance to godlike figures. When he tells

his reason for returning to the house, he could be the angry Yahweh about to let a Deluge cover up past mistakes: "This was my mission. . . . : to clear away the weeds, expose the crimes, settle accounts, so that this young couple [the Student and Adèle] might start a new life in this home that I have given them" (191). Hummel is simultaneously a ruthless, unscrupulous real estate speculator and Yahweh, the capricious demiurge. Behind the play's surface realism, the conflicts set in motion are on a scale beyond the merely human, and this is evident in the brilliant, tumultuous final moments of the street scene. After a brief absence, the old Man returns like some grotesque Thor.

> JOHANSSON: Look, look at him, in his war chariot, drawn in triumph by the beggars. . . .
>
> OLD MAN [*enters standing in the wheelchair, drawn by one beggar and followed by others*]:
> Hail the noble youth who at the risk of his own life rescued many in yesterday's accident! Hail Arkenholz!
>
> [*The beggars bare their heads but do not cheer.* . . . .]
>
> OLD MAN: . . . although I'm not a Sunday child, I possess the spirit of prophecy and the gift of healing, for I once brought back to life someone who drowned . . . yes, it was in Hamburg on a Sunday afternoon just like this one . . .
>
> [*The Milkmaid enters, seen only by the Student and the Old Man. She stretches up her arms like a drowning person and stares fixedly at the Old Man.*]
>
> OLD MAN [*sitting and shrinking in terror*]:
> Johansson, get me out of here! Quickly! . . . Arkenholz, don't forget *The Valkyrie*!
>
> STUDENT: What is all this?
>
> JOHANSSON: We'll just have to see! We'll just have to see! (172–173).

As they did in *To Damascus* and *A Dream Play*, myth and dream intermingle to represent the movement of the forces of the unconscious. But while the prevailing dream mood in *A Dream Play* was the melancholy of reverie, in *The Ghost Sonata* (witness the scene above) the mood is the confusing horror of nightmare. It is nightmare, however, mitigated by black,

absurd humor, which is especially apparent in the opening of
the scene in the round drawing room. As if in a parody of the
typically cumbersome exposition of a French well-made play,
two servants discuss their curious, respective employers.

JOHANSSON:	Will it be a musical evening, or what?
BENGTSSON:	Just the usual ghost supper, we call it. They drink tea, never say a word, or the Colonel talks by himself. And then they nibble cookies, all together, so that it sounds like rats in the attic storeroom.
JOHANSSON:	Why is it called the ghost supper?
BENGTSSON:	They look like ghosts . . . And it's been going on for twenty years, always the same people, who say the same things, or else keep quiet to avoid embarassing themselves (174–175).

The sparseness and matter-of-factness of Bengtsson's description belie the haunted atmosphere that is created. This is the
land of the dead, or at any rate the living dead. An attic storeroom, we recall, is also mentioned in *The Father*; Bertha hears
the sound of singing coming from there, from the place where
the cradle is stored (*23, 51*). House of the dead and house of the
Great and Terrible Mother. In *The Father* Laura's mother calls
from offstage; in *The Ghost Sonata* the maternal figures include
the Mummy, who sits offstage in a closet, and a bizarre Cook,
who waits in the kitchen.

Part of the tension in this marvelous scene comes from the
fact that metaphors threaten to become concrete. "She thinks
she's a parrot," Bengtsson says about the Mummy, "and maybe
she is" (*45*, 176). He points out to Johansson a black Japanese
screen standing near a chaise longue: "It's called the death
screen. It's put out when someone's going to die, just like in the
hospital." No matter how terrible the powers Hummel
possesses, we sense that he will find more here than he bar-
gained for. "This is a dreadful house," Johansson observes in a
mythic simile, "and the Student longed to come here, as if to
paradise" (177).

The Mummy confronts Hummel before the others arrive for
the "ghost supper" and, like a fairy tale oracle, issues a stern

warning: the Old Man must spare her husband, the Colonel, during the vengeful exposé he has planned.

OLD MAN: No!

MUMMY: Then you must die; in this room; behind this screen. . . .

OLD MAN: Then so be it . . . Once I have my teeth in something, I can't let go (182).

As he promised, Hummel is unrelenting. At the supper he sits like a lord high executioner, revealing one by one each poor, naked wretch who hides behind an invalidated military rank or a false aristocratic title, behind a wig or a fake mustache. He clears away the "weeds" and settles accounts. The hour of reckoning becomes Judgment Day.

OLD MAN: Listen to the clock ticking, like a deathwatch beetle in the wall! Do you hear what it's saying? "Times' up! Times' up!" . . . When it strikes—in a little while—then your time will be up, then you can go, but not before. But the clock sends a warning before it strikes! . . . Listen! Now it's threatening: "The clock can strike. . . ." And I can also strike . . . [striking the table with his crutch] You hear?

Suddenly, after a period of silence, mythic time replaces realistic time. The Mummy rises, crosses to the clock, stops the pendulum, and speaks in a normal voice; she is Amalia again. It is as if the compassion and concern she showed by trying to protect her husband from Hummel's cruelty has broken the wicked spell under which she was suffering.

MUMMY: I can stop time in its course. I can wipe out the past, undo what has been done. Not with bribes, not with threats—but through suffering and repentance. [crossing to the Old Man] We are wretched creatures, we know that. We have erred, we have sinned, like everyone else. We are not what we seem, for we are better than we are, since we condemn our faults. But that you, Jacob Hummel, with your false name, should sit in judgment, proves that you are worse than we wretches! You too are not what you seem to be! . . . You steal people. You stole me once with false promises.

> [*The Old Man tries to rise to speak, but falls back in his chair and shrinks down. During the following, he shrinks down more and more.*] (191–192).

Amalia rings for Bengtsson to have him reveal what she suspects is a "black spot" in Hummel's past. Without warning, the apparition returns:

> [*The little Milkmaid appears in the door to the hall, unseen by everyone except the Old Man, who cringes in terror; the Milkmaid disappears when Bengtsson enters.*] (193).

After the servant relates the story of Hummel as an accused murderer, the Old Man is forced to return the promissory notes he used to gain power over the people in the house, and the scene takes on the quality of the exorcism of a demon.

MUMMY [*stroking the Old Man on the back*]:
      Pretty polly! Is Jacob there?
OLD MAN [*like a parrot*]:
      Jacob's here! Cockatoo! Atoo!
MUMMY: Can the clock strike?
OLD MAN [*clucking*]:
      The clock can strike! [*imitating a cuckoo clock*] Coo-coo, coo-coo, coo-coo! . . .
MUMMY [*opening the closet door*]:
      Now the clock has struck! Stand up and enter the closet. . . . There's a rope hanging in there. It represents the one you used to strangle the Consul upstairs. . . . Go! [*The Old Man enters the closet.*] Bengtsson! Put out the screen! The death screen. [*Bengtsson places the screen in front of the door.*] It is finished! May God have mercy on his soul!
ALL: Amen!
      [*a long silence*] (194–195).

The power of this moment inspired Dürrenmatt to pay a tribute that also includes an implicit criticism of the play: "Modern drama has come out of Strindberg: we have never gone beyond the second scene of *The Ghost Sonata*."[10] A number of critics and directors have found the last scene in the hyacinth room anticlimactic and static. Hummel, one argument runs, seems so obviously the villainous central character, what is there left to say after he is dead? But this is to forget the careful preparation in the street scene for the meeting between the Student and the Young Lady and the prospect established of their living together happily ever after. Even a fairy tale manqué is incomplete without a full view of the moment in which the hero and heroine come together. The moment, however, turns out to be disappointingly brief and is followed immediately by tragedy: Adèle withers and dies before our eyes. More than one audience has been left stunned and bewildered by what appears to be a gratuitous and unnecessarily cruel sequence of events.

An important element keeps the final scene from being gratuitous: the relationship between Hummel and the Student. When the Old Man dies, the focus of attention shifts naturally to the young one. The two have in common unusual powers not shared by other characters in the play. Only they, for example, are able to see the Milkmaid. As Hummel says: "Our destinies are intertwined through your father . . . and in other ways too" (163). If the Old Man resembles the demiurge of the creation play, the Student represents the fulfillment of Lucifer's promise to send "his only son" (2, 318) to teach "truth to men" and to bring "the gift of deliverance from the anguish: the joy of death"(315). There are several resonances in the character of the Student which suggest either Christ or an avatar of the "only son": the similarity already mentioned between the scenes involving him and the Milkmaid, Jesus and the Samaritan woman; and the oblique connection in statements by the Student that his "father ended up in a madhouse" (45, 208) and that Christ descended into "this madhouse . . . of a world" (209). Hummel, like the demiurge, is forced to learn that even he must answer to a higher authority, an invisible Eternal One. In the moments after the Old Man's death, the Student sings in Strindberg's revised version of the Icelandic song:

> I saw the sun
> so it seemed
> that I beheld the Hidden One (195).

The demiurge Hummel is made to yield and the light-bringer Arkenholz forwards Lucifer's dark message of deliverance.

The implications in Hummel's passing of the demise of a

divine figure are amplified through polyphonic mythology. Amalia's line "It is finished" repeats Christ's last words on the cross,[11] a speech, as Carl Reinhold Smedmark has pointed out, Strindberg used in several contexts.[12] And the fact that Hummel hangs himself brings to mind that Odin also hanged himself. A verse in the *Havamål* from the *Poetic Edda* has the god relate how he hung for nine nights in Yggdrasil, the World Tree:

I ween that I hung on the windy tree,
Hung there for nights full nine;
. . . and offered I was
To Odin, myself to myself.[13]

In a book on Norse mythology owned by Strindberg, Sophus Bugge's *Studier over de nordiska gude- og heltesagns oprindelse*, the following passage is marked in the margin: "Odin, hanging on the Tree, had thus sacrificed himself to Odin. Jesus sacrificed himself on the Tree to God."[14]

A number of mythologies describe how an old god must be killed in order to make room for a new one, and this resonance too is present in Hummel's death. Frequently, such transferral of divine power from one generation to another involves the violence of mutilation. In Greek mythology Kronos castrates his father Ouranos. Hummel's change of voice to that of a parrot suggests emasculation. We are reminded as well of the eloquent passage from *The Father* in which the Captain wonders what happens to men "when they grow old and stop being men. The dawn was sounded not by roosters, but capons, and the hens that answered didn't know the difference"(23, 68).

Mythically, the passing of an old order usually makes room for a new beginning, the coming of another age, the promise of something better arising from the dissolution of decadence and corruption. The scene in the hyacinth room contains that promise, even if it is subsequently aborted. The Student and Adèle become the "first couple." The fact that things deteriorate so rapidly indicates that the tempo of the metaphysical rhythm has been accelerated. In only a matter of minutes the two young people arrive at insights about the world of lies which took their elders half a century to realize. The destructive work of the World Weaver is accomplished in record time.

Part of the problem in interpreting the purpose and meaning of the action in the hyacinth room lies in the ambiguous effect that is produced. As in the final moments of *The Father*, we have a combination murder/love scene. Ingmar Bergman recognized this in his 1973 production of the play. According to the published text of this version, at one point the Young Lady is dragged by the Student across the floor, "during which her dress is ripped apart and falls off her. . . . Under the dress she wears a tattered and dirty, high-necked, gray-white slip with red stains in the area of the groin."[15] The implication is that Adèle's deflowering and her terminal illness are one and the same; the fruit of desire is death. Although some critics and scholars regarded Bergman's symbolism as unsuitably pessimistic and heavy-handed, his approach did not depart radically from the spirit of the original. No matter how serene the author indicates the effect he wants produced by the final moments—the stage directions call for sorrowful music, but "gentle" and "agreeable" (*45*, 211)—the identity of the pale liberator is still death.

As the controlling image pattern in a scene of new beginnings, Strindberg chose, appropriately, an old favorite: vegetation. The Student's name, Arkenholz, relates him to the German *Arche* and *holz*, or "ark of wood," and consequently to two first couples; the Biblical Noah and his wife, and the Norse Ask and Embla, who were actually created out of wood.[16] Other vegetation images appear in the stage directions.

> [*A room decorated in a somewhat bizarre style, with oriental motifs. Hyacinths are everywhere, in every color. On the porcelain-tiled stove sits a large statue of Buddha, with a flat root in its lap. Out of it rises the stem of a shallot (Allium ascalonium), bearing its spherical inflorescence with white star flowers!*]

The flowers symbolize sensuality and hope, but the statue implies the message Strindberg found so compelling in Buddhism: that sensuality is but the lure of māyā and that the only hope is resignation in the face of the nothingness of existence.

Other signs point to the transitoriness of this world. The old couple, the Colonel and Amalia, can be seen upstage through a door into the round drawing room, where they sit "idle and silent"; "a portion of the death screen is visible"; and Adèle is playing a harp (196), the instrument that heroes in the *Edda* chose to have buried with them to expedite their passage to the other world.

As in the grotto scene in *A Dream Play*, which the scene in the hyacinth room resembles, the opening contains an inventory of correspondences in a chain of symbolic associations that leaps back and forth from microcosmic detail to macrocosmic context: from flower to soul to cosmos to snowflake.

YOUNG LADY: Sing now for my flower.
STUDENT: Is this the flower of your soul?
YOUNG LADY: My very own! Do you love the hyacinth?
STUDENT: I love it above all others—its virginal figure rising so slim and straight from the bulb.

But first its meaning. The bulb, whether floating on water or buried in soil, is our earth. The stem shoots up, straight as the axis of the world. And at its top are the six-pointed star flowers.
YOUNG LADY: Above the earth the stars! Oh, that's magnificent! Where did you get this, how did you see it?
STUDENT: Let me think—in your eyes!—And so, it is an image of the cosmos. . . .

YOUNG LADY: Aren't snowflakes also six-pointed, like the hyacinth lily?
STUDENT: Of course! Then snowflakes are falling stars . . .
YOUNG LADY: And the snowdrop is a snow star . . . risen from the snow.

Have you seen the shallot bloom?
STUDENT: Yes, certainly! It carries its flowers in a ball, a globe that resembles the sphere of heaven, strewn with white stars (196–198).

The inventory ends in a beautiful moment of mutual recognition, an exchange of soulful sentiments that recalls a similar moment between Agnes and the Poet in the grotto scene.

YOUNG LADY: God, how magnificent! Whose idea was this?
STUDENT: Yours!
YOUNG LADY: Yours!
STUDENT: Ours! Together we have given birth to some-
            thing. We are wed.

Then, again as in the earlier play, the moment of sharing is shattered. When the Student talks of being wed, Adèle demurs:

YOUNG LADY: Not yet . . .
STUDENT: What else remains?
YOUNG LADY: The waiting, the trials, the patience (198–199).

The golden poetry of love once more evolves into the leaden prose of domestic life. Adèle's home resembles the Lawyer's home in *A Dream Play*: the trials, imperfections, and deadly monotony of everyday life turn the transcendent into the banal. And the greatest trial of all is another woman who is part real and part apparition.

YOUNG LADY: The cook is coming . . . Look at her! How big
            and fat she is. . .
STUDENT: Who is this giantess?
YOUNG LADY: She belongs to the Hummel family of vampires;
            she's devouring us (199–200).

Surely among the most disagreeable servants in dramatic litera-ture, the Cook prepares meals so that she saves all the nutrients for herself and serves the dregs to the family.

STUDENT: Why don't you discharge her?
YOUNG LADY: She won't go! We have no control over her.
STUDENT: Drive her away!
YOUNG LADY: We can't!
STUDENT: Why not?
YOUNG LADY: We don't know! She won't go! No one has any
            control over her—she's drained all our strength!
STUDENT: May I send her away?
YOUNG LADY: No! Things are probably as they should be!

STUDENT: What a strange house. It's bewitched! (200–
            201).

The house is indeed bewitched, and we recognize the cause. The Cook may be a member of the Hummel family of vampires, but she is also a member of the Strindberg family of Terrible Mothers. The Student sees what has to be done—get rid of her—but Adèle and her family cannot accomplish this. The Terrible Mother hangs on. In recent years it has been fashionable among Swedish critics to find social significance in the plight of Adèle's family: it represents the decadence of upper-middle-class society. Certainly this aspect is present; the bourgeoisie were always one of Strindberg's favorite targets, which explains why he was virtually persona non grata in his native land for many years. But in this instance he balanced his attack and judgment through a view that is essentially tragic: Adèle is both oppressor and victim, and so is the Cook. The latter sums up the situation neatly: "You suck the juices out of us, and we out of you" (205). The pain in this world of lies and illusions is not simply the result of social injustice, it is existential. Social evils must be remedied, but the great round of life creates and devours in a rhythm that is not governed by human concepts of order and justice. Schopenhauer's comment on the irony of the Great Round is fitting: "Compare the feelings of an animal engaged in eating another with those of the animal being eaten."[17]

The Cook appears only briefly, but the character, as we see, introduces several levels of meaning: social, philosophical, and—as the Student with his gift of second sight comes gradually to recognize—mythic. "Now," he says in the final moments of the play, "I can feel that vampire in the kitchen beginning to drain me. I believe she's a Lamia who sucks the blood of children. It's always in the kitchen that a child's seed leaves are nipped, if it hasn't already happened in the bedroom" (209). The Lamia is a traditional image of the devouring mother in Greek and Roman mythology, where her name means "gluttonous" and "lecherous," thus connecting her with both the kitchen and the bedroom. In ancient Greek carvings she is depicted as kidnapping newborn babies.[18] That Strindberg was aware of the Lamia as symbol of a primary obstacle the hero must battle is clearer in a passage from *Inferno* than in the Student's speech. In the novel the narrator, after reading some occult books, fears that he is being persecuted by "elemental and elementary spirits, Incubi, Lamias, who were trying with all their might to prevent me from completing my alchemical Great Work" (28, 152).[19] As Jung so eloquently demonstrated, in psychological terms, the "alchemical Great Work" is analogous to the mythic hero's quest for self-realization, in which the first enemies to overcome are often representatives of the Terrible Mother.[20]

The Student's reference to seed leaves being nipped returns us to the context of vegetation imagery that was established on an apparently hopeful note at the beginning of the scene. The hope is only apparent because, although Adèle is the hyacinth girl, the Student learns that she is ignorant of the tragic implications of the story of Hyacinthus. In the myth as told by Ovid in *Metamorphoses*, Hyacinthus is a young man beloved by Apollo but fatally injured in an accident while he and the god are discus throwing. Just as flowers in a garden hang and wither once their stems are broken, "so did the head of the dying Hyacinthus droop." Apollo, grief-stricken, feels responsible and promises that Hyacinthus's name will not be forgotten: "When I strike the chords of my lyre, and when I sing, my songs and music will tell of you. You will be changed into a new kind of flower and will show markings that imitate my sobs." At this, the young man's blood, which stains the grass where he is lying, is transformed into the lily-shaped hyacinth, with the mournful words "Ai, Ai," printed upon it.[21]

The tragic irony of a love that kills is also present in the Student's longing for Adèle.

STUDENT: There's nothing I wouldn't do to win your hand.
YOUNG LADY: Don't talk like that!—You can never have me!
STUDENT: Why not?
YOUNG LADY: You mustn't ask.
             [*pause*]
STUDENT: But you dropped your bracelet through the window . . .
YOUNG LADY: Because my hand has grown so thin (45, 204–205).

As Evert Sprinchorn has pointed out,[22] the hyacinth girl's illness "at the source of life" takes on additional meaning in a Strindberg reference to the same flower in a *Blue Book* essay. "The hyacinth is beautiful to look upon: consummate, its fragrance sweet to inhale. Perhaps it perceives something resembling pain or joy; but without reason, self-consciousness, and free will, the life of the soul cannot begin, and to be without a soul is to be almost dead . . ." (*48*, 847).

Psychologically, Adèle's inability to throw the Cook out marks a failure to battle the Terrible Mother, and the will she lacks is the will to live. When the Student brings her the challenge of life, she is not equal to it.

STUDENT: Do you know what I'm thinking now about you?
YOUNG LADY: Don't! If you say it, I'll die!
STUDENT: I must, otherwise I'll die! (*45*, 207).

For Adèle, the Student's gift of second sight becomes a curse, forcing her to face the truth concealed by the world of lies. He becomes the Gnostic messenger, the alien one, who brings the light into a world of darkness.

STUDENT: There are poisons that blind and poisons that open the eyes. I must have been born with the second kind in me, for I can't see beauty in ugliness or call evil good—I can't! Jesus Christ descended into hell—that was His pilgrimage on this earth—into this madhouse, this dungeon, this morgue of a world. And the madmen killed him when he tried to liberate them, but the bandit was released; the bandit always gets the sympathy! (209–210).

As was Hummel, the Student too is a creditor who finds the corpse in the cargo.

STUDENT: There's something rotting here! And I thought this was paradise the first time I saw you enter here . . . On a Sunday morning I stood looking in. I saw a colonel who wasn't a colonel. I saw a generous benefactor who was a bandit and had to hang himself. I saw a mummy who was no such thing and a maiden—speaking of that: where can virginity be found? Where is beauty to be found? In nature and when it is dressed in Sunday clothes in my own mind. Where are honor and faith to be found? In fairy tales and children's entertainments! Where is anything

that fulfills its promise? . . . In my imagination!
(208–209).

The revelations are fatal to Adèle, and she droops as Hyacinthus did.

[*The Young Lady has shrunk down and is evidently dying. She rings;
Bengtsson enters.*]
YOUNG LADY: Bring the screen! Quickly—I'm dying!
[*Bengtsson returns with the screen, which he opens and places in front of
her.*]
STUDENT: The Liberator comes! Welcome, you pale and
             gentle one! (210).

The Student who came to the house as liberator arrived like a
Kāma deva, the Hindu god of love, whose weapons to pierce the
heart with desire are five flower-arrows, tipped with fragrant
blossoms. But *Kāma* has other names as well, one of which is
Māra, literally "he who kills, or makes 'die' (*mar*)", according to
Heinrich Zimmer.[23] The scene in the hyacinth room thus becomes a recapitulation in brief of primal rhythms, a microcosm
of life's relentless cycle of the birth, ripening, and death of love.
"We made poetry," says the Student, "sang and played, and
then in came the Cook" (209). His farewell to Adèle is simultaneously grim and tranquil, a coda of the themes of life's
essence as māyā and eternal metamorphosis: "Poor little child,
child of this world of illusion, guilt, suffering, and death; this
world of endless change, disappointment, and pain! The Lord
of Heaven be merciful to you on your journey" (211).

Like Eleonora and Agnes before him, the Student suggests
the godhead incarnate, the immanent deity who is "the Christ
within man," and who comes on a mission of reconciliation.
The fact that he is more an angel of death than his predecessors
points to the climax of a somber progression in Strindberg's
later works. The message of reconciliation is alive in Eleonora,
fading in Agnes, and dead in the Student. In this world of māyā
nothing is what it seems to be, and the final victory belongs to
the World Weaver, she of nets and webs and ropes, at once
creator and destroyer, the vampire who constantly threatens to
stunt life's aspirations by nipping them in the bud in the kitchen
or in the bedroom. Instead of reconcilation, what is left is
resignation in the face of the great mystery: "the rest is silence."

Conclusion

In a sense we are back where we started. Assembled in *The Ghost Sonata* are references and allusions to all the images in the small, mythic cluster that fascinated Strindberg from the beginning: creation play, maiden and tower, and Great Mother. In Hummel are echoes of Thor, the deity suggested in Strindberg's first produced play, *In Rome*. Every writer, says Northrup Frye, has "his own imagery, ranging from a preference for certain vowels and consonants to a preoccupation with two or three archetypes."[1] But of course the effect produced by the mix and balance of the archetypes in *The Ghost Sonata* is unique, as it is in all the other plays discussed. Strindberg's virtuosity in developing new variations on the same mythic themes is probably best exemplified in his treatment of the Hercules figure: as it appears in the Captain in *The Father*, the result is tragedy, and in the Officer in *A Dream Play*, comic pathos. In both instances the character has its own integrity and the play its own special tension.

The special tension in *The Ghost Sonata* is the product of a conflict between two of the archetypes—the hero quest and māyā—and it is because the climactic moments of this conflict take place in the hyacinth room that the purposes served by the final scene are so important to the design of the play. As they did in *A Dream Play*, the two archetypes—the first Western and optimistic, the second Eastern and pessimistic—collide because, while the quest stresses the potential of self-realization and affirms the inherent significance of the individual, māyā implies the necessity of repudiating an ego-centered, earthly existence. As Strindberg treats them, the first archetype offers the hope of reconciliation, of opposites complementing each other; and the second urges acceptance of the message that the only liberation to be sought is release from the veil of māyā.

A number of critics have characterized the mood of *The Ghost Sonata* as black misanthropy, and certainly the paltry and deceitful creatures the author puts on parade are deserving of contempt. But they are also, to reiterate the theme of *A Dream Play*, deserving of pity as victims of the painful contradiction between the hope raised by the quest dream and the disillusionment aroused by the realization of the truth of māyā.

Strindberg's experimentation with the themes of māyā and the quest reveals one of the reasons why he was an important precursor of subsequent developments in modern drama and theatre. Implied in the conflict between the images are two contrasting ideas of theatre, Eastern and Western. Two decades after Strindberg's death, Antonin Artaud called for a rejection of the narrowness of the occidental theatre's emphasis on psychology and acceptance instead of the broader, more comprehensive, oriental, metaphysical vision. "The true purpose of the theatre," he wrote, "is to create Myths, to express life in its immense, universal aspect, and from that life to extract images in which we find pleasure in discovering ourselves."[2] Brought to mind is Strindberg's assertion made almost half a century earlier that he found "the joy of life in its cruel and powerful battles," and his enjoyment came "from being able to know something, being able to learn something" (*23*, 101). In context, his reference was to a naturalistic view of the cruel and powerful battles, but as we have seen, like Artaud, he dreamed of evoking mythic resonances on a grander stage than that of simple fourth-wall illusionism. It was no coincidence that two of the plays

Artaud conceived of as appropriate for his "theatre of cruelty" were *A Dream Play* and *The Ghost Sonata*.

Like other artists—Yeats, for example—Strindberg began by borrowing imagery from the great mythologies and ended by creating his own mythic world, a world with a unique landscape and inhabitants. It is interesting that although the character of the Cook in *The Ghost Sonata* was added late in the writing process, almost as an afterthought, she belongs there.[3] She is a familiar feature of Strindberg's mythic landscape, and she emerges, so to speak, of her own free will.

In all the plays discussed in his volume the clarion call has been the yearning and search for liberation. We saw how in *Master Olof* the search involved an interpenetration of psychological and political considerations. Olof's literary, artistic concern with the freeing of the people of Israel from the slavery they must endure at the hands of their Babylonian captors is transformed into a real concern for the spiritual freedom of his own people. But Gert tries to teach him that slavery can take many forms, that spiritual liberation is inseparable from political liberation. If in succeeding chapters the focus has been more on Strindberg's involvement with psychological rather than political themes, it is partly because of the plays chosen for discussion. In his later history plays Strindberg brilliantly analyzed the complex relationship between personal and public responsibilities. But there is another reason for my emphasis on the psychological. Although Strindberg never defined liberation in a narrow sense, in *Master Olof* especially, he suggested that the realization of an inner psychic freedom is the requisite of an outward political one. And the symbolic language he used to express this order of importance was that of myth; the hero cannot remake the world unless he first agrees to follow his destiny by faithfully answering an inner call. As Gert's warnings imply, the revolution fails on the day one denies the Holy Spirit.

Notes

Introduction

1. *Brev* 14:51.

2. *Brev* 1:19.

3. See, for example, John R. Milton, who concludes that Strindberg's dream plays "as they stand, fail to combine subjectivity with the correct dramatic techniques to arrive at the proper esthetic distance" ("The Esthetic Fault of Strindberg's 'Dream Plays,' " *The Tulane Drama Review* 4 [March 1960]: 116).

4. The word *mythic* is used throughout this book to describe Strindberg's direct references to specific myths, sagas, legends, or fairy tales—in *The Ghost Sonata*, for example, Hummel is likened to the Norse god Thor—as well as the evocative qualities possessed by figures like the Mummy or the Milkmaid in the same play. The latter are charged with energies that are addressed, to use Kierkegaard's definition of mythical, not "primarily to the understanding but to the imagination." Their presence permits the reader or spectator to experience what Bert O. States has expressively described as

> the fundamentally creative nature of myth-seeing—that
> mystery or "uprush of feeling" that takes place when you

suddenly, or gradually, perceive that the text you are reading is in some devious or hidden sense "oscillating" (as
Kierkegaard says) with something else, being in effect fore-
ordained, though the point of ordination is nowhere to be
seen. It does not have to be a bona fide myth that is inform-
ing the fiction . . . (*The Shape of Paradox* [Berkeley, Los
Angeles, London: University of California Press, 1978],
p. 25).
See also Søren Kierkegaard, *The Concept of Irony*, trans. Lee M.
Capel (Bloomington: Indiana University Press, 1968), pp. 136–
137).

5. Erik Hedén, *Strindberg: En ledtråd vid studiet av hans verk* (Stockholm: Tidens förlag, 1926), p. 235.

6. "Strindberg seems to have realized that the older forms of narrative—romance, fairy tale, and myth—harboring as they do the
archetypes of the collective unconscious, are depositories of human
wisdom concerning the workings of the psyche" (Eric O. Johannesson, *The Novels of August Strindberg* [Berkeley and Los Angeles:
University of California Press, 1968], p. 21).

7. See Pavel Fraenkl, *Strindbergs dramatiske fantasi i Spöksonaten* (Oslo:
Universitetsforlaget, 1966); my articles "Ambiguity and Arche-
types in Strindberg's *Romantic Organist*," *Scandinavian Studies* 48
(Summer 1976):256–271, "The Unknown Painter of Myth," *Scandinavian Review* 64 no. 3 (September 1976):32–38, and "Strindberg och mytologierna—en studie i 'Påsk,' " trans. Herbert
Grevenius, *Signum* 4 no. 3 (1978):73–77; and Sven Delblanc,
"Korngudinnan madam Flod och den falske samhällsbyggaren
Carlsson," *Dagens Nyheter*, 29 July 1978. Delblanc calls Strindberg
"a creator of myths, like Hesiod, sufficiently many-faceted and
rich to be always a bit misunderstood. . . . On the whole, one risks
being led astray through a realistic reading of Strindberg: the
primordial, mythic perspective is continually mixed with a description of social conditions, even before the 'Inferno' [crisis]."
    In 1979 three books and an article, all emphasizing Strindberg's
interest in myth, were published in Stockholm, several months
apart: first, the Swedish version of this book, *Strindberg och myterna*
trans. Sven Erik Täckmark (Författarförlaget); then, Stephen A.
Mitchell, " 'Kama-Loka' and 'Correspondences': A New Look at
Spöksonaten," *Meddelanden från Strindbergssällskapet* no. 61–62
(May):46–51, Delblanc's collection of critical essays, *Stormhatten*

(Bonniers); and Olof Lagercrantz's biography, *August Strindberg* (Wahlström & Widstrand).

8. In the autobiographical fragment, *The Cloister*, Strindberg has the narrator say that not until years after assuming "the pseudonym of 'Son of a Servant Woman' " did he identify himself consciously with the son of Hagar. At the same time, the narrator wonders: "Or had someone whispered to him secretly that this was to be his destiny?" (*The Cloister*, reconstructed as a novel, *Klostret*, by C. J. Bjurström [Stockholm: Bonniers, 1966], p. 10). Another reference to the Son of a Servant Woman appears at the end of Strindberg's last play, *The Great Highway*, where the protagonist, the Hunter, speaks his own epitaph:

> Here rests Ishmael, Hagar's son,
> who was once called Israel,
> because he fought a battle with God
> and did not break off the struggle until he was laid low,
> conquered by His almightly goodness (*51*, 100).

It was not Ishmael, of course, but Jacob who was named Israel after wrestling with the angel at Penuel (Gen. 32:31). But Strindberg was too astute a student of the Bible to be guilty here of a simple mixup; the contrapuntal effect produced by the merging of the different mythic resonances is typical of his polyphonic approach.

Chapter 1

1. *Brev* 10:177–179.

2. Strindberg's familiarity with the Indic Śiva and the Zoroastrian Ormuzd and Ahriman dates from at least as early as 1876, when he did research for an article, "The Devil," published in *Nordisk familjebok* ([Stockholm: *Expeditionen af Nordisk familjébok*, 1880] 3:1286–1288), a standard Swedish encyclopedia. See Gunnar Brandell, *Strindberg in Inferno*, trans. Barry Jacobs (Cambridge: Harvard University Press, 1974), p. 39.

3. Brandell, *Strindberg in Inferno*, p. 161.

4. Eric O. Johannesson, *The Novels of August Strindberg* (Berkeley and Los Angeles: University of California Press, 1968), p. 22.

5. "Doesn't Goethe say in *Aus meinem Leben* that his entire authorship is a Confession? Isn't *Faust* a diary?" (Strindberg to Emil Schering, his German translator, 1902, in *Brev* 14:223, 224, n.7). Goethe's

statement is marked in the margin of Strindberg's copy of *Aus meinem Leben* (Strindberg 1912 Library, catalog number 97, part 2, pp. 48–49) and is quoted in the novel *Alone* (*38*,198–199). See *Inferno, Alone and Other Writings*, trans. Evert Sprinchorn (Garden City, N. Y.: Anchor Doubleday, 1968), pp. 415–416.

6. "It seems to me," Strindberg wrote in 1887 after completing *The Father*, "as if I am walking in my sleep; as if fiction and life were mingled. I don't know if *The Father* is a fiction or if my life has been one. . . ." *Brev* 6:298.

7. The narrator in Strindberg's roman à clef *Jacob Wrestles* says: "As long as Swedenborg in *Arcana* and *Apocalypsis* confined himself to revelations, prophecies, and interpretations, he made me religious, but when in *Vera Religio* he began to argue dogma, he became a freethinker and a Protestant. He chooses his own weapons when he crosses swords with reason, and they are bad weapons" (*28*,390).

8. Among the more than 300 religious books, magazines, and pamphlets in the Strindberg Museum Library in Stockholm are two dozen Bibles, several of which contain many marginal notations. An excellent survey of his lifetime habits as a bibliophile is Hans Lindström's *Strindberg och böckerna* (Uppsala: Skrifter utgivna av svenska litteratursällskapet, 1977), which contains catalogs of libraries owned by Strindberg during three different periods: 1883, 1892, 1912.

9. See Allan Hagsten, *Den Unge Strindberg* (Stockholm: Bonniers, 1951), 2:38–42.

10. Värend is the old name of an area in southern Sweden whose inhabitants long retained ancient customs and beliefs. Hans Lindström has noted that *Värend and the People of Värend* (*Wärend och wirdarne* [Stockholm: Norstedts, 1863–68]) was one of only fourteen books that were included in each of the three libraries Strindberg owned in his lifetime (*Strindberg och böckerna*, p. 13). See Bengt af Klintberg, *Svenska folksägner* (Stockholm: PAN/Norstedts, 1977), p. 66; and Nils-Arvid Bringéus, *Gunnar Olof Hyltén-Cavallius* (Stockholm: Nordiska museets handlingar, no. 63, 1966), p. 7.

11. *Brev* 11:347.

12. *Wärend och wirdarne*, 1:498–499, Strindberg 1912 Library, catalog number 4443.

13. Brandell, *Strindberg in Inferno*, p. 160.

14. *Brev* 11:347.

15. Martin Lamm, *Strindberg och makterna* (Stockholm: Svenska kyrkans diakonstyrelses bokförlag, 1936), p. 158.
16. See Erich Neumann, *The Great Mother*, trans. Ralph Mannheim (Princeton: Princeton University Press, 1974), pp. 235–236.
17. Torsten Eklund, *Tjänstekvinnans son: En psykologisk Strindbergsstudie* (Stockholm: Bonniers, 1948), p. 287.
18. *Före Roda rummet: Strindbergs ungdomsjournalistik*, ed. Torsten Eklund (Stockholm: Bonniers, 1946), p. 231.
19. Eklund, *Tjänstekvinnans son*, p. 288.
20. Arthur Schopenhauer, *The World As Will and Representation*, trans. E. F. J. Payne (New York: Dover, 1969), 2:628–629.
21. Arthur Schopenhauer, *Essays and Aphorisms*, trans. and ed. R. J. Bellingdale (Baltimore: Penguin, 1970), p. 49.
22. Ibid., p. 49.
23. *Brev* 11:109.
24. Schopenhauer, *Essays*, p. 62.
25. *Brev* 11:376.
26. Emanuel Swedenborg, *The Worship and Love of God*, trans. A. H. Stroh and F. Sewall (Boston: Massachusetts New-Church Union, 1956), p. 174.
27. August Strindberg, *Ockulta Dagboken* (Stockholm: Gidlunds, 1977), cover page.
28. Éliphas Lévi, *The Key of the Mysteries*, trans. Aleister Crowley (New York: Weiser, 1972), pp. 34, 51.
29. *Brev* 11:295.
30. Strindberg, *Ockulta Dagboken*, entry for 1 August 1896.
31. *Brev* 11:376.
32. French version of *Inferno*, trans. Marcel Réja, ed. C. G. Bjurstrom (Paris: Mercure de France, 1966), pp. 17–26; English version of *Inferno*, trans. David Scanlon, *The Tulane Drama Review* 5 (November 1961): 128–131.
33. Schopenhauer, *Essays*, p. 48.
34. For an analysis of the image of the artist as demiurge in Strindberg's novel *By the Open Sea*, see Sven Delblanc, *Stormhatten* (Stockholm: Bonniers, 1979), pp. 11–27.
35. Cf. Hyltén-Cavallius's observations on the significance of mythological thinking as "a primary factor in human nature": "the development of the intellectual and spiritual life of the human race takes

the same course, under the same conditions, as that of the individual in human history" (*Wärend och wirdarne*, 1:499).

36. Among the studies I found especially useful and stimulating in the preparation of this book were the following: Gaston Bachelard, *The Poetics of Reverie* (Boston: Beacon, 1971); Bruno Bettelheim, *The Uses of Enchantment* (New York: Knopf, 1976); Maud Bodkin, *Archetypal Patterns in Poetry* (London: Oxford University Press, 1934); Joseph Campbell, *The Hero with a Thousand Faces* (Princeton: Princeton University Press, 1968); J. E. Cirlot, *A Dictionary of Symbols*, trans. Jack Sage (New York: Philosophical Library, 1962); Edward Edinger, *Ego and Archetype* (Baltimore: Penguin, 1973); Mircea Eliade, *The Myth of the Eternal Return*, trans. W. P. Trask (Princeton: Princeton University Press, 1965); Lillian Feder, *Ancient Myth in Modern Poetry* (Princeton: Princeton University Press, 1977); Sigmund Freud, *On Creativity and the Unconscious*, trans. Alix Strachey (New York: Harper & Row, 1958); Northrop Frye, *Anatomy of Criticism* (Princeton: Princeton University Press, 1957); Hans Jonas, *The Gnostic Religion*, 2d ed. (Boston: Beacon Press, 1963); C. G. Jung, *Symbols of Transformation*, trans. R. F. C. Hull, 2d ed. (Princeton: Princeton University Press, 1967); Erich Neumann, *The Origins and History of Consciousness*, trans. R. F. C. Hull (Princeton: Princeton University Press, 1970); and Alan W. Watts, *Myth and Ritual in Christianity* (Boston: Beacon, 1968).

37. The werewolf is discussed as a familiar theme in Swedish folklore by Hyltén-Cavallius, *Wärend*, 1:348–349.

38. August Strindberg, *Getting Married*, trans. Mary Sandbach (New York: The Viking Press, 1972), p. 207. For further discussion of the influences of Lafargue and Bachofen, see Hagsten, *Den unge Strindberg*, 1:36–37, Martin Lamm, *Strindbergs dramer* (Stockholm: Bonniers, 1924), 1:278–282; Hans Lindström, *Hjärnornas kamp* (Uppsala: Appelbags boktryckeri, 1952), pp. 112, 242; and Børge Gedsø Madsen, *Strindberg's Naturalistic Theatre* (Copenhagen: Munksgaard, 1962), p. 51.

39. *Myth, Religion, and Mother Right: Selected Writings of J. J. Bachofen*, trans. Ralph Manheim (Princeton: Princeton University Press, 1973), p. 93.

40. Ibid., p. 76.

41. Strindberg, *Getting Married*, p. 30.

42. Strindberg sought to borrow a copy of *Mother Right* in a letter dated 19 May 1886 (*Brev* 5:327). In an essay series published in January

and February 1887, "The Last Word on the Woman Question," he
mentioned Lafargue as a student of Friedrich Engels, Lewis Henry
Morgan, and Bachofen (54,269).

43. Neumann, *The Great Mother*, pp. 43–44.

"Bachofen's thesis, that
we find an older layer of matriarchal religion underneath the more
recent patriarchal religion of Greece, seems to me to be established
by him beyond any doubt" (Erich Fromm, *The Forgotten Language*
[New York: Grove Press, 1957], p. 210).

44. Joseph Campbell, "Introduction," in *Myth, Religion, and Mother
Right*, p. 1v. See also James Mellart, *Çatal Hüyük: A Neolithic Town
in Anatolia* (New York: McGraw-Hill, 1967).

45. *Myth, Religion, and Mother Right*, p. 179.

46. Ibid., p. 190.

47. Ibid., p. 181.

48. Ibid., p. 114.

49. Ibid., p. 192.

50. Ibid., pp. 191–192.

51. Ibid., p. 115.

52. See Fromm, *The Forgotten Language*, p. 205.

53. Joseph Campbell, *The Masks of God: Occidental Mythology* (New
York: The Viking Press, 1970), p. 25.

Chapter 2

1. C. G. Jung, *Symbols of Transformation*, trans. R. F. C. Hull, 2d. ed.
(Princeton: Princeton University Press, 1967), p. 125.

2. See Erich Neumann, *The Origins and History of Consciousness*, trans.
R. F. C. Hull (Princeton: Princeton University Press, 1970), especially pp. 152–169.

3. For analyses of this novella, see Eric O. Johannesson, *The Novels of
August Strindberg* (Berkeley and Los Angeles: University of California Press, 1968), pp. 109–120; and my article "Ambiguity and
Archetypes in Strindberg's *Romantic Organist*," *Scandinavian Studies* 48 (Summer 1976):256–271.

4. *August Strindbergs Master Olof*, ed. Carl Reinhold Smedmark
(Stockholm: Bonniers, 1957), 3:19, 26, 25.

5. John 14:24–26.

6. John 16:1–2, 8–10, 13–14.

7. *August Strindbergs Mäster Olof*, 3:127.

8. Mark 3:29–30.

Chapter 3

1. Robert Brustein, *The Theatre of Revolt* (Boston: Little, Brown, 1964), p. 111.

2. Jane Harrison, *Prolegomena to the Study of Greek Religion* (New York: Meridian, 1959), p. 320.

3. Carl Reinhold Smedmark, "Inledning till Fadren," *August Strindbergs dramer* (Stockholm: Bonniers, 1964), 3:194.

4. *Brev* 6:282.

5. Charles F. Lyons, "The Archetypal Action of Male Submission in Strindberg's *The Father*," *Scandinavian Studies* 36 (August 1964) :228.

6. Borge Gedso Madsen, *Strindberg's Naturalistic Theatre* (Copenhagen: Munksgaard, 1962), p. 59. An exception to this approach appears in Hillewi Paulin's sympathetic and perceptive article "Prometevs i bojor," *Horisont* 9, no. 5–6 (1962):43–48.

7. F. L. Lucas, *The Drama of Ibsen and Strindberg* (New York: Macmillan, 1962), p. 345.

Chapter 4

1. Tennessee Williams, *A Streetcar Named Desire* (New York: New Directions, 1947), p. 155.

2. "As a demonstration of the skill with which a genius manipulates his material there is nothing more dazzling in dramatic literature than this series of works (unless it be the works Strindberg wrote a decade later). And few authors have let us examine so closely the creative process itself—the process by which 'real experiences' are subjected to the pattern-making genius of the artist to produce different versions of the truth" (Evert Sprinchorn's introduction to *A Madman's Defense* [Garden City, N. Y.: Anchor Doubleday, 1967], p. xxii).

3. August Strindberg, *En dåres försvarstal*, trans. (from French) Hans Levander (Stockholm: Forum, 1976), p. 121. The long-missing manuscript of this version of the novel was discovered in a safe at the University of Oslo in 1973.

4. See J. E. Cirlot, *A Dictionary of Symbols*, trans. Jack Sage (New York: Philosophical Library, 1962), p. 142.

5. C. G. Jung, *Four Archetypes*, trans. R. F. C. Hull (Princeton: Princeton University Press, 1970), pp. 109–132.

6. Ibid., 3:303. The passage is also missing from the standard edition of Strindberg's collected works. It is restored in Carl Reinhold Smedmark's 1964 edition (*August Strindbergs dramer* [Stockholm: Bonniers, 1964], 3:303).

7. Milton May, "Strindberg's *Ghost Sonata*: Parodied Fairy Tale on Original Sin," *Modern Drama* 10 (September 1967): 189–194.

8. Strindberg, *En dåres försvarstal*, trans. Levander, p. 53.

9. August Strindberg, *En dåres försvarstal*, trans. (from French) Tage Aurell (Stockholm: Bonniers, 1962), p. 63.

10. Letter cited by Jacques Chwat, "Introduction," in August Strindberg, *A Dream Play*, trans. Evert Sprinchorn (New York: Avon, 1974), p. 11.

11. Dante Alighieri, *Dantes gudomliga komedi*, trans. Edvard Lidforss (Stockholm: Fahlcrantz, 1902), 1 (*Helvetet*):127. Strindberg 1912 Library, catalog number 2275.

12. Strindberg, *En dåres försvarstal*, trans. Aurell, p. 43.

13. Ibid., p. 128.

14. *August Strindbergs dramer*, ed. Carl Reinhold Smedmark (Stockholm: Bonniers, 1964), 3:343.

Chapter 5

1. *Brev* 7:105.

2. Carl Reinhold Smedmark, "Inledning till Fordringsägare", *August Strindbergs dramer* (Stockholm: Bonniers, 1964), 3:370.

3. See *Brev* 7:261.

4. Ibid., 7:259.

5. Ibid., 10:76.

6. See *August Strindbergs dramer*, 3:517.

7. Sigmund Freud, "The 'Uncanny,'" in *On Creativity and the Unconscious*, trans. Alix Strachey (New York: Harper & Row, 1958), pp. 122–123.

8. Ibid., p. 141.

9. James Joyce, *The Critical Writings of James Joyce*, ed. Ellsworth Mason and Richard Ellmann (New York: The Viking Press, 1959), p. 40.

10. C. G. Jung, *Memories, Dreams, Reflections*, recorded and ed. Aniela Jaffé, trans. Richard and Clara Winston (New York: Vintage, 1965), p. 344.

Chapter 6

1. Gunnar Brandell, *Strindberg in Inferno*, trans. Barry Jacobs (Cambridge: Harvard University Press, 1974), p. 312.

2. Egil Törnqvist, "Strindberg and the Drama of Half-Reality: An Analysis of *To Damascus, I*," in *Strindberg and Modern Theatre*, ed. Carl Reinhold Smedmark (Stockholm: The Strindberg Society, 1975), p. 120.

3. *Brev*, 12:279.

4. Brian Johnston, "The Corpse and the Cargo," *The Drama Review* 13 (Winter 1968):62.

5. *Brev* 10:153, n. 10. For an examination of the implications of Swedenborg's influence on Strindberg's work, see Göran Stockenström, *Ismael i öknen: Strindberg som mystiker* (Uppsala: Acta Universitatis Upsaliensis, no. 6, 1972).

6. *Brev* 14:51.

7. Ernst Cassirer, *The Philosophy of Symbolic Forms: Mythical Thought*, trans. Ralph Manheim (New Haven and London: Yale University Press, 1955), 2:46.

8. In a similar vein Kenneth Burke complains, "Shakespeare tends to bludgeon us at times with the too frequent use of metaphor, until what was an allurement threatens to become an obstacle. We might say that the hypertrophy of metaphor is Shakespeare at his worst, and fills in those lapses of inspiration when he is keeping things going as best he can until the next flare-up" ("The Poetic Process," *Five Approaches of Literary Criticism*, ed. Wilbur Scott [New York: Collier Books, 1962], p. 81, n. 1). On Strindberg's use of metaphor, see also Karl-Åke Kärnell, *Strindbergs bildspråk* (Stockholm: Almqvist & Wiksell, 1962); Göran Lindblad, *August Strindberg som berättare* (Stockholm: Norstedt, 1924); and *Strindbergs språk och stil*, ed. Goran Lindstrom (Falköping, Sweden: 1964).

9. Matt. 23:12.

10. Joseph Campbell, *The Hero with a Thousand Faces* (Princeton: Princeton University Press, 1968), p. 63.

11. *Brev* 11:311.

12. Ibid., 11:315, 322.

13. Gunnar Ollén, *Strindbergs 1900-talslyrik* (Stockholm: Seelig, 1941), p. 259, n. 4.

14. August Strindberg, *Vivisektioner* (Stockholm: Bonniers, 1958), p. 9.
15. C. G. Jung, *Mandala Symbolism*, trans. R. F. C. Hull (Princeton: Princeton University Press, 1972), p. 73.
16. "St. Elizabeth," *The Encyclopedia Britannica* 11th ed. (1911), 9:287.
17. Dickens's influence on Strindberg is well documented. See Kärnell, *Strindbergs bildspråk*, pp. 191–194, 196–199 passim; Martin Lamm, *August Strindberg*, trans. and ed. Harry G. Carlson (New York: Benjamin Blom, 1971), pp. 61, 62 passim; and Lindblad, *berättare*, pp. 79–118.
18. Erich Neumann, *The Great Mother*, trans. Ralph Manheim (Princeton: Princeton University Press, 1972), p. 284.
19. The *mara* is another Swedish folklore theme, like that of the werewolf, which is discussed by Hyltén-Cavallius, *Wärend och wirdarne* (Stockholm: Norstedts, 1863–68) 1:349–351.
20. Gen. 3:6.
21. Isaiah 14:12.
22. Acts 9:4.
23. Compare the advice given to Dorothy in *The Wizard of Oz*: "Follow the yellow brick road."
24. Dr. Eliasson, who recognized easily the description of Strindberg's visit to his home in *Inferno*, was appalled by the author's portrait of him: "The brief episodes and anecdotes that . . . are supposed to characterize me are all lies" (Letter cited by Nils Ludvig, "Strindberg på vägen till Inferno," *Svensk litteraturtidskrift* [1964], p. 64).
25. *Brev* 11:205.
26. See J. E. Cirlot, *A Dictionary of Symbols*, trans. Jack Sage (New York: Philosophical Library, 1962), p. 350.
27. Rom. 12:20.
28. See discussion in Lamm, *Strindberg*, p. 309.

Chapter 7

1. Martin Lamm, *August Strindberg*, trans. and ed. Harry G. Carlson (New York: Benjamin Blom, 1971), p. 367.
2. Erich Neumann, *The Great Mother*, trans. Ralph Manheim (Princeton: Princeton University Press, 1972), pp. 318–319.
3. Edith Hamilton, *Mythology* (New York: The New American Library, 1953), p. 54.

4. See Aage Kabell, "Påsk og det mystiske teater," *Edda* 54 (1954):164.

5. See Neumann, *The Great Mother*, p. 307.

6. *Brev* 14:57.

7. Mircea Eliade, *Patterns in Comparative Religion* (New York: Meridian, 1963), p. 296.

8. See Hans Jonas, *The Gnostic Religion*, 2d ed. (Boston: Beacon Press, 1963), pp. 301–303, on the passion of Sophia.

9. *Brev* 14:16.

10. Ibid., 11:253.

11. Ibid., 15:88.

12. Ibid., 14:34.

13. Ibid., 13:329.

14. Ibid., 14:58.

Chapter 8

1. *Brev* 14:31–32.

2. Arthur Schopenhauer, *Werke* 8:220–225, cited by Joseph Campbell, *The Masks of God: Creative Mythology* (New York: The Viking Press, 1970), pp. 343–344.

3. See Helmut Müssener, "Ett drömspel: tillkomst och textproblem," *Meddelanden från Strindbergssällskapet*, no. 36 (December 1964):26.

4. Ibid.

5. Ahnfelt's two-volume survey was another of the fourteen works to which he returned for inspiration throughout his life (see Hans Lindström, *Strindberg och böckerna* [Uppsala: Skrifter utgivna av svenska litteratursällskapet, 1977], p. 13).

6. Arthur Schopenhauer, *The World As Will and Representation*, trans. E. F. J. Payne (New York: Dover, 1969), 1:352.

7. Erich Neumann, *The Great Mother*, trans. Ralph Manheim (Princeton: Princeton University Press, 1972), p. 227.

8. Arvid Ahnfelt, *Verldslitteraturens historia* (Stockholm: 1875), 1:37. Strindberg 1912 Library, catalog number 4149.

9. *Brev* 11:99.

10. Ibid., 15:354.

11. Evert Sprinchorn, "The Logic of *A Dream Play*," in *A Dream Play*, trans. Evert Sprinchorn (New York: Avon, 1974), p. 160.

12. Ejnar Thomsen, "Bidrag til tolkningen af 'Ett drömspel,' " *Orbis Litterarum* 1 (1943):87.

13. Viktor Rydberg, *Undersökningar i germanisk mythologi* (Stockholm: Bonniers, 1889–90), 2:441–442; 2:76, 79.

14. *Brev* 11:151.

15. G. de Lafont, *Le Buddhisme* (Paris: Chamuel, 1895), p. 43. Strindberg 1912 Library, catalog number 2847.

16. The Sanskrit names for these elements are ākāśa (ether), vāyu (wind), agni (fire), āpah (water), and pṛthivī (earth).

17. Quoted by Martin Lamm in *August Strindberg*, trans. and ed. Harry G. Carlson (New York: Benjamin Blom, 1971), p. 292.

18. Thomsen, "Bidrag," p. 105.

19. August Strindberg, *Ockulta Dagboken* (Stockholm: Gidlunds, 1977), entry for 1 June 1898.

20. *Pistis Sophia. Ouvrage gnostique de Valentin*, trans. (into French) E. Amélineau (Paris: Chamuel, 1895), p. vi. Strindberg 1912 Library, catalog number 2869.

21. C. G. Jung, *Answer to Job*, trans. R. F. C. Hull (Princeton: Princeton University Press, 1973), p. 52.

22. M. Matter, *Emanuel Swedenborg: Hans lefnad, hans skrifter och hans lära* (Stockholm: 1864), pp. 67–68. Strindberg 1912 Library, catalog number 2073.

23. See *Larousse Encyclopedia of Mythology* (London: Paul Hamlyn, 1959), p. 346.

24. Robert Graves, *The White Goddess* (New York: Noonday, 1966).

25. See Selma Lagerlöf's version of the story, "Valdemar Atterdag brandskattar Visby," in *Sägnernas ö Gotland i vers och prosa*, ed. Valton Johansson (Stockholm: Fahlcrantz & Gumaelius, 1950), pp. 86–92.

26. Lamm, *August Strindberg*, p. 394.

27. Frida Uhl, *Strindberg och hans andra hustru*, trans. (from German) Karin Boye (Stockholm: Bonniers, 1933–34), 1:359.

28. See Lamm, *August Strindberg*, p. 389.

29. Sprinchorn, "Logic of *A Dream Play*," p. 158.

30. Lamm, *August Strindberg*, p. 400.

31. Hans Jonas, *The Gnostic Religion*, 2d ed. (Boston: Beacon Press, 1963), p. 44.

32. See my translation, "Hercules," *Scandinavian Review* 64 (September 1976):25–26.

33. For a stimulating discussion of Strindberg's use of the Greek god in this novel, see Eric O. Johannesson, *The Novels of August Strindberg*

(Berkeley and Los Angeles: University of California Press, 1968), pp. 168–171.

34. *Brev* 11:107.

35. Guy Vogelweith, *Le Psychothéâtre de Strindberg* (Paris: Klincksieck, 1972), p. 231.

36. Neumann, *The Great Mother*, p. 226.

37. Graves, *The White Goddess*, p. 53.

38. *Brev* 11:307.

39. Cf. Sven Delblanc, who presents a different view: "The Officer represents a correct love, in contrast to that practiced in the prison of marriage" (*Stormhatten*, [Stockholm: Bonniers, 1979], p. 87).

40. Maurice Valency, *The Flower and the Castle* (New York: Macmillan, 1963), p. 331.

41. I am indebted to my former student and colleague Peter Goslett for calling to my attention the rich suggestiveness of *quarantaine*.

42. O. B. Hardison, *Christian Rite and Christian Drama in the Middle Ages* (Baltimore: Johns Hopkins University Press, 1965), p. 97.

43. August Strindberg, *Ockulta Dagboken* (Stockholm: Gidlunds, 1977), entry for 15 April 1907.

44. See Gunnar Brandell, *Strindberg in Inferno*, trans. Barry Jacobs (Cambridge: Harvard University Press, 1974), p. 99.

45. Uhl, *Strindberg och hans andra hustru*, 2:252.

46. Schopenhauer, *The World As Will and Representation*, 2:169.

47. *Brev* 15:368.

48. Letter 11 August 1894 in ibid., 10:207. In another letter two years later he chided the same correspondent, his theosophist benefactor, Torsten Hedlund:

> You meddle with metaphysics without having passed through physics. (You know that ever since Aristotle metaphysics is so called because it comes after physics. I am a Naturalist/occultist, like Linnaeus, my great teacher. First physics, then meta-. I want first to see with my outward eyes, then with my inward ones. "True to oneself, even in growth and change." Don't want to spit upon Naturalism and sensualism, because when they were accepted, they were justified as phases. But proceed further! (ibid., 11:219).

49. de Lafont, *Le Buddhisme*, p. 120.

50. Ibid., pp. 107–109.
51. Ibid., p. 109.
52. " 'The sense of duty,' we read in a classic Vedāntic text, 'is of the world of relativity. It is transcended by the wise, who are of the form of the void, formless, immutable and untainted' " (Campbell, *The Masks of God: Oriental Mythology*, p. 287.)
53. Campbell, *The Masks of God: Creative Mythology*, p. 259.
54. *Brev* 10:221.
55. de Lafont, *Le Buddhisme*, pp. 81–82.
56. Lamm, *August Strindberg*, p. 404.
57. August Strindberg, *En dåres försvarstal*, trans. Hans Levander (Stockholm: Forum, 1976), p. 245.
58. Mircea Eliade, *The Two and the One*, trans. J. M. Cohen (New York: Harper & Row, 1969), p. 100.
59. Gaston Bachelard, *The Poetics of Reverie* (Boston: Beacon, 1971), p. 79.
60. *Faust*, (*Part One*), trans. Bayard Taylor (New York: Modern Library, n.d.), p. 124.
61. Campbell, *The Masks of God: Oriental Mythology*, p. 431.
62. Heinrich Zimmer, *Myths and Symbols in Indian Art and Civilization*, (ed. Joseph Campbell (Princeton: Princeton University Press, 1972), p. 152. According to Joseph Campbell, "in the Sāṅkhya of Kapila, the five [elements] are linked to the five senses: respectively space or ether to hearing; wind or air to touch; fire to sight; water to taste; earth to smell" (*The Masks of God: Oriental Mythology*, p. 431).
63. de Lafont, *Le Buddhisme*, p. 53.
64. J. E. Cirlot, *A Dictionary of Symbols*, trans. Jack Sage (New York: Philosophical Library, 1962), p. 27.
65. Zimmer, *Myths and Symbols*, p. 102.
66. Campbell, *Masks of God: Oriental Mythology*, pp. 21–22.

Chapter 9

1. See John Northam, who also stresses the journeylike structure of the play in "Strindberg's Spook Sonata," *Essays on Strindberg*, ed. Carl Reinhold Smedmark (Stockholm: The Strindberg Society, 1966), pp. 41, 48.

2. Brian Rothwell makes a similar point when he speaks about "a constant theme in Strindberg since the Inferno; that this life may really be hell or purgatory. Life is perhaps only māyā (illusion)" ("The Chamber Plays," in *Essays on Strindberg*, p. 35).

3. Egil Törnqvist, *Bergman och Strindberg* (Stockholm: Prisma, 1973), p. 81.

4. Stephen A. Mitchell has pointed out Hummel's resemblance to still another Norse deity, the trickster Loki, "who attends a feast of the gods and verbally abuses each of the gods and goddesses in turn, revealing secrets and facts about them and throwing this information in their faces in the form of taunts and insults" (" 'Kama-Loka' and 'Correspondences': A New Look at *Spöksonaten*," *Meddelanden från Strindborgssällskapet* [May 1979]:49). Mitchell also suggests (p. 47) that in the course of Strindberg's investigations into word correspondences between several languages, he could have come into contact with the Old Icelandic stem *kám-* and its forms: "A compound such as '*kama-loka*' might have been identified by Strindberg, however imperfectly from a philological point of view, as meaning something like 'the defiling of Loki' or the 'debasement of Loki.' "

5. Mircea Eliade, *Patterns in Comparative Religion* (New York: Meridian, 1963), p. 81.

6. Stephen C. Bandy, "Strindberg's Biblical Sources for *The Ghost Sonata*," *Scandinavian Studies* 40 (August 1968): 203.

7. Gen. 29:9–11.

8. Joseph Campbell, *The Masks of God: Creative Mythology* (New York: The Viking Press, 1970), p. 489.

9. Pavel Fraenkl, *Strindbergs dramatiske fantasi i Spöksonaten*," (Oslo: Universitetsforlaget, 1966), p. 127.

10. Quoted by Thomas Whitaker in *Fields of Play in Modern Drama* (Princeton: Princeton University Press, 1977), p. 58.

11. John 19:30.

12. See, for example, the last line in the history play *The Saga of the Folkungs*—"It is finished"—spoken by the Christ-like figure, King Magnus (*31*,129).

13. *The Poetic Edda*, trans. Henry Adams Bellows (New York: The American-Scandinavian Foundation, 1923), p. 60.

14. Sophus Bugge, *Studier over de nordiska gude- or helte-sagns oprindelse* (Christiania [Oslo]: Cammermeyer, 1881–89), p. 297. Strindberg 1912 Library, catalog number 1307.

15. Törnqvist, *Bergman och Strindberg*, p. 172.

16. In an 1896 letter Strindberg stated that he found everything he was groping for in Rydberg's *Teutonic Mythology*: "The World Tree . . . and the creation of the first couple out of wood." In another letter several months later he wrote that he could see the likeness of Ask and Embla in walnuts (*Brev* 11:295, 358).

17. Arthur Schopenhauer, *Essays and Aphorisms*, trans. and ed. R. J. Bellingdale (Baltimore: Penguin, 1970), p. 42.

18. As in the cases of Śiva, Ormuzd, Ahriman, and other mythic figures, the significance of the Lamia is discussed in Strindberg's early article, "The Devil," published in 1880 in the encyclopedia *Nordisk familjebok* (Stockholm: Expeditionen af Nordisk familjebok, 1880), 3:1286–1288.

19. In the autobiographical work *Legends*, Strindberg makes a direct association between the Incubus and the *mara* (*28*,223).

20. See C. G. Jung, *Symbols of Transformation, Psychology and Alchemy*, trans. R. F. C. Hull (Princeton: Princeton University Press, 1968); and *Alchemical Studies*, trans. R. F. C. Hull (Princeton: Princeton University Press, 1967).

21. Ovid, *Metamorphoses*, trans. Mary M. Innes (Baltimore: Penguin, 1955), p. 250.

22. Evert Sprinchorn, "Introduction," *The Chamber Plays by August Strindberg* (New York: Dutton, 1962), p. xxii.

23. Heinrich Zimmer, *Philosophies of India*, ed. Joseph Campbell (Princeton: Princeton University Press, 1969), p. 144, n. 4.

Conclusion

1. Northrop Frye, *Anatomy of Criticism* (Princeton: Princeton University Press, 1971), p. 268.

2. Antonin Artaud, *The Theater and Its Double* (New York: Grove Press, 1958), p. 116.

3. See Egil Törnqvist, *Bergman och Strindberg* (Stockholm: Prisma, 1973), p. 31.

Index

Designer: Linda Robertson
Compositor: Trend Western Technical Corp.
Printer: McNaughton & Gunn, Inc.
Binder: McNaughton & Gunn, Inc.
Text: 10/12 Janson
Display: Janson